ESCAPE FROM THE MAZE:

9 STEPS TO PERSONAL CREATIVITY

James M. Higgins

Crummer Graduate School of Business
Rollins College
James M. Higgins & Associates Inc.

THE NEW
MANAGEMENT
PUBLISHING COMPANY
400 North New York Avenue, Suite 215
Winter Park, Florida 32789

http://www.jhiggins.com

i

This book is available at a special discount when ordered in bulk quantities. For information, contact New Management Publishing Company, Inc., 400 North New York Avenue, Suite 215, Winter Park, Florida 32789.

PRODUCTION EDITOR: Susan Novotny
WORD PROCESSOR: Susan Crabill
COPY EDITORS: Steven Garnett & Louise Hanson
DESIGNER/ILLUSTRATOR: Dean Dorman
COVER DESIGN: Keri Caffrey & Dean Dorman

New Management Publishing Company, Inc.
400 North New York Avenue, Suite 215
Winter Park, FL 32789

Publisher's Cataloging in Publication Data
(Prepared by Quality Books, Inc.)
Higgins, James M.
Escape From the Maze: 9 Steps to Personal
Creativity/ James M. Higgins.
p. cm.
Includes bibliographical references.
Preassigned LCCN: 95-69950.
ISBN 1-883629-02-0
1. Creative Ability.   2. Intuition.   I. Title.

BF408.H54 1995
153.3'5
QBI95-20350

PREFACE

The Age of Innovation is upon us. Business leaders are now heralding innovation as a key ingredient in achieving future economic success. These leaders recognize that innovation is <u>the</u> most important single skill that an organization can possess if it is to be competitive. And for the individual who is creative and innovative, personal competitiveness also accrues. Furthermore, the individual seeking empowerment and an improved quality of work life, can find both in an organizational culture that promotes creativity and the innovation to which it leads. And finally, our society is confronted with a large number of problems, most of which demand creative and innovative solutions. The message for the organization is innovate or evaporate; for the individual, innovate or stagnate; for the society, innovate or degenerate. Since creativity leads to innovation, the first step for the individual is to acquire creativity skills. This book tells you how to acquire those skills.

ESCAPE WAS WRITTEN PRIMARILY FOR THE PERSON JUST GETTING STARTED IN THE FIELD OF CREATIVITY

This book was written primarily for the person just getting started in the field of creativity, the person who wants to understand the key steps involved in becoming more creative. For the person experienced in creativity, *Escape* offers the first overview of the major streams of thought in the field. This overview will assist the experienced creative in understanding other perspectives and in opening the possibilities for the expansion of his or her own creativity skills.

The authors of most books on creativity proclaim that their books contain <u>the</u> key to achieving higher levels of creativity. Each of these authors is right in his or her own way, but more importantly, they are all collectively correct. My research has uncovered nine distinct action steps which enable you to achieve higher levels of creativity. By using many or preferably all of these steps, you will become much more creative than through the use of just one or a few of these approaches.

Preface

Escape discusses these nine steps to personal creativity in sufficient detail to enable you to get started improving your skill levels for each technique. Appendix 2 of *Escape* lists a number of books which can further enhance your skills for each of the nine steps. *Escape's* chapters are based on these steps and follow along numerically with the steps as they are identified in Chapter 1—Chapter 2 discusses Steps 1 and 2; Chapter 3 discusses Step 3; Chapter 4 discusses Step 4; Chapters 5, 6, 7, 8, and 9 discuss Steps 5 and 6; and Chapter 10 discusses Steps 7, 8, and 9.

THE INNOVATION TRILOGY

In most organizations, especially in businesses, creativity is a means to an end—innovation. **Creativity** is the process of originating something new that has value to an individual, a group, an organization, an industry or a society. **Innovation** is the process of originating something new that has significant value to an individual, a group, an organization, an industry or a society. The key word that distinguishes creativity from innovation is *significant*. The perspective of this book is that innovation is ultimately what the creative person in business is seeking. Being creative is fun, but innovation results in profits, and profit is what it is all about in business.

An innovation is the result of the innovation process. There are two basic types of innovations—product innovation and process innovation. The relationships between creativity and innovation, from an organizational perspective, can be readily described using the **Innovation Equation:**

C + ROC = I. Creativity occurring in the Right Organizational Culture results in Innovation.

The innovation trilogy consists of three books which explain the three parts of this equation. Two books explain the creativity part of the equation, and the third book explains the organizational culture and innovation parts of the equation. *Escape* describes the nine steps to personal creativity. One of those steps is so vital to the creativity process, and offers the biggest bang for the buck of any of these actions, that a whole book has been devoted to Step 4, creativity processes—*101 Creative Problem Solving Techniques:*

Escape

from
the Maze

The Handbook of New Ideas for Business. As its title suggests, it describes 101 creativity processes and provides many business examples of their use. Learning such techniques adds a tremendous capacity for creativity in a relatively short time period and for a relatively small amount of energy and resource commitment. The third book in the trilogy is *Innovate or Evaporate: Test and Improve Your Organization's IQ—Its Innovation Quotient.* This book provides an in-depth guide to the forty-nine characteristics of the organizational culture that turns creativity into innovation. Numerous business examples of these characteristics are provided.

THE AGE OF INNOVATION

The Age of Innovation is here. The needs of the individual, the organization, and the society are now, more than ever, best obtained through an emphasis on innovation.

Individuals are seeking more of a voice in the organization at the same time that organizations find it beneficial to empower employees. The consequence of the convergence of these two events is that individuals are being required to become better problem solvers. Creativity is a critical part of the new perspective on problem solving emerging in organizations, the kind of creativity that leads to innovation. Hence, enhancing personal creativity skills is critical to being successful in the organization today. To compete in the workplace, the individual needs a skill that helps differentiate him or her from the rest of the competition. Creativity will be such a skill for some time. Furthermore, as people seek to achieve more self-actualization, learning to be more creative is a natural action to take. The two go hand-in-hand. Creativity can add value to anyones personal life as well as ones professional life, from planning parties to decorating a home. Finally, being creative is fun, and we all deserve some fun.

All types of organizations, but especially corporations, are focusing on innovation as a necessary skill for success. Corporations, having pretty much exhausted the opportunities for restructuring and reengineering, are now turning to revenue growth as the new strategic mantra. Revenue growth results from four primary strategies: geographic expansion; alliances, acquisitions and mergers; market penetration; and product development and enhancement. About half of the growth of high growth firms has been shown to

Preface

come from the combination of market penetration, and product development and enhancement. Product development and enhancement ultimately depend on product innovation as their foundation. Market penetration highly depends on marketing innovation for its success, with product development and enhancement, and cost advantages contributing greatly. Obtaining cost advantages also depends on innovation—process redesign and continuous improvement are process innovation activities. And, the related process of management innovation is a virtually untapped vital resource which can help companies improve the value they add to the value chain of key organizational processes.

At the most fundamental level, all competition in some way depends on creativity and innovation. To compete firms either attempt to differentiate themselves from their competitors and/or they attempt to achieve some relative low cost position compared to their competitors. In both cases, innovation is the key. Product innovation generally leads to some degree of relative differentiation and process innovation generally leads to relative low cost. For the first time in business history, the importance of innovation is now being understood.

Organizations are also confronted by a large number of strategic challenges that require creativity and innovation in order to meet these challenges successfully. Among these are accelerating rates of change in all aspects of business, increasing globalization of business, rapidly changing technology, a more diverse work force than ever before, a transition from an industrially based economy to one based on knowledge, and increasing demands of virtually all stakeholders from government to environmentalists to customers.

Finally, our national society is faced with a myriad of complex problems, such as technological unemployment on a scale never before seen. We also have an educational system which is turning out students who are not globally competitive. Welfare is in shambles, although efforts are beginning to be made to correct its weaknesses. We have an aging population which poses a number of health care and social security related problems. And, crime and drugs are major problems in most parts of the country. For virtually all of these problems and a host of others, old solutions simply

Escape

from

the Maze

have not worked. New solutions are needed. Creativity and innovation are required at the national, state and local levels in order to solve these problems.

When individual, corporate, and societal interests are examined, it becomes obvious that creativity and innovation are mandatory. The Age of Innovation is upon us. So innovate or stagnate.

SPECIAL THANKS

No book is the work of the author alone. I want to thank several people for their critical inputs into this book. First, Dean Dorman has illustrated and designed this book in a masterful way. As you can see from his art work, he is a very creative individual. His patience in my seemingly endless, last-minute changes is greatly appreciated. Keri Caffrey continues the excellent work she has done for us with her very clever front cover. Susan Novotny managed the project from word processing through final printing in a most professional manner. Susan Crabill word processed much of the original manuscript, often on a very tight schedule. Steven Garnett and Louise Hanson, *Escape's* copy editors, did an outstanding job of making this book accurate and grammatically correct. Several hundred Roy E. Crummer Graduate School of Business MBA students and Crummer Management Program students provided important feedback about the various questionnaires, as did employee groups from several companies. My business reviewers provided excellent input. I especially want to thank those who so graciously allowed me to use their comments on the back cover— Malcolm Hughes, CEO, Proudfoot, PLC; Stan Starr, Art Director Walt Disney attractions; and Joyce Wycoff, Executive Director, Innovation Network.

The Roy E. Crummer Graduate School of Business at Rollins College, is a special place in the universe. Innovation has been a driving force there for many years, commencing with the deanship of Martin Schatz, and continuing through the deanships of Sam Certo, Alan Nagle, and Ed Moses. Working in an environment with faculty members similarly inclined toward innovation is a prerequisite to a work such as this book. Many of my colleagues have produced creative and innovative products, services, and processes of their own.

Preface

Part of the research for this book was funded by a faculty research grant from the Crummer School. I want to thank the Dean, Ed Moses, for his continued support of my work.

I want to thank Philip Crosby Associates, Inc. for their alliance with my firm, James M. Higgins & Associates, Inc., thereby enabling my works to become part of the corporate cultures of a large number of client organizations. I especially want to thank Beeler Gauz, President of the Quality College of Philip Crosby Associates, Inc., for the confidence he has shown in my works and philosophies.

Our golden retriever, Macmillan, spent as many hours by my PC as I did in front of it. He helped me keep a sense of perspective about life. He demanded that I take two or three breaks a day to throw his frisbee for him. It was just what I needed.

And finally, my wonderful wife, Susan, has always believed in the innovation trilogy and has provided constant encouragement throughout its writing and publication. It has been her enthusiasm that has kept me going when it seemed like I might never finish this six year project.

Escape

from
the Maze

ABOUT THE AUTHOR

Dr. Higgins is an author, consultant, professor, and entrepreneur. He is the author of the Innovation Trilogy—three trade books on creativity and innovation; and the author of 6 college texts on strategy, management, and human relations. His first trade book, *101 Creative Problem Solving Techniques: The Handbook of New Ideas for Business*, was published in 1994. The second book of the trilogy, *Innovate or Evaporate: Test and Improve Your Organization's IQ—Its Innovation Quotient*, was published in 1995; and the third book, *Escape From the Maze: 9 Steps to Personal Creativity* was published in August of 1996. He is the author of over 30 articles and 40 cases.

Dr. Higgins is an experienced consultant, working with people and firms since 1985, to increase levels of creativity and innovation as well as to solve particular problems. Dr. Higgins has consulted with organizations since 1973, on strategic planning and has given development seminars in behavioral areas such as motivation, leadership, communication, and stress management since that time. His clients have included several divisions of Walt Disney Companies; SunTrust Bank; The Kirchman Corporation; Olsten-Kimberley Quality Care; Cincinnati Bell Information Systems; Skopbank of Helsinki; Philip Crosby Associates, Inc.; and Akerman, Senterfitt, & Eidson (a major law firm). Dr. Higgins is president of James M. Higgins & Associates, Inc., consultants specializing in strategic management and innovation management. He is also an expert consultant on innovation for Philip Crosby Associates, Inc.

Dr. Higgins is Professor of Management at the Roy E. Crummer Graduate School of Business at Rollins College in Winter Park, Florida.

To Macmillan, Brandy and Mookie–
friends present and past.

TABLE OF CONTENTS

CHAPTER 1

Ideas are the currency of success. They separate you from your competition.
Dr. Edward de Bono,
noted author and
consultant on creativity

Boom, flash; boom, flash; boom, flash.[1] Within the brain biochemical-electrical thought energy is moving from one neuron to hundreds, maybe even thousands, of others. This energy seems chaotic, but it actually moves in meaningful ways. This energy exists in both sides of the brain, and often travels from one side of the brain to the other, across the connecting tissue of the corpus callosum. When neurons connect with others they have not connected with before, associations are made and ideas are born. Creativity and insight often result.

Managing your brain—managing those boom, flashes in order to increase your creativity—is primarily what this book is about. This book is also about fun. And, it's about escaping from the maze. So let's manage those boom, flashes; have some fun; and escape from the maze at the same time. In the following maze, start at point X and try to find your way out. Go ahead, try to find your way out, let us see how good you are at this game.

*Boom,
Flash*

Chapter 1

1

THE MAZE

Escape

*from
the Maze*

Shame on you if you drew straight lines through the maze. This book is about escape. It is about thinking in new ways. This book is not about following old ways of thinking; it is about breaking through thinking barriers and gaining thinking freedom.

Based on past experience, I know that about 95 percent of you drew the lines through the maze in the traditional mouse manner. This book will help you awaken and strengthen a new and important skill, escape thinking. For the 5 percent of you who jet-packed out, jumped out, flew out, dynamited your way through the maze's walls, tunneled out, helicoptered out, pogo sticked out, climbed out, or pole vaulted your way to freedom, congratulations. You have captured the spirit of what this book is all about. You will find that what you read here will help you grow stronger in a skill you already have begun to possess. *So escape, don't just do what you've always done.*

THE MAZE AND WHAT IT REPRESENTS

It is easy to see that escaping from a traditional maze puzzle could be done in more creative ways. But that maze, of course, just represents the maze of problems that you face every day, at work, at home, at play. This book teaches you creative ways of solving that maze of problems. At a deeper level, the maze represents always using rational analytical thought to the detriment of new ideas, not thinking outside the box, always following the rules, never trying anything new, never taking risks, just doing the same old thing over, and over, and over again.

How important is the skill of escaping? Consider this— Japan is a nation literally trapped in the maze. The Japanese thinking style causes them to be not particularily innovative when it comes to creating new products, thus they are less competitive in many industries than they would like to be.

Boom, Flash

Chapter 1

3

HOW TRAPPED IN THE MAZE ARE YOU?

Before you begin to really learn about creativity, it is useful to assess how creative you might be. In this way you will discover just how trapped in the maze you might be before your answers are influenced by what you read in this book. We can assess creativity in two main ways: Personality testing specifically for creativity,[2] and inventorying and evaluating your actual creations. We will do both in this chapter.

Three Surveys on Creativity Potential

On the next few pages are three surveys. The first survey will give you some insight into your level of potential creativity. It examines for personality factors related specifically to the characteristics of highly-creative people. A second survey for related characteristics follows. The third

Escape

from

the Maze

4

survey examines other factors apparently inherent in creativity. Now please complete the brief survey "How Creative Are You?" in the Where Are Your Now 1.1 feature which follows.

WHERE ARE YOU NOW? 1.1
How Creative Are You?

How creative are you? The following test helps you determine if you have the personality traits, attitudes, values, motivations and interests that usually characterize the creative person. It is based on several years' study of attributes possessed by men and women in a variety of fields and occupations who think and act creatively.

For each statement write in the appropriate letter:
A = Agree; B = In-Between or Don't Know; C = Disagree
Be as frank as possible. Try not to second-guess how a creative person might respond.

___ 1. I always work with a great deal of certainty that I am following the correct procedure for solving a particular problem.

___ 2. It would be a waste of time for me to ask questions if I had no hope of obtaining answers.

___ 3. I concentrate harder on whatever interests me than do most people.

___ 4. I feel that a logical step-by-step method is best for solving problems.

___ 5. In groups I occasionally voice opinions that seem to turn some people off.

___ 6. I spend a great deal of time thinking about what others think of me.

___ 7. It is more important for me to do what I believe to be right than to try to win the approval of others.

___ 8. People who seem uncertain about things lose my respect.

___ 9. More than other people, I need to have things interesting and exciting.

___ 10. I know how to keep my inner impulses in check.

___ 11. I am able to stick with difficult problems over extended periods of time.

Boom,
Flash

Chapter 1

5

___ 12. On occasion I get overly enthusiastic.
___ 13. I often get my best ideas when doing nothing in particular.
___ 14. I rely on intuitive hunches and the feeling of "rightness" or "wrongness" when moving toward the solution of a problem.
___ 15. When problem solving, I work faster when analyzing the problem and slower when synthesizing the information I have gathered.
___ 16. I sometimes get a kick out of breaking the rules and doing things I am not supposed to do.
___ 17. I like hobbies that involve collecting things.
___ 18. Daydreaming has provided the impetus for many of my more important projects.
___ 19. I like people who are objective and rational.
___ 20. If I had to choose from two occupations other than the one I now have, I would rather be a physician than an explorer.
___ 21. I can get along more easily with people if they belong to about the same social and business class as myself.
___ 22. I have a high degree of aesthetic sensitivity.
___ 23. I am driven to achieve high status and power in life.
___ 24. I like people who are most sure of their conclusions.
___ 25. Inspiration has nothing to do with the successful solution of problems.
___ 26. When I am in an argument, my greatest pleasure would be for the person who disagrees with me to become a friend, even at the price of sacrificing my point of view.
___ 27. I am much more interested in coming up with new ideas than trying to sell them to others.
___ 28. I would enjoy spending an entire day alone, just "chewing the mental cud."
___ 29. I tend to avoid situations in which I might feel inferior.
___ 30. In evaluating information, the source is more important to me than the content.
___ 31. I resent things being uncertain and unpredictable.
___ 32. I like people who follow the rule, "Business before pleasure."
___ 33. Self-respect is much more important than the respect of others.
___ 34. I feel that people who strive for perfection are unwise.

Escape

from
the Maze

6

__ 35. I prefer to work with others in a team effort rather than solo.

__ 36. I like work in which I must influence others.

__ 37. Many problems that I encounter in life cannot be resolved in terms of right or wrong solutions.

__ 38. It is important for me to have a place for everything and everything in its place.

__ 39. Writers who use strange and unusual words merely want to show off.

__ 40. Below is a list of terms that describe people. Choose 10 words that best characterize you.

___energetic	___factual
___courageous	___persuasive
___open-minded	___efficient
___observant	___tactful
___helpful	___fashionable
___inhibited	___perceptive
___self-confident	___enthusiastic
___quick	___persevering
___innovative	___original
___good-natured	___thorough
___poised	___acquisitive
___cautious	___habit-bound
___impulsive	___alert
___practical	___realistic
___determined	___curious
___resourceful	___independent
___egotistical	___stern
___modest	___absent-minded
___organized	
___involved	___flexible
___unemotional	___formal
___predictable	___sociable
___clear-thinking	___dynamic
___understanding	___dedicated
___informal	___restless
___well-liked	___forward-looking
___self-demanding	___retiring
___polished	

How do you rate? See next page.

Boom,
Flash

Chapter 1

To compute your score, circle and add up the values assigned to each item. The values are as follows:

	A Agree	B In-Between or Don't Know	C Disagree
1.	0	1	2
2.	0	1	2
3.	4	1	0
4.	-2	0	3
5.	2	1	0
6.	-1	0	3
7.	3	0	-1
8.	0	1	2
9.	3	0	-1
10.	1	0	3
11.	4	1	0
12.	3	0	-1
13.	2	1	0
14.	4	0	-2
15.	-1	0	2
16.	2	1	0
17.	0	1	2
18.	3	0	-1
19.	0	1	2
20.	0	1	2
21.	0	1	2
22.	3	0	-1
23.	0	1	2
24.	-1	0	2
25.	0	1	3
26.	-1	0	2
27.	2	1	0
28.	2	0	-1
29.	0	1	2
30.	-2	0	3
31.	0	1	2
32.	0	1	2
33.	3	0	-1
34.	-1	0	2
35.	0	1	2
36.	1	2	3
37.	2	1	0
38.	0	1	2
39.	-1	0	2

40. The following have values of 2:

energetic	dynamic
perceptive	dedicated

resourceful	flexible
innovative	courageous
original	observant
curious	self-demanding
enthusiastic	independent
persevering	involved

The following have values of 1:

determined	self-confident
informal	forward-looking
thorough	restless
alert	open-minded

The rest have values of 0.

Now compare your scores to the following guidelines:

95-116	Exceptionally Creative
65-94	Very Creative
40-64	Above Average
20-39	Average
10-19	Below Average
Below 10	Noncreative

Source: Eugene Raudsepp, "How Creative Are You?" *Nation's Business* (June 1985), pp. 25–26. Reprinted by permission, *Nation's Business*, June 1985. Copyright ©1985, U.S. Chamber of Commerce.

Eugene Raudsepp, the creator of the above survey, is a well-known consultant who has examined various studies of creative people to arrive at this excellent questionnaire.

However, I always think its's best to examine more than one set of characteristics if possible. Therefore, Where Are You Now? 1.2 contains a second questionnaire examining creative

characteristics developed by me from material written by David H. Lyman, founder and director of the Maine Photographic Workshops. The Workshops was founded in 1973 as a center for creative imagemakers and story tellers. Each year more than 2,600 photographers, writers, film makers, actors, and producers attend more than 200 one-week workshops and Master Classes at TheWorkshops in Rockport, Maine. The founder, David H. Lyman welcomes each new class with a

Boom, Flash

Chapter 1

9

lecture on creativity each Monday morning. The lectures help explain the process by which artists and other creative people grow, mature and master their craft and articulate the messages that pass through them. Giving them permission to be creative, to be different is his first order of business.

Rate yourself on a scale of one to ten to see to what degree you possess these characteristics.

WHERE ARE YOU NOW? 1.2
How Creative Are you?

Creative People:	Extent to which you possess this characteristic:
	Low High
Are different and don't mind being different	1 2 3 4 5 6 7 8 9 10
Are playful	1 2 3 4 5 6 7 8 9 10
Do not play by the rules	1 2 3 4 5 6 7 8 9 10
Are adventurous	1 2 3 4 5 6 7 8 9 10
Have trouble being accurate, punctual, and proper	1 2 3 4 5 6 7 8 9 10
Are funny	1 2 3 4 5 6 7 8 9 10
Are spontaneous	1 2 3 4 5 6 7 8 9 10
Are independent	1 2 3 4 5 6 7 8 9 10
Are sensitive to art and beauty in more than art and beauty	1 2 3 4 5 6 7 8 9 10
Are enthusiastic, idealistic and responsive	1 2 3 4 5 6 7 8 9 10
Are bold	1 2 3 4 5 6 7 8 9 10
See things where others do not	1 2 3 4 5 6 7 8 9 10
Take action	1 2 3 4 5 6 7 8 9 10

Push beyond, around or through the wall	1 2 3 4 5 6 7 8 9 10
Are driven, they are passionate	1 2 3 4 5 6 7 8 9 10
Are not content with the obvious, the mundane, the mediocre, the cliche	1 2 3 4 5 6 7 8 9 10
Know when to let go and how to do it	1 2 3 4 5 6 7 8 9 10
Are patient	1 2 3 4 5 6 7 8 9 10
Have faith in their vision, craft and the creative process	1 2 3 4 5 6 7 8 9 10
Have courage and willpower	1 2 3 4 5 6 7 8 9 10
Possess concentration and an ability to focus their energy on a single goal	1 2 3 4 5 6 7 8 9 10

Source: Created by the author from text material in David H. Lyman, "Being Creative," *Training & Development Journal* (April 1989), pp. 45-47. Reprinted by permission of American Society for Training & Development. All rights reserved.

Now add your scores for all 21 questions. A score of 158 or higher suggests a high potential for creativity. From 116–157 shows above average potential. From 54–115 shows average potential. A score below 54 suggests a low potential.

Some other factors also affect creativity. Where Are You Now? 1.3 examines these. Please complete this set of questions now.

WHERE ARE YOU NOW? 1.3
You and the Characteristics of Creative People

Boom, Flash

Intelligence and Creativity—Do you have enough intelligence to be creative? (An IQ of 100, 120 in the sciences, is sufficient.)
Experience and Creativity—Do you have enough knowledge and experience (a data base) to be creative in your field?
Fantasy and Creativity—Do you have a rich fantasy life?

Chapter 1

Encouragement and Creativity —Did someone in your life encourage you early-on to be creative?
Creativity and Exercise —Do you get a sufficient amount of heart-lung exercise to help stimulate the brain? (Twenty minutes, four times a week.)
Creativity and Your Environment —Do you have a stimulating work environment? Home environment?
Creativity and Food —Do you eat the proper diet for the creative personality? (See Exhibit 1 in Appendix 1.)
Creativity and Drugs —Do you use alcohol in a moderate way or not at all? (All other drugs are viewed as negative as far as creativity is concerned.)
Motivation— Are you a self-starter, are you motivated by the work itself?

Source: This list of questions is derived from the material in Appendix 1.

The questions asked here help identify the potentially creative person. They ask about factors that have been shown to increase creativity potential. The more of these you can answer positively, the more likely you are to be creative.

> *Work should be fun–the ultimate oxymoron.*
> —Lindsay Collier, author and creativity consultant

The three surveys you just completed suggest whether or not you might be creative. They are not in themselves conclusive, but rather just indications of potential. They indicate to what degree you match the characteristics that we know most creative people tend to have.

The Truest Test of Your Creativity

Another way of finding out about your level of creativity is to look at your track record. When was the last time you came up with a creative product—the result of a creative effort, whether it was a product, a service, some process, or an idea?

1. This morning. _____
2. Yesterday. _____
3. Last week. _____
4. Last month. _____
5. Last year. _____
6. Before that, never._____

Escape

from the Maze

What was this creative product (product, service, process or idea)?

To be truly creative it must be original and have value. Does your creative product satisfy these requirements?

Now list the ten major creative products (products, services, processes, ideas) of your life to this point in time. Also please indicate why you think each was creative. They don't have to be job related. They can be related to homelife, hobbies, and so on.

ITEM	WHY
1.	
2.	
3.	
4.	
5.	
6.	
7.	
8.	
9.	
10.	

Think about your creativity for a second. Do you come up with more ideas than you realize, or fewer than you ever thought possible?

Your Creativity and These Surveys

The first two surveys tell us whether or not you have managed to maintain a creative personality despite efforts by schools and work organizations to cause you to unlearn how

Boom, Flash

Chapter 1

13

to be creative. As you will explore further in Chapter 2, we are all born with an innate capacity for creativity, but organizations pound it out of most of us. In Chapter 2, you will learn ways to unlearn what you have been taught about how *not* to be creative.

With respect to the truest test—how much you have created—*it too is biased by what you have been allowed to do creatively.* Performance levels for most readers should rise as you complete this book and apply what you learn.

Schools and employers can help you develop your creativity. They can establish certain practices that help the creative create as described in Escape Routes 1.1.

ESCAPE ROUTES 1.1

Nabisco's "Skunk" Works

At Nabisco, each operating company has its own product development staff. While product developers spend most of their time on approved projects, they also want them to work outside the box.

When developers wear a shirt with a skunk on it, it means they're spending the day in the blue sky. No one can bother them on their "skunk" days.

Once a year, Product Development stages "skunkworks," a science fair for adults. Most of the creations don't pan out. Still, a couple of the most successful new SnackWell's cookies came directly out of Skunkworks.

Source: Ray Verdon, "Innovation May Be Wonderful, But Naught Without User Demand," *Brandweek* (December 12, 1994), p. 17.

Escape

from
the Maze

ESCAPE THINKING

The secret to becoming more creative is **escape thinking**—a perspective on problem solving that requires you to fully use your creative capacity by focusing on improving and using your intuition. Despite all of the books which offer <u>the</u> way to be creative, *becoming more creative does not result from any single action, but rather nine of them.* Escape thinking is a synthesis of several major streams of thought on increasing creativity. The nine actions involve both the conscious and subconscious parts of your mind as shown in Figure 1.1.

You'll always do what you've always done if you always think the way you've always thought.
—Larry Wilson, president, Pecos River Learning Center

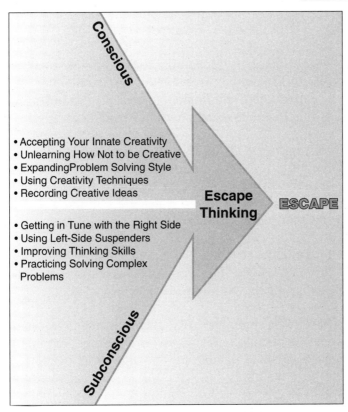

Figure 1.1 The Nine Steps to Escape

Boom, Flash

THE NINE STEPS

1. Accepting your innate creativity—realizing you are creative; consciously using your imagination, subconscious, and intuition.

2. *Unlearning* how *not* to be creative—overcoming the roadblocks to creativity that schools, work organizations, people and other organizations have put in your path.

> *It is not enough to have a good mind. The main thing is to use it well.*
> —Rene Descartes

3. Expanding your problem solving style—when it comes to solving problems, people can be either information oriented, intuition oriented, or possess some combination. The best style is to use both information and intuition to solve problems. Most people predominantly use one style or the other. So expand your style.

4. Using creativity techniques—using some or all of the over 100 creative problem-solving techniques such as brainstorming, mindmapping, and storyboarding which will help you unleash your intuition and creativity.

5. Getting more in tune with the right brain—learning to use your right brain more effectively in creative problem solving. This includes engaging in **brain aerobics**—exercises for increasing right-brain thinking skills, and for improving left-brain, right-brain integration.

6. Learning to suspend your left side—taking advantage of those occasions when your left brain falls asleep, such as when jogging, putting your right side in charge.

7. Improving thinking skills—learning new ways of thinking, for example, using lateral thinking—digging more holes, instead of digging the same hole deeper.[3] This means searching for solutions in unusual places rather than following the same old problem solving path.

Escape

from the Maze

8. Practicing solving complex problems—the more complex problems you solve, the more likely you are to develop

your intuition. The more you practice thinking and being creative, the more likely you will become more creative.

9. Recording the ideas of your creative self—keeping a notebook, note cards, dictaphone or personal digital assistant handy at all times to record ideas you have.

Using the Nine Steps

The nine steps do not have to be accomplished exactly in order, but if steps 1, 2, and 3 are not achieved before the others, then the other steps may not be as effective as they might otherwise have been. You can, of course, perform any of steps 4 through 9 without first accomplishing steps 1, 2, and 3. Using creativity techniques (step 4) without unlearning how not to be creative, accepting your innate creativity, or expanding your problem solving style causes little damage, and step 9 can be used at any time.

If you do not expect the unexpected, you will not find it.
—Heraclitus, Greek philosopher, 535-475 BC

ASSESSING YOUR CURRENT LEVELS OF PERFORMANCE

Now that you understand, at an introductory level, the nine actions you must take to increase your intuition in order to increase your creativity, rate yourself on the wheel in Where Are You Now 1.4 as to how well you currently do each of these nine actions.

Boom, Flash

Chapter 1

Think back to the nine steps. Now rate yourself as to how well you do each. A score of 1 means not very well (NVW) and 10 would be very well (VW). Darken all the blocks from the circle's edge up to and including the one that is your score. This gives you a quick visual reference of your standing in all nine areas. When you have completed this book, I'll ask you to do this exercise again.

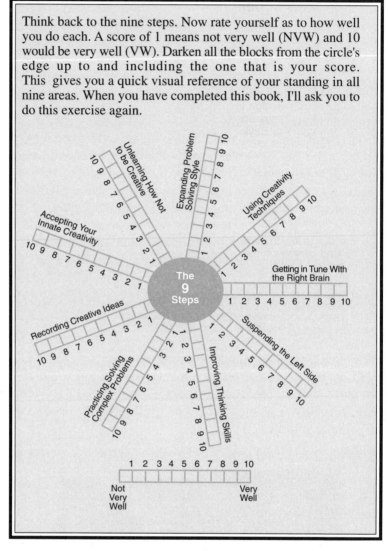

The purpose of these actions is to increase your intuition—your ability to have those "Ah ha" experiences, and to take advantage of intuition when it occurs. This chapter's Great Escapes 1.1 describes one such experience that you will readily identify with if you have ever flown a paper airplane.

Escape

from
the Maze

Innovate or die.

—Michael Sinyard, inventor of the mountain bike, president of Specialized Inc.

YOUR ESCAPE ROUTE

This book is aimed at helping you raise your levels of **creativity**—the skill of creating something new that has value. To be creative, you must escape from the maze. Throughout this book, you will find four principal devices aimed at helping you escape from the maze:

1. Questionnaires to help you find out where you are on your journey to escape.
2. Information which tells you where you ought to be and describes how to get there.
3. Exercises to help you get started toward where you ought to go, some within the chapter and some at the end of most chapters called Brain Aerobics.

Boom, Flash

Chapter 1

4. Lots of examples, both personal and corporate to help you identify more personally with the material in the text. In particular, three boxed features will occur throughout— Great Escapes, Escape Routes, and Trapped in the Maze.

Great Escapes describe how certain individuals or companies have escaped from the maze. These case studies are normally associated with some great innovation. Great Escapes 9.2 discusses how Thomas A. Edison managed his sleep periods to invent the light bulb. Escape Routes describe various means used by individuals and companies to try to help themselves or employees escape from the maze. Escape Routes 6.2 discusses why and how Siemens is trying to help employees unleash their creativity. Finally, the Trapped in the Maze feature describes problems individuals and organizations face in escaping from the maze. Trapped in the Maze 2.1 describes how a little boy lost his creativity at school.

> *Just as energy is the basis of life itself, and ideas the source of innovation, so is innovation the vital spark of all man-made change, improvement, and progress.*
> —Theodore Levitt, former editor, *Harvard Business Review*

The first chapter of *Escape* provides background so that you will understand where you are relative to your pursuit of escape. The remaining chapters largely provide information, exercises, techniques, descriptions or activities to help you improve your escape skills.

This chapter's Escape Routes 1.2 follows. It describes what one company has done to help its employees escape.

Escape

from
the Maze

ESCAPE ROUTES 1.2

IBM Suggestion Program Goes On-Line

IBM's suggestion program is over 60 years old. Employees have never been shy about offering suggestions on improving the company and their own work. However, Thomas J. Dupre, policy manager for the IBM Ideas Department at the Workforce Solutions Division, felt that not enough suggestions were being generated, and those that were took too long to be evaluated. His suggestion—"IBM Ideas," an on-line computer system that makes it easier for employees to submit suggestions, and enables the firm to process them faster.

"To survive and thrive in an increasingly competitive world, every business must strive for continuous improvement in both quality and customer satisfaction," Dupre comments. "Such improvement is possible only if all employees actively seek better ways of doing business."

Employees receive cash awards for cost-saving ideas, ranging from $50 to $150,000 depending on the value of the suggestion. Since going on-line, employee responses have increased 25 percent despite a downsizing program which eliminated about 25 percent of IBM's work force in this division. Award costs have been reduced from 14 percent to 5 percent of savings since going on-line. The company has established a response time reduction of 50 percent, and it is well on its way having cut average response time from 51 days to 39 days since going on-line.

Source: Bob Smith, "Winning Innovations in Human Resources," *Management Review* (July 1,1994), p. 49.

> *We must never forget that in the individual is the origin of the great creative act.*
> —Chester Carlson, co-founder of Xerox

HAVE FUN, ESCAPE

Roger VonOech, noted creativity author and consultant, describes creativity as the "sex of our mental lives." He says, "Ideas, like organisms, have a life cycle, they are born, they develop, they reach maturity and they die. So we need a way to generate new ideas. Creative thinking is the means and like its biological counterpart, it is also pleasurable."[4]

Boom, Flash

Chapter 1

TO BE CREATIVE, OR NOT TO BE CREATIVE; THAT—TO PARAPHRASE SHAKESPEARE—IS THE QUESTION

Almost every facet of everyone's life is changing at warp speed. Companies are changing, technology is changing, competition for the individual and the company is increasing. The market place is going global. Jobs are changing and sometimes being lost, job locations are changing and thus friends are changing too. Marital status is changing, and the world children face today is far different from that of twenty years ago. This constant change leads to both problems and opportunities. Even tried and true approaches may not work in new situations, such as how to meet friends in a new city or how to use the Internet to help you in your business. The way to bring about the best resolutions to these changes is through innovation, which stems from creativity. Defined briefly, **innovation** is significant creativity. As such, it is the process of creating something new, or turning someone else's creation into something, that has significant value to an individual, group, organization, industry, or society. It is creativity that makes money.

Innovation is about solving problems, and improving life. It's about competition in business and in your personal life for raises and promotions. If you follow the same old paths as everyone else, then what have you gained? How have you differentiated yourself in the market place? In business the paradigm is "innovate or evaporate." In personal life, it is "innovate or be dissatisfied with your life." *So follow the nine steps and escape.*

BRAIN AEROBICS

Escape

from

the Maze

A good way to begin your escape is through using Brain Aerobics. In many ways, your brain is like your body. If you sit around all day and don't get any exercise, your body gets out of shape. You lose heart-lung conditioning, muscle tone, and agility. If you don't challenge your brain, your brain gets mentally out of shape. If your brain sits around all day "without ever working up a sweat, your mental muscles become sluggish. This lack of conditioning can lead to hardening of the attitudes, poor circulation of ideas, gain in mental flab, excessive tension, boredom, and worst of all, mental constipation."[5] Fortunately, it's never too late to get started. To help you get into mental shape, Brain Aerobics are included at the end of each chapter. These are mental exercises designed to help you improve your escape thinking.

BRAIN AEROBICS 1
Visualization—The
First Step

One of the most important skills to learn in becoming more creative is visualization. Visualization is a means to ideate. Most importantly, it is an ideation method which allows you to "see" new ideas. The ability to visualize ideas is critical to creativity. Visualization also provides a way for you to become more holistic in your perspective, another important factor in increasing creativity. Visualization helps give you access to the right (more visual and creative) side of your brain. Visualization helps you achieve your objectives because the mind and body cannot tell the difference between what is imagined, and what is real. For some, visualization is easy, for others, it is difficult. With practice, it will eventually become easy, even for those who at first experience difficulty. Research clearly shows that visualization and imaging are at the heart of the creative process.[6]

Vision seems to be a critical ingredient in many creative acts. Albert Einstein attributed much of his creative success to his ability to visualize the "effects, consequences, and possibilities which can be voluntarily reproduced and combined." James Watson, who shared the Nobel Prize for biology with Francis Crick, for their discovery of the shape of the genetic code, reported that he had a vision of the rotation of the molecules which led him to the discovery of the actual code.

Boom,
Flash

Chapter 1

Nikolas Tesla, inventor of the self-starting electric motor, was reciting a poem by Goethe at sunset, when a blinding vision of a magnetic field brought into rotation by a circle of electromagnets came to him. This vision led to both the self-starting electric motor and our current concept of alternating current.[7]

The late Maxwell Maltz, noted plastic surgeon and student of psychology, first asserted that "the mind cannot distinguish between what you imagine and reality."[8] A number of scientific studies have verified this fact and have demonstrated its centrality to the creative process.[9]

Visual imagery is part of the more encompassing mental imagery process in which all five of the senses might be employed. Imagine yourself at the ocean. What do you hear, see, smell, taste, feel? You can use visualization to increase your awareness of how your brain works; or for personal skill development, such as rehearsing an interpersonal skill such as assertiveness, or "seeing" yourself becoming more creative. Even more fundamentally, visualization of your problem, of potential solutions, of successful solving of your problem, aid the creative process tremendously. The ability to globally perceive problems, solutions and success that visualization brings is essential. Verbalization cannot accomplish the same end—"a picture is worth a thousand words," and perhaps in this context, an infinite number of words. Just visualizing, fantasizing, seems to improve your overall creative ability, presumably because you are honing a skill for later use in the creative context.

You are what you think you are. Whatever you "see" yourself being or becoming, you are or you will be. Take a check of yourself right now. Do you see yourself as successful, or a failure? Do you see yourself solving that problem, or not. You are what you think you are.

Getting Started

Escape

from
the Maze

To begin, find a pleasant, relaxing and quiet place, one preferably with a comfortable lounge chair. Later, you will be able to visualize in any situation, but when first learning how to visualize, it is best to work in this environment. For the first visualization, lean back, close your eyes, and relax. Count backwards from ten to one, and as you say each number, relax a little more deeply. As you say each number in a slow, drawn out way, you will relax. Use your eyelids as if they were movie screens. For your first visual trip, see yourself in a zoo. See all of the animals there, one by one, in detail. See their habitats. See the crowds. How do the crowds act? Note what else you see. Now quietly open your eyes.

Your second visual trip will incorporate visualization in a more active mode. Close your eyes, relax, count down again from ten to one, and then see yourself being creative. Choose a problem that you are currently pondering. Next go through the motions of the actual creative act. See the problem. Then see the idea, the product or the process that will solve that problem. See yourself and others using it. Ask yourself how you feel about your creation. Then return to a full waking state.

The third and final visualization in this chapter will show you the extent to which you can use this process in many different endeavors. It is therefore not directly related to creativity. Think of someone with whom you have recently had a confrontation, or someone with whom you have an ongoing unpleasant dialog. Close your eyes and prepare for visualization. Visualize how that interaction takes place, or took place. Think of a proper response in that situation. Now visualize saying that response and otherwise acting in the proper way. Now open your eyes. Do this visualization at least ten times, always speaking and behaving in exactly the right way. The next time this interaction occurs, you will automatically say the right words and behave in the right way because your mind and body cannot tell the difference between what is real, and what you have imagined.[10]

Boom,
Flash

Continue practicing visualization until you feel comfortable with it. Use it. Eventually, you will begin to "see" solutions to your problems.

Chapter 1

REFERENCES

1. For a description of the brain's creativity see Pierce J. Howard, *The Owner's Manual for the Brain* (Austin, Texas: Leornian Press, 1994); and David Gelman, et.al., "Mapping the Brain," *Newsweek* (April 20, 1992), pp. 66–72. This dialog suggested by Joseph Conlin, "Brainstorming: It's Not as Easy as You Think," *Successful Meetings* (September 1989), p. 30.

2. For a review of six other such tests, see Eileen Cooper, "A Critique of Six Measures for Assessing Creativity," *The Journal of Creative Behavior* (Third Quarter, 1991), pp. 194–204.

3. Edward de Bono, *Serious Creativity* (New York: Harper Business, 1992), pp. 52–53. Pages 52–56 provide a lengthy description of lateral thinking.

4. Roy Rowan, *The Intuitive Manager*, (Boston: Little, Brown & Co., 1986), p. 10.

5. Tom Wujec, *Pumping Ions: Games and Exercises to Flex Your Mind* (New York: Doubleday, 1988), p. 3.

6. For a review of related research see: E. Nicholas Maddox, William P. Anthony, Walter J. Wheatley, "Using Visualization Techniques in Human Resource Development: Tapping the Intuitive Mind of the Organization," *Proceedings: Southern Management Association* (Orlando, Florida, November 15, 1985), pp. 6–7.

7. Roger N. Shepard, "The Kaleidoscopic Brain," *Psychology Today* (June 1983), p. 67.

8. Maxwell Maltz, *Psycho-Cybernetics: The New Way to a Successful Life* (Englewood Cliffs, NJ: Prentice-Hall, 1960).

9. Nicholas Maddox, William P. Anthony, and Walter J. Wheatley, loc. cit.

10. This aspect of visualization comes from Maxwell Maltz, *Psycho-Cybernetics* (Englewood Cliffs, New Jersey: Prentice-Hall, 1960). For an updated perspective see Bobbe Sumer, with Mark Falstein, *Psycho-Cybernetics 2000* (Englewood Cliffs, New Jersey: Prentice-Hall, 1993).

Escape

from
the Maze

Wizards or Not– Steps 1 and 2

CHAPTER 2

Creativeness is a fundamental characteristic inherent in human beings at birth.
—Abraham Maslow,
noted psychologist and author

Are creative people wizards? Do they sit and whisper incantations over a crystal ball or a magic potion? Well a few might, but most do not. In fact, creative people are not much different from you and me, because the truth is, we are all creative to some degree. But, we have been made much less creative by the lessons learned about creativity taught by the organizations in our lives. Unlearning those lessons and accepting our innate creativity are the focal points of this chapter.

YOUR INNATE CREATIVITY

Research studies reveal quite clearly that we are all born with an innate ability to be creative, but that this ability diminishes as we succumb to the regimen of organizations, starting with school.

Futurist George Land provides us with a keen insight into the impact of organizations on our innate creativity. "In 1965, we developed a test for NASA to select the most creative engineers and scientists. It was a pretty good test and it was very predictive of people's success in NASA as innovators. In 1968, we decided it would be interesting to find out if creativity is a function of nature or if it is a function of nurture. (We were having the nature/nurture argument— is creativity something that some people get and some people do not? Is it something learned? Is it nature. Is it nurture?)

We gave that test to 1600 five-year-old pre-school kids that represented a good stratified random sample of the American population. What percentage of those kids do you think were predicted to have high creativity potential? 98 percent were in the very high category. We went back five years later and tested the same kids. How many do you think then fell into that category? It was about 30 percent. The last time we tested them they were 15 and there were just 12 percent in the very high category. Now, we've given that test over the years to 280,000 adults and the very high category percentage is running 2 percent. What we have concluded is that non-creative behavior is learned."[1]

> *Non-creative behavior is learned.*
> —George Land, Futurist

To summarize, children are extremely creative, but once they enter school, their creativity drops significantly. Several similar studies confirm Land's research. One showed the drop in creativity to be as much as 90 percent between ages 5 and 7.[2] Why? Because in school, children are socialized to no longer be creative but rather to do it "the right way." Children are literally taught how not to be creative. Trapped in the Maze 2.1 poignantly describes just how this occurs.

Escape

from
the Maze

TRAPPED IN THE MAZE 2.1

The Little Boy
by Helen E. Buckley

Once a little boy went to school.
He was quite a little boy.
And it was quite a big school.
But when the little boy
Found that he could go to his room
By walking right in from the door outside,
He was happy.
And the school did not seem
Quite so *big* any more.

One morning,
When the little boy had been in school a while,
The teacher said:
"Today we are going to make a picture."
"Good!" thought the little boy.
He *liked* to make pictures.
He could make all kinds:
Lions and tigers,
Chickens and cows,
 trains and boats—
And he took out his box of crayons
And began to draw.

But the teacher said: "Wait!
It is not time to begin!"
And she waited until everyone looked ready.

"Now," said the teacher,
"We are going to make flowers."
"Good!" thought the little boy.
He *liked* to make flowers,
And he began to make beautiful ones
With his pink and orange and blue crayons.

But the teacher said: "Wait!
And I will show you how."
And she drew a flower on the blackboard.
It was red, with a green stem.
"There," said the teacher,
"Now you may begin."

The little boy looked at the teacher's.
Then he looked at his own flower.
He liked his flower better than the teacher's.
But he did not say this.
He just turned his paper over
And made a flower like the teacher's.
It was red, with a green stem.
On another day, when the litlc boy had opened
The door from the outside all by himself,
The teacher said:

Wizards or
Not–
Steps 1 and 2

Chapter 2

29

"Today we are going to make something with clay."
"Good!" thought the little boy.
He *liked* clay.
He could make all kinds of things with clay.
Snakes and snowmen.
Elephants and mice,
cars and trucks—
And he began to pull and pinch
His ball of clay.

But the teacher said:
"Wait! It is not time to begin!"
And she waited until everyone looked ready.

"Now," said the teacher,
"We are going to make a dish."
Good!" thought the boy,
He *liked* to make dishes,
And he began to make some
That were all shapes and sizes.

But the teacher said, "Wait!
And I will show you how."
And she showed everyone how to make
One deep dish.
"There," said the teacher,
"Now you may begin."

The little boy looked at the teacher's dish.
Then he looked at his own.
He *liked* his dishes better than the teacher's.
But he did not say this.
He just rolled his clay into a big ball again
And made a dish like the teacher's.
It was a deep dish.

And pretty soon
The little boy learned to wait,
And to watch
And to make things just like the teacher.
And pretty soon
He didn't make things of his own anymore.

Then it happened
That the little boy and his family
Moved to another house,
In another city,
And the little boy
Had to go to another school.

This school was even bigger
Than this other one,
And there was no door from the outside
Into his room.
He had to go up some big steps,
And walk down a long hall
To get to his room.

Escape

from
the Maze

30

And the very first day
He was there
The teacher said:
"Today we are going to make a picture."
"Good!" thought the little boy,
And he waited for the teacher
To tell him what to do.
But the teacher didn't say anything.
She just walked around the room.
When she came to the little boy
She said, "Don't you want to make a picture?"
"What are we going to make?"
"I don't know until you make it," said the teacher
"*How* shall I make it?" asked the little boy.
"Why, any way you like," said the teacher.
"Any color?" asked the little boy.
"Any color," said the teacher.
"If everyone made the same picture,
And used the same colors,
How would I know who made what,
And which was which?"
"I don't know," said the little boy.
And he began to make pink and orange and blue flowers.

He liked his new school...
Even if it didn't have a door
Right in from the outside!

Source: "The Little Boy" by Helen E. Buckley first appeared in *School Arts Magazine* in October 1961. Reprinted in *Young Children*, November 1989. Copyrighted 1961 by Helen E. Buckley. Used with permission.

And what little creativity remains in us after school is pounded out of us by the work organizations we enter. Work organizations typically reinforce ways of not being creative through rules, policies, procedures, and norms—such as "We don't do it that way around here," or "Nice idea, but it will never work." Some companies, however, are beginning to understand that creativity can lead to improved problem solving. Most importantly, it leads to innovation, and thus to competitive advantage—which ultimately depends on innovation for new or enhanced products, services, or processes.[3] So these organizations are beginning to change their cultures to encourage creativity and innovation. For instance, creativity training programs are becoming more common, and some firms have taken really bold steps to encourage creativity. Escape Routes 2.1 describes how Fluor Corporation puts childlike creativity back into the workplace.

Wizards or Not– Steps 1 and 2

Chapter 2

ESCAPE ROUTES 2.1

Fluor Corporation Puts Childlike Creativity Back Into Problem Solving

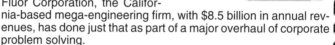

Ann McGee-Cooper, a Dallas-based creativity consultant, often advises her clients to use children as part of the creative problem-solving process. This helps the firm take advantage of the innate creativity of children, and therefore their spontaneity and lack of inhibition when it comes to throwing out ideas. Fluor Corporation, the California-based mega-engineering firm, with $8.5 billion in annual revenues, has done just that as part of a major overhaul of corporate problem solving.

Much of the firm's efforts have been aimed at changing corporate culture to more openness and creative collaboration, a difficult task in a firm ruled by technical precision and rigid rules and procedures. "We've always had brilliant engineers," says Marilyn Coil, a Fluor executive, "but now they're learning to apply themselves in new, creative ways."

In one training seminar, McGee-Cooper brought in a group of bright children from a local school to problem solve with managers. A competing group had only managers. At the end of the day the mixed group of executives and children had far more good new ideas than the group that only had executives. One of the key ideas that came from the mixed group and that was later used in the company's engineering division was a Vision Room—a sort of war room with "master schedules, team goals and engineering models for dozens of projects."

Overall, Fluor's innovation program has proven quite successful. Projects are being finished faster and cheaper, and customer satisfaction ratings are up. And, employees say they are having a lot more fun.

Source: "Companies Bring Creativity in Vogue," *Orange County Register*, as reprinted in *The Orlando Sentinel* (May 7, 1995), p. D1.

In the search for new materials, you must keep trying new—even crazy things.
— Sungho Jin, supervisor at the Materials Science & Engineering Division, Bell Labs

---

Managers set the tone for the organization's culture with phrases like,"It's against company rules," or "We've never done it that way before," or "Not around here you don't," or with phrases like "Let's give it a try," "Why not?" or "Wow, what a good idea." Escape Routes 2.2 examines how a change in management style can lead to a change in organizational culture, and ultimately to a change in organizational creativity, innovation, and profits.

Escape

from
the Maze

32

ESCAPE ROUTES 2.2

Eisner Shows Disney the Way Out

When Michael Eisner became CEO of Walt Disney Companies in 1984, the firm was trapped in a maze of rules and regulations. For a supposedly creative company, it wasn't getting many ideas from its employees. Furthermore, most of its top managers in recent years hadn't asked for any new ideas from its employees, and most of those that were offered were squelched. Some pundits claimed that the company hadn't had any new ideas since Walt (Disney) died in 1966, 18 years earlier.

One of the primary reasons that Eisner had been hired was that he was an idea person—he had lots of ideas, and he was good at getting them from his people. One of the first things he did was to let employees know that he wanted them to think, to be creative, to take the initiative. Typical of the employee reaction was that of Stan Starr. You probably wouldn't recognize Stan if you saw him—he's not a celebrity—but you would recognize his handiwork. He is one of Disney's art directors who use their imagination to create the Disney magic. One of his individual works that you would recognize is the Mickey Mouse hot air balloon which flys all over the world. Stan has worked on many other major projects, such as the castle-in-the-sky balloon and national television advertising.

Who the hell wants to hear actors talk?
—Harry M. Warner, president of Warner Brothers Pictures, 1927

Many of Stan's ideas, including the Mickey balloon, had been thwarted under the previous administration, but under Eisner, Stan's ideas were allowed to blossom, the Mickey hot air balloon became reality. "It was like night and day," Stan recounts. "Once Eisner came on board, ideas were back in fashion. I have had numerous opportunities to use my creativity since then. I get paid to be creative, so it was nice that someone finally let me." Stan Starr's experience reveals how a top manager can show a firm the way out of the maze.

Source: Interview with Stan Starr, Art Director, Walt Disney Attractions.

But you can not wait for a Michael Eisner to become CEO of your company. And even if one did, you still have to accept your innate creativity in order for such a CEO to be fully effective.

Wizards or Not– Steps 1 and 2

Chapter 2

ACCEPTING YOUR INNATE CREATIVITY—
THE FIRST STEP TO ESCAPE

The first step to escape, the first step to increasing your creativity, is to recognize that *you are innately creative and that the main reason you have not demonstrated your creativity more than you have is that you have been taught not to.*

Until you take that step, none of the other steps you take will be as effective as they could have been. One study of executives in a major oil company found that the only major difference between creative executives and those who were not, was that the creative executives thought they were, the non-creative executives did not.[4] Think you are creative —and you will be, because you already are. Let it out. *Escape by accepting your innate creativity.*

Two actions which can help you once again believe in your creativity are affirmation and visualization.

Affirming Your Creativity

Affirmations are positive statements about your abilities, for example, saying to yourself "I am creative." One of the women who had attended one of my seminars on creativity wrote "I am a very creative woman," in bold letters on a piece of paper and put it on her mirror. Every morning when she would be getting ready to go to work, she would see that statement and read it to herself over and over. She later reported that she had been extremely creative in her job, coming up with several new processes which greatly improved patient care in the clinic which she managed. She admits that some of the ideas she had were not all that good, but enough were to earn her a nice raise in salary.

Visualizing Being Creative

In this use of visualization, you see yourself being creative. You need not necessarily envision the actual process of creativity but you can merely envision yourself as being creative at some particular project or at no project in particular but rather feeling the feelings and emotions of being creative.

Escape

from
the Maze

34

See yourself over and over having created something, something you are working on now or some new problem.

You may be creative without believing in your creative abilities, but it is unlikely. Why, because you probably will not even try to be creative if you do not believe in your abilities. *So escape—affirm and visualize.*

UNLEARNING HOW NOT TO BE CREATIVE— THE SECOND STEP TO ESCAPE

A major hindrance to the process of acceptance of your innate creativity consists of all of the **blocks to creativity** that organizations, other people, and you, yourself, have put in your path. These blocks have conditioned you to not be creative. By unlearning how not to be creative, you can be creative like a child again. To do so, you have to go back to when there were not any blocks, to a time and attitude when it was okay to be creative. If you will unlearn these blocks, you will be well on you way to escape. These blocks are described in Exhibit 2.1.

Exhibit 2.1

> ### The Five Fundamental Types of Blocks to Creativity
>
> James L. Adams, who for years has taught a course in creativity to engineering students at Stanford University and has consulted with businesses on increasing creativity, has identified five fundamental **types of blocks to creativity:** perceptual, emotional, cultural, environmental, and intellectual.[5] Professor, author, and consultant on creativity, J. Daniel Couger, building on Adams' work, and the works of Min Basadur, Eugene Raudsepp, Doris J. Shallcross, and Morris I. Stein, describes these five blocks as discussed in the following paragraphs (except for the discussion of environmental blocks which follows my own materials).[6] (For a fun and funny, but less extensive examination of blocks than found in the above works, read Roger von Oech's, *Whack on the Side of the Head*.)[7]

Wizards or Not–
Steps 1 and 2

Chapter 2

Perceptual blocks "are obstacles that prevent the problem-solver from clearly perceiving either the problem itself or the information needed to solve the problem."[8] Typical examples include accepting as facts information that is really unsubstantiated assumption, recognizing that you have a problem without identifying the true underlying causal problem, coming to the problem with a set notion of what the problem really is about despite information you might encounter to the contrary, focusing on only a small part of the problem or too much of the problem, focusing on solutions rather than defining the problem, assuming that you can apply what works in one discipline to another when in a particular case it does not apply, information overload, and failure to use all of your senses.

Emotional blocks are those that "interfere with the freedom with which we explore and manipulate ideas, with our ability to conceptualize fluently and flexibly—and prevent us from communicating ideas to others in a manner which will gain them acceptance."[9] Doris J. Shallcross labels these as psychological barriers.[10] These are very common and often serious blocks. They include: the fear of failure, of making a mistake, and of risk-taking; the inability to tolerate ambiguity, having no appetite for chaos; being too quick to judge; the inability to relax, incubate ideas, or sleep on it; distrust; inflexibility; and negative attitudes towards new ideas.

Cultural blocks are those acquired when we are exposed to a set of cultural patterns. They are the do's and don'ts of a culture. They include taboos, the belief that fantasizing and reflecting are wastes of time, beliefs that logic and reason are inherently good while intuition and qualitative judgments are inherently bad, the belief that any problem can be solved by scientific thinking and enough money, too much conformity, the belief that it is not good to be too inquisitive, the desire for the safety of the known, stereotyping, and the belief that problem solving is serious business and that humor and having fun are to be avoided.

Environmental blocks are those imposed by our immediate physical and social environments. From a business perspective, the organization's culture is the primary consideration. As I have described in, *Innovate or Evaporate: Test and Improve Your Organization's IQ—Its Innovation Quotient*, the organization's culture is the difference between creativity and innovation.[11] If you have creativity and put it in the right organizational culture, then an organization will be innovative. The absence of either

Escape

from
the Maze

creativity or the right culture precludes innovation from taking place. There are at least eight areas of concern: organizational—strategy, structure, management systems, leadership style, staff, resources, shared values and organizational skills. Each of these helps define the culture. Although I have identified forty-nine characteristics of innovative organizations, among the more critical issues to a blockage of creativity and innovation are: the absence of objectives for creativity and innovation, both organizationally and individually; a rigid, mechanistic, authoritarian structure; no or few rewards for being creative or innovative; autocratic managers who value only their own ideas; an absence of training; no or little organizational support for creativity and innovation; no successes to build on.

Intellectual blocks result from an inappropriate choice of mental approaches or an unwillingness to use new solution approaches. Because of this, our ability to generate alternatives is limited. These roadblocks include using only techniques which worked before; over reliance on logical, left-brain thinking; reluctance to use intuitive techniques; and the inability to abandon the unworkable approach.

The remainder of this chapter discusses five very common roadblocks. At the end of the chapter several more are listed and you are asked to take actions to turn them around. You can identify many such blocks for yourself, and take actions on these as well.

If in the last few years, you haven't acquired a new idea, check your pulse, you may be dead.
—Gillette Burgess

Follow the Rules (A Cultural Block)

Everywhere you go there are rules—most well-intended, most effective, but many ineffective. Sometimes you just have to break the rules. It is not that you want to break the rules just to break the rules. It is just that sometimes you have to break the rules in order to make something positive happen. Columbus broke the rules. People told him the earth was flat. He said he didn't think so. People told him that he needed to stay near the shore, or his ship would fall off the edge. He said he didn't think so. The Wright brothers broke the rules too. The scientific rules of the day showed clearly that heavier than air flight was impossible. Most people

Wizards or Not–
Steps 1 and 2

Chapter 2

37

believed them and followed them. That's why if you were Lord Kelvin, you could never be a Wright brother. (See margin quote.) Steven Jobs and Stephen Wozniak, founders of Apple Computer, also broke the rules. People told them there was no market for a personal computer. They thought there was. This chapter's Great Escapes 2.1 describes another man who broke the rules, just horsing around.

GREAT ESCAPES 2.1
Horsing Around With Innovation

125 participants from the Innovative Thinking Network's Annual Convergence stand spellbound, staring down into an oval arena watching Monty Roberts "break a horse," without "breaking" her. Before the event is over, many of us will shed a tear or two for all the horses bludgeoned into submission, when they could have been made into friends and willing partners with man. And some of those tears will be shed for our fellow human beings, who like horses, have been, not physically, but mentally bludgeoned into submission in our organizations. Roberts, who is an excellent storyteller, likens what happens to horses in the breaking process to what happens to people when they join an organization with an employment contract that reads, "submission for security."

Horses have more or less been brought into man's world for the same way for over 3000 years. But Monty Roberts, owner of the Flag Is Up Farms, about a forty-five minute drive north, over the mountains from Santa Barbara, has developed an innovative way of training horses that allows them to be partners rather than subjugated dumb animals. Tired of watching his father and others break a horse's spirit in order to control him, Monty intuitively perceived a better way. In watching the horses on his father's farm relate to each other, he recognized that they communicated with each other through looks, and body positioning. This "body language" was the key ingredient in determining acceptance and power within the herd. Roberts began using a horse training method—whereby a young horse would willingly accept a bridle, a saddle, and a rider, without bucking—through the use of this body language. His father refused to let Monty work the horses in this new way, so Monty had to wait until he had his own farm before he could use this innovative approach. But his day came and in the past few years he has trained several thousand horses in this manner.

Escape

from the Maze

And so it was on this evening that, as he often does, Monty demonstrated his method to the uninitiated. In just over 30 minutes, he took a two-year old filly, who had had only a lead around her neck before this night, and turned her into a professional athlete, willingly accepting her trainer-jockey's body on her back, ready to begin training for horse racing. She never once bucked. He never once hit her or struck her with a rope, nor did her eventual jockey ever kick her with spurs. Rather, he began a socialization ritual with her that is as old as horses, but this time, a man participated in that ritual. By merely turning his head and body, looking or not looking in her eyes, and gently waving a rope in her direction, she accepted him as a friend, and one she would work with willingly. At each important point he explained the whys of his actions, and predicted what he expected her to do. And of course, she always did what he predicted. At the end of 35 minutes, to a rousing ovation, she left the ring with her jockey on board. She had, as Monty puts it, "joined up."

A person who never made a mistake, never tried anything new.
—Albert Einstein

Throughout the evening, Monty philosophized that horses and people would both be better off if we all worked together. As he interacted with the horse, he drew parallels to organizational management practices. Having written a best-selling textbook on management, I can tell you that his homespun philosophy is right on the leading edge of current management practice.

Source: Author's personal experience on April 26, 1995.

Look around. What rules are there that you could break that would lead to a positive result?

Don't Mix Work and Play (A Cultural Block)

You are supposed to be serious at work. After all, this is serious business. Wrong. Work should be fun. Research studies have shown that laughter can lead to increased levels of creativity.[12] Not having fun makes work dull, and less productive.

The universe plays its way into existence.
—Margaret Wheatley

Research shows that as we grow older, the number of laughs we have per day decreases, and we already know that as we grow older, creativity goes down. Finally, as we grow older, the number of questions we ask in a day also decreases. All of these changes contribute to reduced productivity. These three changes occur in a rather dramatic fashion as Table 2.1 suggest.

Wizards or Not–
Steps 1 and 2

Chapter 2

39

Table 2.1 What Happens As We Age?

	Age of Those Studied		
	5 yrs	8 yrs	44 yrs
Percentage with Creative Potential	98%	32%	2%
Number of Laughs per Day	113 laughs	83 laughs	11 laughs
Number of Questions Asked in a Day	65 ?s	41 ?s	6 ?s

Source: Chic Thompson, speech entitled "Being The Change You Seek in The World" (Santa Barbara, California: Innovative Thinking Convergence), February 28, 1996.

> *I like nonsense. It wakes up the brain cells.*
> —Dr. Seuss

Sometimes, the use of humor and fun are themselves creative. As this chapter's Escape Routes 2.3 suggests, it is OK to have fun, and more than that, it is also productive.

ESCAPE ROUTES 2.3
The Big Squeeze

David Andrews, head of Andersen Consulting's Financial Services Division, wanted to use a two-day conference to plot the division's future. How do you get 400 consultants to plot together? David Andrews tried Plasticine, the child's clay-like toy for, in this case, adults. Each person had five minutes to mold a ball of the brown squishy stuff into a model of his or her vision of the division's future. The consultants had to keep in mind the Andersen mission statement: To be the best organization in the world at combining strategy, process, technology and people in ways that create superior performance. For one female consultant this resulted in her creating a model of an oyster with a pearl inside, signifying for her that change management was not getting enough visibility from Andersen.

At the end of the conference, Andrews had the answer he was searching for—to double the division's size in three years. The Plasticine had worked. The models, and the discussions about them which

> *Ours is the age that is proud of machines that think and suspicious of men who try to.*
> —H. Mumford Jones

Escape

from the Maze

40

Don't Make Mistakes (An Environmental Block)

In April of 1996, the regional branch manager of a major computer systems management and consulting firm delivered the following message to his assembled staff of 127 programmers, systems analysts and consultants. "This quarter's numbers do not look very good. There's going to be a downsizing. Do not make any mistakes. Those who make mistakes in the next few weeks will be let go." Six weeks later, twenty-seven mistake makers were downsized right out of the organization. Talk about negative motivation.

A mistake is an opportunity the full value of which we have yet to realize.
—Edwin Land, founder of Polaroid Corporation and inventor of the Polaroid camera

You may say that this is an extreme example, but in most organizations, this block is just as pronounced, it just is not as plainly stated. The truth is, if you want to move forward, you have to take chances. If you take chances, you will make mistakes. Yes, we want to minimize mistakes, but we do not want to preclude the opportunity for success by precluding the opportunity for failure. Babe Ruth hit 714 home runs, but he also struck out over 1300 times. The average entrepreneur fails in at least two businesses before he or she succeeds. Go take some chances, and if you make some mistakes, so be it.

The biggest block to living a creative life is the voice of blame and criticism within each of us: the voice of judgment, or VOJ for short.
—Daniel Coleman, Paul Kaufman, and Daniel Ray, *The Creative Spirit*

Be Rational—Listen to Reason (Partly Cultural, Partly Intellectual Block)

Our whole system of thought is aimed at improving rationality. You already know the story—our educational systems and organizational cultures promote rationality. Rationality is primarily based on narrowing down the choices—"Let's find the answer." "What's politically acceptable?" "Which solution will make the numbers?"–rather than on intuition

Wizards or Not–
Steps 1 and 2

Chapter 2

41

and broadening the list of alternatives— "What are the possibilities?" "What's new?" "What else can we try?" The focus of problem solving ought to include creativity, not just rationality based on getting to a solution.

Think of a recent experience in problem solving at your organization. Was it broadening or narrowing oriented? How could it have been improved with a broader number of ideas? What can you do to broaden perspectives in the future—for your organization and for yourself?

Fear (An Emotional Block)

People fear many things in life. Fear limits our creativity potential. Do you have:

Fear of not being creative.
Fear of success.
Fear of failure.
Fear of embarrassment.
Fear of upsetting your boss.
Fear of upsetting your boss's boss.
Fear of change.
Fear of being an individual.
Fear of being rejected by the group
Fear of losing your investment.

There has to be a lack of fear. The most creative ideas start coming when people just say the first thing that comes into their head.
—John Cleese, comedian and actor

Why do you have any of these fears? What other fears do you have? Why?

Put these fears to rest. In a very methodical, yet creative way, visualize each fear going away; or consistently create and state affirmations to put these fears to rest.

Remember "It won't be on your tombstone."

BREAK THROUGH MORE BLOCKS

Escape

In addition to the above blocks, identify others. *Escape by breaking through those blocks.*

from
the Maze

BRAIN AEROBICS 2

Part 1—Killing the Idea Killers

Idea killers are those phrases that destroy ideas.
Most of these phrases are roadblocks to creativity.
For example, "We don't do it that way around here,"
or "We tried that once," or "It's not in the budget," or "Don't
be foolish," or "That's not logical." In the following box on
the left side are killer phrases. On the right-hand side, write
down how to overcome each one.

50 IDEA KILLERS	NOW, TURN 'EM AROUND
Are you kidding me	
Be real	
Doesn't conform to standards	
Don't be ridiculous	
Engineering won't approve it	
Good thought, but it'll never work	
I can't sell it to top management	
I agree except...	
Impossible	
It won't stand up to the test of time	
It will set a bad precedent	
It won't work in my department	
It won't work in this industry	
It won't work, not here	
It's too far out	
It's not in the budget	
It's never been done before	
I'm not convinced	
Let's give it some more thought	
Let's form a committee to study it	
Not feasible	
Not for us, not now, not ever	
Not right now	
Not that same old song again	
Not permitted by our plans	
Our overhead is already too high	

Wizards or
Not–
Steps 1 and 2

Chapter 2

43

Production won't buy off on it	
Takes too much time and money	
That's not my job	
That's against company policy	
Too technical	
Too difficult	
Too hard to sell	
Too hard to administer	
Too much work	
Top management will never go for that	
We don't have the personnel	
We have too many new ideas now	
We don't do it like that here	
We don't have the authority	
We don't have enough facts	
We don't have enough help	
We'd lose money in the long run	
We'll be the laughing stock	
We've tried that once before	
We've got something even better	
Where'd you get such a ridiculous idea	
Why change what we have, it works	
You should have been there	
You're right, but...	

Part 2—Affirmations

Write three affirmations that will provide specific emotional support for your confidence in your creativity.

1. _____

2. _____

3. _____

Escape

from
the Maze

Now place these on some visible surface where you'll be reminded of them throughout the day, for example, on 3x5 cards taped to the refrigerator. Keep them there for a month. Believe them. Make them happen. After a month, replace them with some new ones.

Part 3—Humor and Creativity

Humor, You, and the Work Place

Work should be fun, otherwise there would not be much creativity. So, are you doing your part to make it that way? Or maybe we should ask—what are you doing to make work fun? More specifically, let us examine what you are doing to make work more fun by making it more humorous. Remember, from the chapter, that humor and creativity are highly correlated.

Think of eight to ten different sets of actions that you could take to make work more fun through humor. For example:

1. You might want to tell jokes.
2. You might want to make up a humorous cartoon that helps people think creatively. (Now, its your turn.)
3.
4.
5.
6.
7.
8.
9.
10.

Now that you have identified ten actions that you could take to bring fun into the work place, actually do these things. First identify what you can specifically do below for each of the ten items noted above.

1. For example, think of a joke you could tell at work—a nice positive one.
2. Or, draw a humorous, contributive cartoon.
3.
4.
5.
6.
7.
8.

Wizards or Not–
Steps 1 and 2

Chapter 2

9.

10.

P.S. If you had trouble identifying ten actions to bring humor to the work place, here are some more suggestions.[6]

- Quotations and quips that provoke insight, like "For every vision, there is a complete and opposite revision"
- Funny signs and slogans, such as a sign outside a bakery which reads, "Get your buns in here."
- Analogies, like "Why is organizational downsizing like liposuction?"
- Display humorous things around you, for instance, light-hearted posters.
- Go to a toy store, be a child again, see things that relate to work, and make up humorous stories or comments, such as "Playdough is the real stuff here."
- Create a humor room, for example, one with all sorts of gadgets, toys, etc., to enable people to have a little fun.

CAUTION: Having fun in the work place may be hazardous to your job tenure. Be humorous with discretion.

Escape

from
the Maze

REFERENCES

1. George Land, "Creativity of the Heart," (Santa Barbara, California: Innovative Thinking Convergence 95) April 12, 1995.

2. Emily T. Smith, "Mix Skepticism, Humor, A Rocky Childhood — And Pronto! Creativity," *Business Week* (September 30, 1986), p. 45.

3. I have described this connection in James M. Higgins, *Innovate or Evaporate: Test and Improve Your Organization's IQ—Its Innovation Quotient* (Winter Park, Florida: The New Management Publishing Company, Inc., 1995), pp. 13–15, 47–56.

4. Ibid.

5. James L. Adams, *Conceptual Blockbusting, 3 ed.* (Reading Massachusetts: Addison-Wesley, 1986).

6. J. Daniel Couger, *Creative Problem Solving and Opportunity Finding* (Danvers, Massachusetts: Boyd & Fraser, 1995), pp. 72—76; Min Basadur, *Creative Problem Solving* (Ancaster, Ontario, Canada: Center for Research in Applied Creativity, 1989), p. 2.0; Eugene Raudsepp, *How Creative Are You?* (New York: Perigee Books, 1981), pp. 100—101; Doris J. Shallcross, *Teaching Creative Behavior* (Buffalo, New York: Bearley, Ltd., 1985), pp. 56—59; Morris I. Stein, *Making the Point* (Buffalo, New York: Bearley, Ltd., 1984), pp. 13–14.

7. Roger von Oech, *Whack on the Side of the Head* (New York: Warner Books, 1983).

8. James L. Adams, op. cit., p. 13.

9. Ibid., p. 42.

10. Doris J. Shallcross, loc. cit.

11. James M. Higgins, *Innovate or Evaporate: Test and Improve Your Organization's IQ—Its Innovation Quotient* (Winter Park, Florida: New Management Publishing Company, 1995).

12. Norman Cousins, *Head First: The Biology of Hope* (New York: Dutton, 1989).

13. Lindsey Collier, *The Whack-A-Mole Theory: Creating Breakthroughs and Transformation in Organizations* (West Henrietta, NY: WHAM Books, 1994), pp. 128–132.

Wizards or Not– Steps 1 and 2

Chapter 2

Escape

from
  the Maze   48

HOW DO YOU SOLVE THE PROBLEM?—STEP 3

CHAPTER 3

Imagination is more important than knowledge.

Albert Einstein

A few years ago, I consulted with a 400 person software firm which was having difficulty with strategic planning. The firm was excellent at day to day operations. Its ability to provide a high quality product, on time, was superior; but it could not figure out where it or its industry was headed. Its leaders could not create a vision and fulfill that vision with the right kind of products. After we tested the entire management staff—40 people, including top management—for their problem-solving styles, the why of this problem became evident. Thirty-nine of the forty managers had the same rational-analytic problem-solving style. This style is past rather than future oriented, day-to-day operations rather than strategically oriented. Only one senior manager, the human resources director, had a forward-looking, potentially creative, problem-solving style.

It takes a considerable amount of time and effort to change such managers' problem-solving styles to include a stronger preference for a more strategic, creative and future-oriented

Problem, Problem, How Do You Solve The Problem? –Step 3

Chapter 3

49

perspective, but eventually through management development and change management, this transition will occur.

Your natural preferences for the way you perceive (gather) and judge (evaluate and come to conclusions about) information has a lot to do with how you solve problems; and therefore, it has a lot to do with your success. This chapter examines these preferences and their implications when you use the creative problem-solving (CPS) process, and when you relate with others as they solve problems. Ultimately these are key issues in personal and organizational success.

PREFERENCES FOR PERCEIVING AND JUDGING INFORMATION DURING THE CPS PROCESS

The reasonable man adapts himself to the world; the unreasonable man persists in trying to adapt the world to himself. Therefore, all progress depends on the unreasonable man.
—George Bernard Shaw

According to psychological type theory developed by Carl G. Jung, a Swiss psychiatrist,[1] people have a preference for how they perceive information and the way they judge that information. This theory was later reconfirmed by researchers and authors Isabel Myers and Katherine Briggs.[2] There are no good or bad preferences. They are simply preferences, like preferring to use your right hand or your left hand to write with. Preferences can be strong or weak, or somewhere in between.

Perceiving Information

According to type theory, people may **perceive information** either through sensing or through intuition. **Sensing** relies on observable facts or happenings which are obtained through one or more of the five senses. **Intuition**, as defined by Myers and Briggs, relies on the less obvious process which relies on meanings, relationships, and possibilities which have been worked out beyond the reach of the conscious mind. This is similar to the definition of intuition used in this book. Just as in type theory, intuition as used in *Escape* is a way of knowing without using the senses, but, as used in this book, intuition is also a way of making decisions not just gathering information. Chapter 4 discusses intuition as a way of making decisions in more detail.

Escape

from the Maze

From this point on until the end of this chapter, the term intuition will have the meaning as defined by Myers and Briggs. Later, I will reintroduce its use in a decision-making context.

Judging Information

Once information is perceived, regardless of whether it was perceived by sensing or intuition, it must then be judged, that is, evaluated and a decision made. People may **judge information** either through thinking or feeling (or through intuition as will be discussed at the end of the chapter). **Thinking** is impersonal decision making on the basis of logical consequences. **Feeling** is based on personal or social values which result in individual personal feelings, that is, evaluating based on the impact a decision has on people.

> *The most common source of mistakes in management decisions is emphasis on finding the right answer rather than the right questions.*
> —Peter Drucker

Type Theory and Creativity

There are two more pairs of preferences in type theory: extroversion and introversion; and judging and perceiving. Extroversion or introversion is a preference you have about where you focus your attention—extroversion, the outside world, or introversion, inside yourself. Judging or perceiving is a preference that describes your way of orienting toward the outer world—judging is organized, perceiving is flexible. Our focus in this book will be on sensor-intuitive, and thinker-feeler preferences since they are the ones involved most directly in problem solving. Persons with certain combinations of these two sets of preferences might typically be expected to be more intuitive, more creative than others. An individual who perceives data in an intuitive manner and judges it by feeling would be expected to be more creative than an individual who perceives data by sensing and judges it by thinking. Type theory does not exclude sensor-thinkers or other combinations from being creative but it does suggest a lower probability of being creative for some types than for others. Unfortunately, from the innovation perspective, many,

Problem, Problem, How Do You Solve The Problem? –Step 3

Chapter 3

if not most, top-level managers in most business organizations are sensor-thinkers. I say unfortunately, because higher-level management positions and many professional/technical jobs often require intuitive thinking for solving complex, unstructured problems. Sensor-thinkers have more difficulty with these than do intuitive-feelers. People can learn to be more intuitive-feeling or they can hire those who are.[3] *So escape and expand your problem-solving style.*

Your Preferences

What preferences do you have? Take the following test and find out. If you score 6 or more in a category, you probably have a preference for that characteristic. The higher the score, the stronger the preference—not necessarily how good you are at it.

WHERE ARE YOU NOW? 3.1

Test for Information Perceiving (Gathering) and Judging (Evaluating) Preferences

Information Perceiving (Gathering)

Which preference do you have—for intuition or sensing? Below are pairs of characteristics. Place a check in front of that characteristic in each pair which most describes you.

Sensors	Intuitives
1__ Prefer specific answers to specific questions	1__ Tend to give general answers to questions, and you don't like it when people push you for specifics.
2__ Prefer a routine to doing something new.	2__ Would rather do new things than do the same thing over and over.
3__ Prefer to concentrate on what you are doing at the moment.	3__ Find the future and its possibilities intriguing, prefer to think about where you are going rather than where you are.
4__ Would rather work with facts and figures than with ideas and theories.	4__ Prefer ideas and theories to facts and figures.

Escape

from
the Maze

52

5___ Work steadily toward a project's completion.	5___ Work in bursts of energy, with a great deal of enthusiasm, and you relax in between these bursts.
6___ Wonder about people who seem to spend too much time indulging their imagination.	6___ Enjoy fantasizing. You have a rich imagination.
7___ Would rather do something than think about it.	7___ Tend to think about several things at once; you are often accused by friends of being absentminded.
8___ Find it easier to see the individual trees than the forest.	8___ Find yourself seeking the connections and inter-relatedness behind most things; you see the forest, the overall perspective.
9___ Use your five senses.	9___ Use your sixth sense.
10___ Like precision.	10___ Don't like to take the time to be precise. You like brainstorming.

Information Judging (Evaluation)

Which preference do you have—for feeling or for thinking? Below are pairs of characteristics. Place a check in front of that characteristic in each pair which most describes you.

Thinkers	**Feelers**
1___ Are able to stay cool, calm and collected when everyone else is upset.	1___ Often have feelings which override your logical self.
2___ Like putting things into a logical order, not that concerned about harmony.	2___ Prefer harmony to order; you don't like conflict, and will either try to avoid it or smother it.
3___ Believe that the important thing is to be right.	3___ Believe that the important thing is to take people's feelings into account.
4___ Tend to step on people's feelings when making a decision (you may not even know it).	4___ Almost always consider people's feelings when making a decision.
5___ May seem hard-hearted to others (you may not even know it).	5___ Are usually sympathetic to others.

Problem, Problem, How Do You Solve The Problem?
–Step 3

Chapter 3

53

6__ Are able to take negative personnel actions, such as disciplining or firing, without a great deal of personal discomfort.	6__ Find it difficult to discipline or terminate people.
7__ Are impersonal when you make decisions.	7__ Often let your needs and the needs of others influence your decisions.
8__ Enjoy proving a point, even if it might hurt someone's feelings.	8__ Won't hesitate taking back something you've said if you believe it hurt someone's feelings.
9__ Are more firm-minded than gentle-hearted.	9__ Will overextend yourself meeting other people's needs.
10__ Pride yourself on your objectivity.	10__ Put yourself in somebody else's shoes.

Sources: These questions were created from descriptions of these characteristics contained in Otto Kroeger with Janet M. Thriesen, *Type Talk at Work: How the Personality Types Determine Your Success on the Job* (New York: Delacorte Press–Bantam Doubleday Dell Publishing Group, Inc., 1992), pp. 19–22; Robert Benfari with Jean Knox, *Understanding Your Management Style* (New York: Lexington Books–Macmillan, Inc., 1991), pp. 155–159; Isabel Briggs Myers, "Introduction to Type, 5th ed," (Palo Alto: Consulting Psychologists Press, Inc., 1993), pp. 4–5. For another, more comprehensive set of questions that also cover the other type preferences see David Keirsey and Marilyn Bates, *Please Understand Me* (Del Mar, California: Prometheus Nemesis, 1978), pp. 5–13.

How many intuitive statements did you check? _____ How many sensing? _____ How many feeling statements? _____ How many thinking? _____

If you checked seven or more of any of these statements, you show a relatively clear preference for that type.

Now place yourself on Figure 3.1 using the numbers you have just calculated. The axis across the top indicates the degree to which you have a preference for sensing or intuition. The vertical axis to the left indicates the degree to which you have a preference for thinking or feeling. Each axis is divided in the middle, and represents a score of 5,5. If you have a higher preference for intuition (7) than for sensing (3), you would

Escape

from
the Maze

place yourself at point 7 on the row of numbers under the word intuition. You would be to the right of the center axis. Conversely, if you had a score of 7 on sensing, you would place yourself to the left of the center axis. Find the number 7 in the row of numbers underneath the word sensing. Now look at your Thinking/Feeling scores. You follow the same procedure placing yourself in either the upper or lower half of the center axis depending on whether or not you had a relatively high degree of feeling or thinking. For example, if you have a score of 7 thinking and 3 feeling, you would place yourself at point 7 on the column of numbers beneath the word thinking. You would be in the upper half of the figure. Or if you had a feeling score of 7, you would place yourself at point 7 on the column of numbers beneath the word feeling. You would be on the lower half of the figure.

Now, intersect the two points to see in which of the four quadrants—problem solving styles—you find yourself, either ST, NT, SF, or NF. Let's suppose you were a 3, 7 on the sensor-intuitive axis, and a 7, 3 on the thinker-feeler axis, then you would be located in the NT style quadrant.

Problem, Problem, How Do You Solve The Problem? –Step 3

Chapter 3

T h i n k i n g	F e e l i n g		Sensing										
			10	9	8	7	6	5	4	3	2	1	0
			Intuition										
			0	1	2	3	4	5	6	7	8	9	10

		T F 10, 0	S N 10, 0	Sensing	S 5	N 5	Intuition	S N 0, 10
10	0	**T h i n k i n g** T 5 F 5		**ST**			**NT**	
9	1							
8	2							
7	3							
6	4							
5	5							
4	6	**F e e l i n g**		**SF**			**NF**	
3	7							
2	8							
1	9							
0	10	T 0 F 10						

Note: N represents Intuition

Figure 3.1 Your Information Gathering and Processing Preferences

DESCRIPTIONS OF THESE FOUR STYLES

Read the following descriptions to see if indeed they seem to characterize you.

Sensor—Thinkers

ST individuals rely primarily on sensing for perceiving and thinking for judging information. STs are focused on the realities of a situation. They like facts—facts that can be verified by the senses. They concentrate on specifics and details. Reality for them is what can be observed, collected, and analyzed by the senses. STs prefer making choices by thinking, by logical analysis. They like step-by-step procedures. They like to proceed logically. They like rules and regulations. The perfect organization for them is hierarchical with everyone's roles well defined. STs tend to be impersonal and matter-of-fact, rather than personal. They tend to be authoritarian rather than democratic. They send information downward, but do not care much for upward or lateral communication.

They are oriented toward the practical. They find their niche in technical skills that deal with objects and facts. Thus, STs often end up in banking, business, production, construction, administration, law enforcement, or applied sciences.

> *In every work of genius, we recognize our own rejected thoughts.*
> —Ralph Waldo Emerson

Sensor—Feelers

SF individuals rely primarily on sensing for perceiving, but they prefer feeling for the purposes of judgment. SFs are also focused on the realities of a situation, and they concentrate on details and specifics. Because they make their decisions using feelings, not rational-analytical behavior, they are much more interested in how decisions impact others and themselves than is the ST. Because they have highly refined sensory input capabilities, they become easily attuned to the feelings and reactions of others. They approach their decisions with personal warmth. They are more interested in facts about people than facts about things. They are usually sociable and friendly. While the ST designs the organization to be a well run, mission accomplishing machine, the SF wants to design the organization for the benefit of its members and others. They communicate in all directions. They tend to be democratic rather than authoritarian. SFs are sympathetic and friendly. They end up in careers that are practical but

Problem, Problem, How Do You Solve The Problem? –Step 3

Chapter 3

helpful such as sales, teaching, health care, office work, supervision, community service, religious service.

Intuitive—Feelers

NF individuals make their decisions like SFs—with their feelings. They are personable and warm, but since they prefer intuition as a way of gathering information, rather than sensing, their interests are on possibilities, not facts. They are attracted to the future, to what might happen, to new projects, to new truths that are not yet known, especially as these deal with people. They are interested in broad, global perspectives, not in specifics. They are concerned with the long-term future of the organization. They are insightful and enthusiastic. They like decentralized, fluid organizations, without fixed roles, rules and regulations. NFs tend to gravitate to work that requires creativity, understanding and communicating with people, and that deals with the future such as teaching, research, literature, health care, art and music, religious service, or behavioral science. They are often inspired by a new idea derived by the subconscious.

> *You have to be with the work, and the work has to be with you. It absorbs you totally, and you absorb it totally.*
> —Louise Nevelson, sculptress

Intuitive—Thinkers

NT individuals are also interested in possibilities, but because they prefer thinking, they are interested in these as interpreted through rational, impersonal analysis requiring the application of objectives and logical criteria, as opposed to feelings. They often subordinate the human element. They often end up in ill-defined work situations. They like to focus on general concepts and ideas. They are less interested in efficiency than in theory. They like organizations to focus on achievement of broad goals. They are not excited by the details of a job, nor by the bureaucratic organization with highly defined rules and regulations. NTs are logical and analytical. They often end up in jobs where they can use their skills at analysis, but one that is theoretical or technical in nature such as law, research, computers, management, engineering, technical work, or physical science.[4]

Escape

from
the Maze

IMPROVE YOUR CREATIVE PROBLEM SOLVING THROUGH YOUR KNOWLEDGE OF YOUR PREFERENCES

To improve your CPS ability, you first need to identify your preferences, which you did earlier in this chapter, and secondly, you need to systematically work to more fully utilize all four preference options. Start with your perception processes. Using both alternatives means gathering information through both senses and intuition. Then, when you evaluate information, use both thinking and feeling. (And in the broader context of the word intuition, as we use it elsewhere in this book, use intuition to make decisions.) As shown in Figure 3.2, you would first gather data through the senses, add information that you intuitively perceived, and then evaluate (make decisions) analytically and intuitively. Finally, evaluate by using your feelings about how the decision impacts you and others. When you have completed this type of problem-solving process, your solution will be improved because you will have considered realities, human values, possibilities, consequences, and subconscious solutions.[5] If you do not use all of the preferences, you become trapped in the maze, as the following feature on Michael Dell points out. (Up to this point, we've used the Trapped in the Maze feature to focus on people who do not use their intuition enough. Here we focus on someone who used it too much without enough rational thinking.)

> *Thinking is the hardest work of all, which is probably why so few engage in it.*
> —Henry Ford

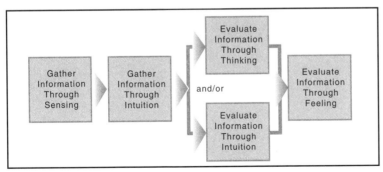

Figure 3.2 Using All Four Preferences, Plus Decision-Making Intuition to Solve Problems

Problem, Problem, How Do You Solve The Problem? –Step 3

Chapter 3

59

TRAPPED IN THE MAZE 3.1

Michael Dell Learns to be More of a Sensor-Thinker

Michael Dell, founder and CEO of the Dell Computer Corporation, had always been an intuitive decision maker. After all, the 1984 decision to sell computers by phone had been intuitive, and so had most of the other major decisions that had grown the firm into the fourth largest PC manufacturer in the United States by the end of 1992, with $2 billion in sales. Then, some of those hunches failed miserably, most notably investments in currency hedging and derivatives. And the problems did not stop there. A decision to release a laptop based on the comparatively slow Intel 386 chip had to be abandoned, with the firm taking a $40 million write-off. Many top managers departed, partly because Dell did not delegate enough.

So Dell is learning to manage, to become more of a sensor-thinker, combining these preferences with his intuition. Eric Harslem, Dell's senior vice president for product development, who had been with Dell Computer Corporation for 19 months when he commented that, "It's a different company, and Michael's changed too." Instead of using a seat-of-the-pants approach, as it did when Harslem first came to the firm, Dell Computer Corporation now makes decisions analytically. Michael Dell now delegates many decisions, and he has added planning and budgeting systems to the firm's approach to management. He has also surrounded himself with older, more experienced managers. Dell comments, "I like to be part of a company and part of a team. I'm very content to hire and delegate." The firm is no longer just growth, growth, and more growth oriented, but it also now has its eye on the bottom line.

Sources: Scott McCartney, "Michael Dell—and His Company—Grow Up," *Wall Street Journal* (January 31, 1995), pp. B1, B4; Dan McGraw, "The Kid Bytes Back," *U.S. News & World Report* (December 12, 1994), pp. 70–71.

Use Your Sensing To:

- face the facts.
- find out what the situation is exactly.
- find out what others have done—what has worked, or not worked.
- do not let wishful thinking or sentiment blind you to the realities.

Escape

from
the Maze

- ask yourself how the situation would look to an impartial observer.

Use Your Intuition (As Defined in Type Theory) To:

- brainstorm all of the possibilities—all the ways in which you might change the situation, your handling of it, or other people's attitudes toward it.
- put aside your natural assumption that you have been doing the one and only obviously right thing.
- ask how this problem relates to something else.
- fantasize the best possible action.

Use Your Thinking To:

- conduct an impersonal analysis of cause and effect.
- make decisions, solve problems[6].
- examine all the consequences of the alternative solutions, both pleasant and unpleasant.
- count the full cost of everything.
- examine every misgiving you may have been suppressing out of loyalty to someone or liking for something, or reluctance to change your stand.

Use Your Decision Making Intuition To:

- have an "Ah ha" experience.
- allow your subconscious to work for you.
- derive solutions from patterns of information without using rational thought.
- make decisions, solve problems.

Use Your Feeling To:

- weigh just how deeply you care about the things that will be gained or lost by each of the alternatives.
- make a fresh appraisal, trying not to let the temporary outweigh the permanent, however agreeable or disagreeable the immediate prospect may be.

Problem, Problem, How Do You Solve The Problem?
–Step 3

Chapter 3

61

- consider how the other people concerned will feel about the various outcomes, even if you think they are being unreasonable.
- include feelings, your own and others, as facts that must be respected[7].

In order to understand the differences between information gathering and decision making intuition, consider the following.

One of the greatest escapes of all time, financially speaking, was that made by Ray Kroc when he purchased McDonald's from the McDonald brothers in 1960, apparently working from an intuitive hunch. Note how this was an intuitive judgement process.

GREAT ESCAPES 3.1

A Funny Feeling

Ray Kroc owned the exclusive rights to the multimixer, a machine that could make six milkshakes at once. In 1952, Maurice and Richard McDonald ordered eight of them. Kroc wanted to know what kind of a restaurant could use that many. So he flew to San Bernardino, California, to see for himself. "When I got there," said Kroc, "I saw more people waiting in line than I had ever seen at any drive-in. I said to myself, 'These guys have got something.'"

Kroc talked the brothers into letting him franchise their outlets nationwide. During the next five years, he organized a chain of 228 stores. But he felt he was not making enough from the deal, so he offered to buy the whole operation in 1960. The brothers quoted him a price of $2.7 million plus the original store. His lawyer advised strongly against the purchase. The price was exorbitant he claimed. Kroc stomped around his office, shouting and cursing. Then it came to him. Buy it anyway. When asked why, he said, "I had a funny feeling." And, the rest, as they say, is history.

Sources: Most of this narrative is taken from Roy Rowan, *The Intuitive Manager* (Boston, Massachusetts: Little, Brown and Company, 1986), pp. 7–8. The part about "a funny feeling" comes from Philip Goldberg, *The Intuitive Edge* (Los Angeles, California: Jeremy P. Tarcher, Inc. 1983), p. 22.

Escape

from
the Maze

ADDITIONAL INFORMATION ON PSYCHOLOGICAL TYPES

While our interest here has been with the two sets of preferences most closely related to problem solving—sensor-intuitive and thinker-feeler—you would find more clues to your CPS ability by further studying type theory. As noted previously, two additional sets of preferences—extrovert-introvert and perceptive-judgment provide additional information as to how you solve problems, and how you relate to the world and other people. Our questionnaires on your two sets of preferences were brief.

For further information on psychological type, see the references at the end of the chapter and in the source notes for the questionnaires. For the beginner on type theory, *Gifts Differing* by Isabel Briggs Myers with Peter B. Myers and *Please Understand Me* by David Keissey and Marilyn Bates are good places to start.[8]

IMPLICATIONS OF YOUR STYLE

Now that you have learned more about your preferences, you can better understand the biases that you may have in problem solving. Your dominant style can greatly affect how you attempt to solve problems. You should attempt to use all preferences in solving problems. Because our society, and our business and educational institutions dwell on it, you should be especially concerned with being overly critical and evaluative as a way of approaching problem solving. Learn to be more open to new possibilites.

Problem, Problem, How Do You Solve The Problem? –Step 3

You should also be interested in matching your preferences with those of your boss, subordinates, peers, family and friends. The key reason for this is that if you do not have the same style as these other people, then you are not speaking the same problem-solving language, are not solving problems the same way and are likely to have difficulties solving

Chapter 3

problems together unless you work out your type theory dynamics. If you are not gathering and processing information in the same ways, you would not even want the same types of information. You must learn to work together, to work with those having other styles and preferences.

If your manager is a sensor-thinker and you are an intuitive-feeler, you are likely to have serious problems working together. He or she may be looking for senses-based, logically presented information—facts and figures–which he or she can evaluate. You may be looking for intuitions which you can have feelings about. You may be giving your manager your intuitive, gut reactions to situations when what he or she really wants is something else entirely. The opposite set of situations may also occur. Working in groups and teams, makes learning these dynamics even more important.

Finally, one would most often believe that the more intuitive one is, as defined by these brief preference surveys, the more likely he would have more potential for being creative than a person who was more of a sensor-thinker. This is not necessarily true. Sensor-thinkers, and sensor-feelers can be very creative, but they must be open to being creative. Usually they are not.

If you want to increase your intuition skill levels and those of people around you, institute a network of interested parties. That is exactly what the OZ Network at DuPont is all about.

Escape

from
the Maze

ESCAPE ROUTES 3.1
The OZ Network

The OZ Network was founded in March, 1986. It was originated by seven DuPont employees. OZ refers metaphorically to the "Wizard of Oz." The Network's primary mission is to assist in creating a culture for creative thinking within the company, principally by providing awareness and education, and in other ways helping the organization be a learning organization. It seeks to challenge the status quo, and promote values that lead to innovation, such as risk taking, unconventional approaches to problem solving, and a spirit of zealous entrepreneurship.

It is formally sanctioned by the DuPont Corporation, but it is not formally funded. Employees are given time off work to attend bi-monthly OZ Network meetings which normally last about three hours. Due to its geographic location, those attending OZ Network meetings consist primarily of DuPont headquarters research and development staff. But, through the use of various media, such as video, these meetings can be attended in absentia by anyone at a DuPont facility who is interested in being a member of the network. There are some 700 members, approximately 100 to 250 of which attend these seminars depending on the applicability of the seminar to their work. Local Network groups meet periodically in between network-wide meetings.

Speakers normally make presentations for about two and a half hours of the three hour sessions. Typically, hands on, implementable subjects are the focal points of these sessions. For example, when I spoke to the group, I taught them creative problem-solving techniques such as storyboarding and excursion. Sometimes the group has more esoteric presentations, such as art, in order to stimulate thought.

Sources: Author's personal knowledge, OZ Network internal documents entitled, "OZ Background/Center History," and "OZ Network Intent."

BRAIN AEROBICS 3
Using All The Preferences

Part 1–Thinking of a Problem

Think of a reasonably complex problem that you are experiencing at work, at home, or elsewhere. Now solve that problem as you normally would. Make notes on your problem-solving effort as you proceed.

Part 2–Identifying Your Actions

Identify actions that you took as they relate to the following preferences:

1. Using your intuition to gather information.
2. Using your senses to gather information.
3. Using your thinking to make decisions.
4. Using your intuition to make decisions.
5. Using your feelings to make decisions.

Now examine to what extent these actions were consistent with your survey results from Where Are You Now 3.1.

Part 3–Resolving the Problem

Resolve the problem, making a conscientious effort to use all five preferences. Again, make notes as you proceed through this process.

Part 4–Identifying Preference Improvements

Identify improvements for each of the five preferences:

1. Intuition (for gathering information)
2. Sensing
3. Thinking
4. Intuition (as a decision tool)
5. Feeling

Part 5–Identifying Decision Improvements

Escape

from
the Maze

Identify improvements in your decision that resulted from the expanded use of your preferences.

REFERENCES

1. Isabel Briggs Myers and Mary A. McCaulley, *Manual: A Guide to the Development and Use of the Myers-Briggs Type Indicator* (Palo Alto, California: Consulting Psychologists Press, 1985), pp. 1–5.

2. Myers and McCaulley, op. cit., throughout.

3. Myers and McCaulley, op. cit., pp. 20–29.

4. These definitions were derived from Isabel Briggs Myers, as revised by Linda R. Kirby and Katherine D. Myers, *"Introduction to Type,"* 5th ed. (Palo Alto, California: Consulting Psychologists Press, 1993), pp. 4, 5, 25, 27; Sandra Krebs Hirsh and Jean M. Kummerow, "Introduction to Type in Organizations," (Palo Alto, California: Consulting Psychologists Press, 1990), pp. 16–31; Isabel Briggs Myers, "Introduction to Type," 4th ed. (Palo Alto, California: Consulting Psychologists Press, 1987), pp. 27–29; Isabel Briggs Myers with Peter B. Myers, *Gifts Differing*, (Palo Alto, California: Consulting Psychologists Press, 1980), pp. 4–6.

5. The first, second, third and fifth paragraphs which follow are quoted from Isabel Briggs Myers, op. cit., p. 30.

6. This item is added to the Myers quote to put it more into our context.

7. The materials on sensing, intuition, thinking and feeling were derived from Isabel Briggs Myers, op. cit., p. 30.

8. Isabel Briggs Myers with Peter B. Myers, *Gifts Differing,* op. cit.; David Keissey and Marilyn Bates, *Please Understand Me*, op. cit., pp.5-13.

Problem, Problem, How Do You Solve The Problem? –Step 3

Chapter 3

BRAIN BREAK 1

Whew! I don't know about you, but I'm tired after all those brain aerobics. What we need is some fun while we "cool down" from our workout. The following is a fun exercise that doesn't require too much mental effort.

a. In the below figure, without lifting your pen, pencil, or other drawing instrument, draw four straight lines that connect all nine dots. If you already know how to perform this exercise, go to part b below.

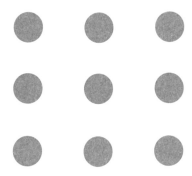

b. 1. Connect all nine dots with three straight lines.
   2. Connect all nine dots with two straight lines.
   3. Ok, this is the really tough one—connect all nine dots with only one straight line.

Escape

from
the Maze

For some (not <u>the</u>) answers to these puzzles, turn to Appendix 3.

Source: James L. Adams, *Conceptual Blockbusting* (Menlo Park, California: Addison-Wesley Publishing, 1986).

CHAPTER 4[1]

Let people develop their own ideas. Give them the freedom to do this. Push down in the organization as far as possible the notion of letting people develop their own ideas. It is important not to stifle an idea. I try not to say "no" to new ideas; rather I try to encourage new ideas. I let them run with it. Reward employees when they get a good idea.

J.Willard Marriott, Jr.,
President
Marriott Corporation

Using creative problem-solving techniques is the fastest way to generate lots of new ideas, and therefore the fastest way to dramatically improve individual and group creativity. Learning and using them offers the biggest bang for the buck. For example, Frito-Lay was able to document savings of $400 million in just six years from teaching its employees the creative problem solving methodology (CPS) and a few CPS techniques.[1]

In my book, *101 Creative Problem Solving Techniques: The Handbook of New Ideas for Business,*[2] I have provided interesting and user friendly descriptions of 101 creativity techniques that provide relatively simple yet practical ways of unleashing your innate creativity. These include well-known favorites such as brainstorming, mind mapping, and storyboarding; and not so well-known but equally effective

Using Creativity Techniques– Step 4

---

[1] Because this is a chapter of techniques, the normal features of Trapped in the Maze, Escape Routes, and Great Escapes have been eliminated.

Chapter 4

techniques such as lotus blossom, excursion, and free association. In this chapter, four of these techniques are presented so that you will have an understanding of how effective they are in raising your levels of creativity.

The first of these is basic brainstorming. I have found that many people are familiar with this technique, but that they also misuse it frequently. So reviewing it will be helpful. Then, mind mapping is discussed. It is probably the second most popular technique in the United States today behind brainstorming. Next, SCAMPER is described. It is an extremely useful technique for improving products and services. Finally, excursion is described. It is a good technique to use when other techniques have not provided many new ideas.

BRAINSTORMING

Brainstorming is one of the most effective, and probably the most widely used, of the group processes.[3] It was created over sixty years ago by Alex Osborn of the advertising firm of Batten, Barton, Durstine and Osborn to increase the quantity and quality of advertising ideas.[4] The process became known as brainstorming because the participants' brains were used to "storm" a problem. Alternative solutions are offered verbally by group members in spontaneous fashion as they think of them. The leader acknowledges each contribution, which is recorded on a board for all to see. Wild and crazy ideas are encouraged. Quantity, not quality, counts at first. In the initial session there is no discussion or criticism. The ideas are evaluated at later meetings of the same group.

The Group: The brainstorming process involves a group of six to twelve people, a leader/facilitator and a secretary, all involved in open generation of ideas about a given topic. The group needs to have at least six people in order to generate enough ideas, but fewer than thirteen because it may be

Escape

from
the Maze

difficult to absorb a large number of ideas and because larger groups tend to intimidate some people, thereby potentially restricting the flow of ideas. Groups may be formed from similar or different work areas or backgrounds, depending on the purpose of the group.

The Rules:

1. No judgments are made about any suggestion.
2. All ideas, even absurd or impractical ones, are welcome.
3. Quantity of ideas is a major objective, since it leads to quality.
4. Ideas may be combined, refined, and piggy-backed.

The Role of the Group Leader: The group leader, usually chosen prior to the session, informs the group, preferably in advance of their meeting, that a given topic will be discussed. He or she sets forth the facts, the issues, the questions involved, and the purposes of the session. These points should be restated at the beginning of the session. The leader then writes the focal question or problem on a whiteboard or other large visible surface. (Open-ended "how" or "what" questions are advisable.) Next the leader calls for solutions to the problem. Once the brainstorming session opens, the leader functions primarily as a facilitator, recognizing contributors, stimulating group members to come up with new ideas, keeping the group focused on the subject at hand, and making sure the four rules of brainstorming are followed. The most important of these rules is that no criticism is allowed. *If criticism occurs while ideas are being generated, the whole point of brainstorming has been lost.* The leader too must refrain from commenting on the value of ideas.

> *Ideas have to be combined and messed with before they work well.*
> —Roger Dow, Vice President, Sales and Marketing Services Marriott Hotels and Restaurants

Sometimes group members begin to tire and the flow of new ideas diminishes. At this time the leader should offer verbal encouragement or call on particular members to suggest solutions. Another method is to give each member thirty seconds to come up with a new idea, moving around the room in order until the time allotted for the session is gone.

Using Creativity Techniques– Step 4

Chapter 4

71

The same leader or a different one may lead the evaluation session. Ideas should be sorted into types and ranked according to priority. As additional research may be necessary, the group may have to convene more than once. In an evaluation session the leader must not allow the group to dismiss ideas simply because they are unusual, but should encourage examination of far-out suggestions, perhaps by asking for different versions or ways to adapt them. Moreover, the leader should not allow ideas to be dismissed because of a lack of funds or other resources. If an idea is a good one, ways should be found to make it happen. The leader's role includes countering unreasonable negativity during the evaluation process.

We trained everyone from top management right down to the shop floor.
—James H. O'Neal, director of Frito-Lay's creativity program

The Secretary: The secretary records each contributor's ideas on some visible surface in front of the group. In small groups the leader and the secretary may be the same person, but it is preferable to have different people performing these functions.

Observations on the Technique

Research has found that brainstorming generates a much greater number of ideas than normal group problem solving. Its features of spontaneity, suspended judgment, and absence of criticism promote an increase not only in the quantity but also in the quality of new ideas. A typical idea generation session, being very intensive, should last no more than thirty to forty minutes. Problem topics should be narrow, and no more than one topic should be covered in a session. For example, don't try to name a product and figure out a distribution system in thirty minutes.

Because the process appears simple, you may be tempted to discount this method. Don't. Thousands of organizations have used brainstorming successfully. I can personally attest to its worth, but must confess that I was a "doubting Thomas" until I used it. You cannot imagine the synergism resulting from this method unless you try it.

Escape

*from
the Maze*

72

Brainstorming can be used for a wide diversity of problems, including not only marketing and product issues but strategy, planning, policy, organization, leadership, staffing, motivation, control, and communication. However, the process is not particularly useful with broad and complex problems. Some of the ideas produced may be of low quality or obvious generalities. Brainstorming is not successful in situations that require trial and error as opposed to judgment. There are no apparent rewards for group members other than the experience of participation and ownership. Group members may not see the final solution implemented and may therefore be reluctant to participate in further sessions.[5] Nevertheless, brainstorming remains a solid technique for generating creative ideas.

Experiences with the Process

Many organizations use brainstorming to solve a wide variety of problems. For example, International Paper Company (IP) has opened a Packaging Innovation Center in Middletown, New York, to help its customers design the best possible packages for their products. The IP center brings customers together with IP's package designers, scientists, technicians and product specialists for brainstorming sessions. In the first few months of operations the Innovation Center's efforts resulted in four new, economically significant, innovative package designs:[6]

The things we fear most in organizations –fluctuations, disturbances, imbalances– are the primary source of creativity.
—Margaret J. Wheatley,
Leadership and the New Science

1. Box & box—intended to replace plastic pails and metal containers,
2. Xpack—a flat-topped liquid container with superior shipping characteristics,
3. Barrier plus—a series of linerless folding cartons with a variety of closures and designs,
4. A new craft paper that decomposes 50 percent faster than previously used papers.

Using Creativity Techniques– Step 4

Federal Express initiated its quality improvement process (QIP) in order to ensure prompt delivery of packages and

Chapter 4

otherwise improve operations. Quality action teams, established in each of its eleven divisions to identify and solve problems, used brainstorming to address these issues.[7]

A group of five faculty members and three administrators from the Crummer Graduate School of Business at Rollins College brainstormed, seeking to improve the marketing of the school's three MBA programs: professional, full-time, and executive. Over 300 ideas were generated in three forty-minute sessions (one session for each of the three programs). The results included the filming of a videotape, which was sent to prospective students; revision of promotional literature to include newly selected features; the creation of a council to work more closely with local businesses; and initiation of opportunities for students to contribute to the promotional literature and the video tape.[8]

> *Nothing, not all the armies in the world, can stop an idea whose time has come.*
> —Victor Hugo, author

Jeffrey McElnea, president of Einson Freeman, Inc., an award-winning and highly profitable New Jersey sales promotion agency, describes a modified version of the brainstorming process as a vital component of his firm's success: "For each new campaign, we flash every established [sales promotion] technique onto a screen. Then we go through each alternative and hypothetically try to fit the product to it—just to see what would happen. Then we start to combine and recombine the techniques, and there's where the unique part comes in. New techniques are created by synthesizing the old." In one of the agency's award-winning campaigns, "The Smaller the Better Sweepstakes," contestants had to walk into a store and listen to the new Sony Super Walkman to find out whether they had won a prize.[9]

Escape

from

the Maze

One Southern Bell manager uses case situations to counter the adverse impact of personalities in brainstorming problem-solving situations. She poses the problem in the form of

74

a case. As moderator, she rewards participation but not ideas, thus avoiding a reward-seeking environment.

SUMMARY OF STEPS

1. Select a group consisting of six to twelve people, a leader and a recorder.
2. The leader defines the problem for the group, preferably in advance of the brainstorming session.
3. The group suggests solutions to the problem in an interactive format, following the four rules of brainstorming:
   a. No judgments are made about any suggestion.
   b. All ideas, even absurd or impractical ones, are welcome.
   c. Quantity of ideas is a major objective, since it leads to quality.
   d. Ideas may be combined, refined, and piggybacked.
4. After twenty-five to thirty-five minutes, the group takes a break and then returns to critique the ideas.

Variations on Brainstorming

There are a number of variations on the basic brainstorming technique. Many of the techniques described in my book, *101 Creative Problem Solving Techniques: The Handbook of New Ideas for Business*, use some of the elements of brainstorming. Most Japanese creativity techniques are derived from some form of brainstorming.[10] For example, Honda engineers attribute a major breakthrough in engine design to a brainstorming exercise that resulted in a 35 percent jump in fuel efficiency in the 1992 Civic VX.[11]

MIND MAPPING

Mind mapping was originated by Tony Buzan of the Learning Methods Group in England.[12] This technique is based on research findings showing that the brain works primarily with key concepts in an interrelated and integrated manner. Whereas traditional thinking opts for columns and rows, Buzan feels that "working out" from a core idea suits the

Using Creativity Techniques– Step 4

Chapter 4

brain's thinking patterns better. The brain also needs a way to "slot in" ideas that are relevant to the core idea. To achieve these ends, Buzan developed mind mapping.

Mind mapping is an individual brainstorming process. To begin a mind mapping session, write the name or description of the object or problem in the center of a piece of paper and draw a circle around it. Then brainstorm each major facet of that object or problem, drawing lines outward from the circle like roads leaving a city. You can draw branches from those "roads" as you brainstorm them in more detail. You can brainstorm all the main lines at once and then the branches for each, or brainstorm a line and its branches, or jump from place to place as thoughts occur. To make the mind map more useful, you might draw each major branch extending from your central thought in a different color. As you branch out, you may notice related topics appearing on different branches. These relationships can be emphasized by circling the items in question, or drawing lines under or between them. Finally, study your mind map and look for interrelationships and terms appearing more than once. A sample mind map is shown in Figure 4.1. This map was drawn by a quality consultant trying to identify a client's causal problems to the issues identified in the center of the map. Next, he would do a mind map of solutions for each major branch. Joyce Wycoff's *Mindmapping*[13] provides additional and very useful business examples of how to use this technique.

> *Chance favors the prepared mind.*
> —Louis Pasteur

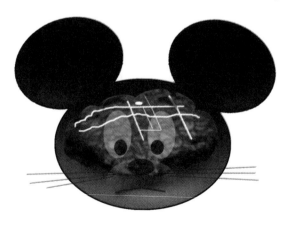

Escape

from
the Maze

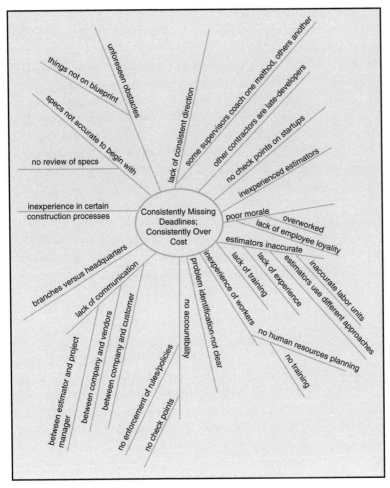

Figure 4.1 A Sample Mind Map

Mind mapping is an excellent technique not only for generating new ideas but also for developing one's intuitive capacity. It is especially useful for identifying all the issues and subissues related to a problem, as well as the solutions to a problem and their pros and cons. The latter is accomplished by making the main branches the solutions and the subbranches from each of these the pros and cons. Mind mapping also works well for outlining presentations, papers, and book chapters. In fact, mind mapping can be used in a wide variety of situations. For example, the extremely successful socio/technical forecasting firm, Inferential Focus, founded by Charles Hess and Carol Coleman, uses mind maps to spot

Using Creativity Techniques– Step 4

Chapter 4

77

trends and predict periods of change before they occur. Hess and Coleman charge a hefty fee for their futurist publications. Their clients include the White House, Chase Manhattan Bank, First Fidelity, and numerous other Fortune 500s organizations.[14]

Numerous managers are using the mind mapping concept. For example, Michael Stanley, the engineer in charge of Boeing's technical publications unit, uses mind maps extensively. He keeps a spiral notebook of mind maps covering the "basic subjects that I've got to know to do my job." He even has a 40 x 4 foot mind map on his wall that he used to show top management about a new process he had designed for developing technical publications.[15] Joelle Martin, head of the agency that created Anheuser-Busch's award-winning "Being Black in America" advertising campaign, uses the technique to help her decide how and when to terminate an employee.[16]

Once you've got the knack of letting your mind flow onto the visual chessboard (a mindmap), you can apply it to anything from business to relationships to your future,
—Jill Neimark, author

About half of the people who learn this process find it extremely useful; the other half find it uncomfortable to use. The latter seem to object to the lack of structure and find it difficult to be as spontaneous as the process requires. But for those who are comfortable with it, it can be a very useful and versatile tool. As author Jill Neimark notes, "Once you've got the knack of letting your mind flow onto this visual chessboard (a mindmap), you can apply it to anything from business to relationships to your future."[17]

SUMMARY OF STEPS

1. Write the name or description of the object or problem in the center of a piece of paper and draw a circle around it.
2. Brainstorm each major facet of that object or problem, placing your thoughts on lines drawn outward from the central thought like roads leaving a city.
3. Add branches to the lines as necessary.
4. Use additional visual techniques—for example, different colors for major lines of thought, circles around words or thoughts that appear more than once, connecting lines between similar thoughts.
5. Study the mind map to see what interrelationships exist and what solutions are suggested.

Escape

from
the Maze

SCAMPER

SCAMPER is an idea generating checklist based on action verbs which suggest changes to an existing product, service or process. This mnemonic was created by Bob Eberle from the verbal checklist orginated by Alex Osborn, a pioneer in creativity technique development.[18] Osborn also orginated brainstorming, a technique discussed earlier in this chapter.

Osborn's original verbal checklist was ordered as follows: put to other uses, adapt, modify, magnify, minify, substitute, rearrange, reverse, combine. Eberle reordered these to make them easier to remember:

S = Substitute?
C = Combine?
A = Adapt?
M = Magnify? Modify?
P = Put to other uses?
E = Eliminate or minify?
R = Rearrange? Reverse?

The idea behind this verbal checklist is that an existing product, service, or process, whether one's own or a competitor's, can be improved if one applies a series of verbs and related questions to it and pursues the answers to see where they may lead. These verbs indicate possible ways to improve an existing product or service by making changes in it. In the case of Osborn's checklist, further alternatives may be suggested by the definitions and related statements accompanying each of the main verbs. For example, if the item under consideration is a laptop PC and you are pursuing the "minify" alternative, you might shrink the laptop into a "notebook" or "palmtop" computer. Eberle kept all of Osborn's questions and added a few more.

Over the years thousands of organizations have used the verbal checklist and derivations such as SCAMPER to create or enhance thousands of products and services. I have utilized it myself in writing some of the most successful books in the

Never leave well enough alone. Others certainly won't, and that affects everybody. That is why it is more important to ask "What's new?" than "How's business?" "How's business?" is about the past. "What's new?" is about the future.
—Ted Levitt, editor, Harvard Business Review

Using Creativity Techniques– Step 4

Chapter 4

college textbook market, including *The Management Challenge,* an introductory management text.[19]   One of my editors found the checklist so useful that he distributed it to the sales force to obtain suggestions for subsequent editions.

To use SCAMPER:

1. Identify the item—the product, service, or process you want to improve.
2. Ask the SCAMPER questions about your item and see what new ideas emerge.

VERB	RELATED ACTION QUESTIONS
SUBSTITUTE?	Who else can be substituted? What else can be substituted? Can the rules be changed? Other ingredient? Other material? Other process or procedure? Other power? Other place? Other approach? What other part instead of this?
COMBINE?	What ideas can be combined? Can we combine purposes? How about an assortment? How about a blend, an alloy, an ensemble? Combine units? What other article could be merged with this? How could we package a combination? What can be combined to multiply possible uses? What materials could we combine? Combine appeals?
ADAPT?	What else is like this? What other idea does this suggest? Does the past offer a parallel? What could I copy? Whom could I emulate? What idea could I incorporate? What other process could be adapted? What else could be adapted? What different contexts can I put my concept in? What ideas outside my field can I incorporate?
MAGNIFY?	What can be magnified, made larger, or extended? What can be exaggerated? Overstated? What can be added? More time? Stronger? Higher? Longer? How about greater frequency? Extra features? What can add extra value? What can be duplicated? How could I carry it to a dramatic extreme?
MODIFY?	How can this be altered for the better? What can be modified? Is there a twist? Change meaning, color, motion, sound, odor, form, shape? Change name? Other changes? What changes can be made in the plans? In the process? In marketing? What other form could this take? What other package? Can the package be combined with the form?

Escape

from
the Maze

80

PUT TO OTHER USES?	What else can this be used for? Are there new ways to use as is? Other uses if modified? What else could be made from this? Other extensions? Other markets?
ELIMINATE OR MINIFY?	What if this were smaller? What should I omit? Should I divide it? Split it up? Separate it into different parts? Understate? Streamline? Make miniature? Condense? Compact? Subtract? Delete? Can the rules be eliminated? What's not necessary? What would a process flow chart reveal?
REARRANGE?	What other arrangement might be better? Interchange components? Other pattern? Other layout? Other sequence? Change the order? Transpose cause and effect? Change pace? Change schedule?
REVERSE?	Can I transpose positive and negative? What are the opposites? What are the negatives? Should I turn it around? Up instead of down? Down instead of up? Consider it backwards? Reverse roles? Do the unexpected?

Source: Created from text in Michael Michalko, *Thinkertoys* (Berkeley, California: Ten Speed Press, 1991), pp. 71–108.

Exhibit 4.1 is an example of SCAMPER used in a service industry—the hotel industry.[20] Consider the traditional check-out prodedure in a hotel. How can SCAMPER help us generate ideas for improving the process?

Exhibit 4.1

A SCAMPER Example

ITEM: Traditional Check-out Procedure

SUBSTITUTE — Check-out by phone, by in-house television channel, by mail; allow check-out at breakfast...

COMBINE — Combine check-out payment with check-in; offer breakfast food at check-out location; combine with services for ground transportation; combine with morning work-out at hotel exercise facility...

ADAPT — Adapt to the location of the guest; accept more credit cards; adapt to the times that guests want to check-out...

Using Creativity Techniques– Step 4

Chapter 4

MAGNIFY	Increase the number of people at the check-out desk; make a big production out of check-out so that the guest enjoys it—have trumpets and encourage employees to weep as the guest leaves; have a very large person at the check-out desk so that the guest will be afraid to complain...
PUT TO OTHER USES	While the guests are waiting to check out, interview them about their stay and how the hotel could be improved; use check-out time as an opportunity to advertise specials that the hotel will be offering in the future; ask the guests if they wouldn't mind washing some windows for you while waiting to check-out...
ELIMINATE	No check-out—the guest leaves a credit card or a large deposit with you upon arrival so that you don't have to collect money upon departure. Or, do not allow any guests to leave the hotel once they come in—this will significantly increase occupancy...
or MINIFY	Have all forms and bills prepared before the guest comes to check out so that the least amount of time is required; cut some steps out of the current process; computerize to increase speed...
REARRANGE	Rearrange the check-out area; rearrange the procedure for check-out...
REVERSE	Come to the guest's room and allow them to check-out there; have guests check out when they arrive and check in when they depart (we don't know, you figure it out)...

Source: Florence Berger and Dennis H. Ferguson, *Innovation: Creativity Techniques for Hospitality Managers* (New York: John Wiley & Sons, Inc., 1990), pp. 25–26.

SUMMARY OF STEPS

1. Identify the product or service to be modified.
2. Apply each of the verbs on the checklist to suggest changes in the product or service, writing the changes in the blank spaces on the form provided.
3. Make sure you use each of the action questions for the listed verbs in identifying possible changes.
4. Review your changes to determine which ones meet your solution criteria.

Escape

from
the Maze

EXCURSION TECHNIQUE

The excursion technique was originally introduced as part of a broader process known as synectics.[21] However, it can and should be used by itself. The excursion technique is especially useful when the group has not arrived at a solution to a problem even after using other creativity techniques. It can be used for either narrowly defined or complex problems, but it probably works best on a more narrowly defined problem for which a conceptual breakthrough is needed. It has been slightly modified here from its original description so as to make it more functional.

The Process

There are four major steps in the excursion process: the excursion itself, the drawing of analogies between the problem and the events in the excursion, the analysis of these analogies to see what creative understanding or solutions can occur, and the sharing of experiences with the group.

1. The Excursion. The leader instructs each member of the group to take an imagined excursion into or through some physical location that has nothing to do with the problem at hand. Normally the leader asks participants to close their eyes and use their imagination for this journey, which may be through a museum, a jungle, a city, or any other kind of place, real or imagined. For example, a Star Trek journey through space and to unknown planets is popular with some problem solvers.[22] The ability to let go and create visual images is critical to the success of this part of the exercise. If the leader is not confident that all members of the group have this ability, he or she might offer some brief instruction and encourage people to give them imagination free rein. Participants are asked to write down what they see during their excursion. The excursion itself need not last more than five or ten minutes, but it is important for participants to record detailed descriptions of what they see. I recommend that they draw three columns on their papers and write what they saw on their excursion in the first

Using Creativity Techniques– Step 4

Chapter 4

83

column. If they prefer, group members can record as they go rather than after the excursion is finished.

2. Drawing Analogies. When the excursion period is over, the leader asks participants to take ten to fifteen minutes to draw analogies between what they saw during the excursion and the problem as defined. Participants are not limited to analogies; they can express the relationships between their visual images and the problem in other ways if they wish. They write their analogies or other relationships in the second column opposite each of the items they saw.

3. Evaluating and Understanding. Now the leader asks the participants to determine what the relationships determined in step 2 really mean in terms of the problem, that is, how understanding these relationships can be used to solve the problem. This is the really challenging part of the process. It requires intuition, insight, and quite often, luck. Participants write their solutions in the third column.

4. Sharing Experiences. Participants are asked to share their excursions, analogies, understandings, and solutions with the group. As with brainstorming, members may piggyback on the ideas of others.

Examples of the Process

A member of a group of bank personnel officers who were experiencing conflicts with other departments described part of her excursion through a natural history museum as follows: "I saw Indians making war on another village. The analogy is obvious. We are at war with the other departments. This tells me just how serious our problem is. I never quite realized it, but, in a way, we are at war and serious measures must be taken to end this feuding before somebody gets killed." Another member of the group found her tour taking her past the section of the museum where rock formations were shown. The various layers of hard and soft rock meant essentially the same thing to her that the Indian warfare had meant to the other woman. When asked how to solve the problem, she said, "We have to take some dynamite (i.e.,

Escape

from
the Maze

84

strong measures) to blow up the hard rock layers separating the departments."

Other analogies are less obvious. One facilitator had worked with NASA personnel for some time to develop a satisfactory device for fastening a space suit. After trying several standard techniques for generating ideas, he had group members take an imaginary excursion through a jungle. One man described his experience as "being clawed at by weeds, trees, and bushes." While describing his experience, he clutched his hands together with his fingers interlaced. While he himself had not made much of his analogy, when the group discussed it they commented on the clutching of his hands. This suggested the overlapping clutching of a Velcro strip and eventually led to the utilization of a Velcro-like fastener for the spacesuit.[23]

Observations on the Technique

The excursion technique is especially useful for a problem that has proved abnormally difficult to solve or calls for really unique solutions as, for example, in developing an advertising campaign or creating product differentiation features in a mature market. The leader needs to encourage participants to let go and to share their experiences. When the process is well explained and understood and participants are properly motivated, really good ideas should emerge.

SUMMARY OF STEPS

1. The leader instructs participants to visualize an excursion into or through some physical location that has nothing to do with the problem at hand.
2. Participants draw analogies between what they saw and the problem.
3. The leader asks participants to determine what the analogies they drew in step 2 suggest in terms of solving the problem.
4. Participants share their experiences and solutions.

Using Creativity Techniques– Step 4

Chapter 4

85

CREATIVITY TECHNIQUES AND CREATIVITY

The four techniques in this chapter are but a few of the 100 plus that are available. Many techniques have very specific usages, for example, for strategic planning. Most are better used in some situations than in others. For example, brainstorming is fine for well-defined, not too complex problems, but for complex problems, storyboarding—which is designed for complex problems—is usually the best technique. Personally, I've used over sixty techniques, but rely on a core of ten to fifteen for most problems. The best action plan is try quite a few and then settle in on those that you generally find most useful. *So escape and use creativity techniques.*

> *The highest form of courage is the courage to create.*
> —Rollo May, author and psychologist

BRAIN AEROBICS 4

Using Creativity Techniques

Reading about creativity techniques is the first step in understanding their usefulness, but the best way is to actually use them. Take some problems that you have been working on and apply the four techniques described here to those problems. Under each technique, desirable problem attributes are listed. Note, while these techniques have been described as being done in groups or individually, most techniques can be done either way.

Escape

from the Maze

Part 1–Brainstorming

With brainstorming, you are looking for a well-defined problem, narrow in scope, and for which solutions can be readily generated. Now try brainstorming on one of your problems.

Question/Problem: _____
Please list below possible solutions:

1. _____	16. _____
2. _____	17. _____
3. _____	18. _____
4. _____	19. _____
5. _____	20. _____
6. _____	21. _____
7. _____	22. _____
8. _____	23. _____
9. _____	24. _____
10. _____	25. _____
11. _____	26. _____
12. _____	27. _____
13. _____	28. _____
14. _____	29. _____
15. _____	30. _____

Using
Creativity
Techniques–
Step 4

Chapter 4

Part 2–Mind Mapping

Mind mapping is useful for complex problems—for identifying issues and then creating solutions—and for narrow scope problems for which solutions can be readily created, with pros and cons of solutions appearing on branches. Now try mind mapping one of your problems.

Escape

from
the Maze

Part 3–Scamper

Some of the verbs in the checklist do not apply as readily to services as they do to products, but each of them should be considered. You may wish to add other verbs to the following list. Be sure to use the expanded definitions of these verbs as guides in changing the product or service in question. If you feel especially creative, you can make up your own checklist—for example, one designed strictly for services. Now try SCAMPER on one of your problems.

ITEM:_____

Substitute _____

Combine _____

Adapt _____

Magnify/Modify _____

Put to other uses _____

Eliminate/Minify _____

Rearrange/Reverse _____

Using
Creativity
Techniques–
Step 4

Chapter 4

Part 4–Excursion

You use excursion when other techniques haven't enabled you or your group to generate enough new ideas. It is useful for simple and complex problems. Now try Excursion on one of your problems.

What I saw on my excursion	Analogy between each thing I saw and my problem	Solution suggested by each analogy
1.	1.	1.
2.	2.	2.
3.	3.	3.
4.	4.	4.
5.	5.	5.
6.	6.	6.
7.	7.	7.
8.	8.	8.
9.	9.	9.
10.	10.	10.

Escape

from
the Maze

REFERENCES

1. Bennett Davis, "Working the Imagination," USAIR (September 1988), pp. 18–27.

2. James M. Higgins, *101 Creative Problem Solving Techniques: The Handbook of New Ideas for Business* (Winter Park, Florida: The New Management Publishing Company, Inc., 1994).

3. David J. Placek, "Creativity Survey Shows Who's Doing What; How to Get Your Team on the Road to Creativity," *Marketing News* (November 6, 1989), p. 14.

4. Alex Osborn, *Applied Imagination* (New York: Charles Scribner & Sons, 1953), pp. 297-304; also see, Robert Kerwin, "Brainstorming as a Flexible Management Tool," *Personnel Journal* (May 1983), pp. 414–418.

5. "Group Techniques: Part 2, Alternatives to Brainstorming," *Small Business Report* (October 1981), p. 15.

6. "IP Offers Creative Partnership," *Purchasing World* (August 1990), pp. 38–41.

7. "Federal Express: Employees Eliminate Problems Instead of Fighting Fires," *Business Marketing* (February 1990), pp. 40, 42.

8. The author was the leader of these sessions.

9. N.A. Howard, "Creativity: A Special Report," *Success*, p. 56.

10. This discussion of Japanese creativity techniques and of the four techniques discussed later in the chapter are taken from: Sheridan M. Tatsuno, *Created in Japan: From Imitators to World-Class Innovators,* (New York: Harper & Row, Ballenger Division, 1990), pp. 104-115; and a summary of these as discussed in Sheridan M. Tatsuno, "Creating Breakthroughs the Japanese Way," *R&D Magazine* (February, 1990), pp. 137–142.

11. Karen Lowry Miller, "55 Miles Per Gallon: How Honda Did It," *Business Week* (September 23, 1991), pp. 82–83.

12. Tony Buzan, *Use Both Sides of Your Brain,* (New York: E.P. Dutton, Inc., 1983).

13. Joyce Wycoff, *Mindmapping*, (Berkley Publishing Group: 1991).

14. Jill Neimark, "Mind Mapping," *Success* (June 1986), pp. 52–57.

Using Creativity Techniques– Step 4

Chapter 4

15. James Braham, "Creativity: Eureka!" *Machine Design* (February 6, 1992), p. 33.

16. Jill Neimark, op. cit., p. 54.

17. Ibid.

18. Robert Eberle, *SCAMPER: Games for Imagination Development* (Buffalo, New York: D.O.K. Press, 1972); Alex F. Osborn, *Applied Imagination* (New York: Charles Scribners & Sons, 1953).

19. James M. Higgins, *The Management Challenge*, 2nd ed., (New York: MacMillan, 1994).

20. Florence Berger and Dennis H. Ferguson, Innovation: *Creativity Techniques for Hospitality Managers* (New York: John Wiley & Sons, Inc., 1990), pp. 25–26.

21 Morris I. Stein, *Stimulating Creativity: Group Procedure* (New York: Academic Press, 1975), Chapter XV, pp. 172–221; William J.J. Gordon and George M. Prince, *The Operational Mechanics of Synectics* (Cambridge, Massachusetts: Synectics Incorporated, 1960), p. 2.

22 Magaly Olivero, "Get Crazy! How to Have a Break Through Idea," *Working Woman* (September 1990), p. 144.

23 As reported in Stan S. Gryskiewicz and J.T. Shields, "Issues and Observations," (Greenville, North Carolina: Center for Creative Leadership, November 1983), p. 5.

Escape

from
the Maze

**Creating, Transcending–
The Purpose of Escape–
All Steps**

CHAPTER 5

*What this power is, I cannot say. All I know is that it exists...and it becomes
available only when you are in a state of mind in which you know exactly what you
want...and are fully determined not to quit until you get it.*
                                                              —Alexander Graham Bell,
                                          describing the "conquering force within"

If you are planning on having open-heart surgery anytime
soon (a half-million are performed each year in the United
States), you are likely to benefit from the creative "hunch" of
Dr. Wesley D. Sherman and Dr. John H. Stevens, founders of
Heartport, Inc., a firm which is revolutionizing such surgery.
The days of major incisions are over. Heartport created port-
access surgery that uses four to seven tiny incisions around
the heart and in other locations, into which tubes are inserted.
These then snake their way through to key areas at and around
the heart. Novel catheters, sophisticated imaging equipment
and special instruments are then inserted into the tubes and
are used for the operation. The heartport system cuts patient
pain and recuperation time and reduces costs dramatically.
The doctors founded their firm on an insight which came to
them during a discussion.[1]

*Creating,
Transcending–
The Purpose of
Escape–
All Steps*

Chapter 5

93

The heart of creativity (no pun intended) is the creative process itself. The creative process is what provides the hunches and insights that give us services such as heartport surgery and products such as compact discs. It is why we have the automobile, the ATM, and the PC. It is why we have every product and service we have. It is what makes creativity, creativity. It is what you have used to come up with new ideas for the problems you have solved at work, at home and elsewhere.

The creative process is described in the first part of this chapter. The chapter then reviews intuition and the fundamental components of two specific types of intuition—mental and transcendent intuition. Intuition is extremely important to the creative process, both as a way of making it happen and as a way of pursuing its results. For example, intuition led to the discovery of the double helix structure of DNA—one of two chemical substances that transmit characteristics from parents to offspring. Intuition also led to the sale of video tape by the Ampex Corporation, although at the time of its invention, no market for it existed. Only the persistance of the firm's president, George L. Long, led to its eventual success.[2]

STAGES IN THE ACTUAL CREATIVE PROCESS

The actual act of creativity, regardless of which stage in the creative problem-solving process it occurs, involves four key stages: preparation, incubation, illumination, and verification.[3]

> The important thing is to never stop questioning.
> —Albert Einstein

Preparation

In preparation, the individual (or group), having recognized the existence of a problem or opportunity, first decides on an objective to be accomplished by solving the problem. Then the problem solver gathers substantive amounts of information and engages in analysis. Creative problem solvers investigate everything—they ask questions, gather data, analyze, and look for the abnormal. Then they concentrate on finding solutions.

Escape

from
the Maze

94

Incubation

Next comes a period of reflection. During incubation, the mind organizes information and insightful reasoning occurs. This stage of the process is not particularly well understood. The problem, having been thoroughly analyzed, is somehow transferred to and processed by the problem solver's subconscious mind. It is this ability to effectively utilize the subconscious that separates the creative thinker from the narrowly rational one.

Incubation is much like a smoldering fire waiting to burst into flame, waiting to achieve illumination. During incubation the problem solver may or may not be consciously working on the problem but his or her subconscious mind is. Sometimes when incubation occurs during concentration, you can almost feel the boom, flashes taking place. Incubation may take minutes, hours, days, months, or even years. Incubation occurs in many ways: while relaxing, while concentrating, while focused on something else, and while sleeping as Great Escapes 5.1 describes.

GREAT ESCAPES 5.1

Dream a Little Dream

Scientists and artists have long known that sleep is a terrific incubation period for creative problem solving. Dreams help free your ideas and solutions can sometimes appear in dreams. Robert Louis Stevenson dreamed complete stories to which he could return to night after night, if he wished to change the endings. In his best-known dream, he saw a criminal being pursued by the police. The criminal drank a potion and changed his appearance. Thus was born the story of Dr. Jekyll and Mr. Hyde.

Inventor Elias Howe worked for many years to perfect the sewing machine. One night he dreamed he was under attack by a savage tribe whose spears had holes in the tips. From this dream the problem of the interlocking stitch, which makes a sewing machine work, was solved— the eye of the sewing machine's needle should be near the tip of the needle.

Creating, Transcending– The Purpose of Escape– All Steps

Chapter 5

Dreams can also represent something we have never seen before. Niels Bohr had a dream of a sun with strings attached to the planets which revolved around it. When the sun cooled and died, everything crumbled away. After awakening, he realized that the sun and its planets were like an atom with a nucleus and electrons. This dream gave him the idea for his model of an atom on which most of atomic physics is based.

Source: Robert Wayne Johnston, "Using Dreams for Creative Problem Solving," *Personnel* (November 1987), pp. 58–59.

Sleep often provides us with a period of incubation. In one study 70 percent of the scientists surveyed reported that solutions to major problems came to them while sleeping.[4]

The next night,...the idea returned. It was the design of an experiment to determine whether or not the hypothesis I had altered 17 years ago was correct.
—Otto Loewi, 1936 Nobel Prize Laureatte in Physiology and Medicine

Illumination

This stage of the process is most commonly characterized by the proverbial light bulb shown above the thinker's head, meaning a solution has been found. Illumination is that sudden inspiration, that spark of enlightenment. It is the insightful problem solution, the idea that follows preparation and incubation. It is the idea of adding special effects to a western script used for a space movie that yields a "Star Wars." It is the realization that time is relative. Illumination is the "Ah ha" experience, the "I've got it," of life. The exact processes of illumination, sometimes referred to as inspiration or intuition, are uncertain. There is intuitive reasoning taking place but exactly how it transpires is uncertain. It is the culmination of incubation but they are not one and the same. Illumination comes without warning and it may occur at any time as Archimedes discovered. "Eureka!" literally, "I have found it," shouted Archimedes, as he ran naked through the streets. He had been sitting in a bath, when the illumination of the principle for discerning a metal's composition by the amount of water

The really valuable thing is intuition. A thought comes and I may try to express it in words afterwards.
—Albert Einstein

Escape

from the Maze

it displaces, occurred to him.[5] Great Escapes 5.2 describes a more recent illumination that has brought the illuminatee and his company significant positive results.

GREAT ESCAPES 5.2

Big Blue's Butterfly

IBM, or Big-Blue as many know it, has developed a mini-laptop that has received accolades from far and wide. The ThinkPad 701C, or the Butterfly as it is more affectionately known, has a keyboard as large as a regular PC. How is this possible while maintaining the notebook size of a regular ThinkPad?—by breaking the keyboard into two parts and collapsing these parts into regular notebook size when not in use.

IBM inventor, John Karides, had been contemplating this seemingly unsolvable problem for months. Consumers wanted a long, rectangular keyboard that would fit into the notebook computer. One day Karides was daydreaming about his three-year-old daughter and how she would create various shapes from her toy blocks. Suddenly it hit him—the keyboard could be broken into two parts, and moved around for collapsing purposes. He ran down the hall, pressed the keypad from his own regular ThinkPad against the copier glass, and made a hundred duplicates. He then sat down on the floor of his office and began to cut and paste a working paper-prototype. By dinner he had one to show his wife.

In April 1993, Karides first showed a working model of his keyboard to Bruce Claflin, general manager of the PC division. After seeing it work twice, Claflin made a decision within a minute to run with the new product. He pulled many key people off other projects, but within two years (a good product development cycle for such products) IBM was selling the Butterfly, too fast in fact, to keep up with demand.

Source: Leslie Kaufman-Rosen, "Big Blue's Butterfly," *Newsweek* (March 20, 1995), p. 46.

Verification

It is one thing to say that "It's an idea whose time has come," it is another for that statement to be true. Following illumination, verification of the idea, or problem solution must occur. The problem-solver must deductively test the validity of his or her ideas. In verification, she is first validating that the act of creativity has resulted in an outcome that really exists, that something works, that something original has been conceived. Second, she is validating that it possesses some utility value either to the person who creates it, or more importantly, to others. What is new is clearly original—you know it's new. It may be a combination of knowns, or something entirely different. It may be an application of something known to a new situation. What has value is something else again.

> *This term (intuition) does not denote something contrary to reason, but something outside the province of reason.*
> —Carl G. Jung, psychologist, researcher, and author

ABOUT INTUITION

Intuition is a way of knowing without using rational thought.[6] It is a way of explaining what goes on during incubation that leads to illumination. Intuition is one of the two main ways of achieving illumination. Rational analytical thinking is the other. Intuition does not depend on the normal five senses—touch, taste, feeling, sight, and smell—or depends on them only in that they have brought experiences for you to call upon subconsciously. Intuition is a sixth sense that everyone possesses in varying degrees.[7]

> *The rational approach to management misses a lot.*
> —Thomas J. Peters and Robert H. Waterman, Jr.

There are at least four levels of intuition: physical, interpersonal, mental, and transcendent. As show in Figure 5.1, you move across a continuum from well understood to less well understood as to how intuition works as you move from physical to transcendent intuition. The first two types of intuition, physical and interpersonal, involve well understood sensory input interpreted (often subliminally) relative to past experiences. Mental intuition involves interpretation and problem solving of current complex situations based on subconscious recognition of similarities to past situations. Transcendent intuition, in which factors such as extrasensory perception or mind reading occur, is related to never before experienced situations. How these occur is not well understood. They involve mysterious processes. We know that something is happening. We have thousands of anecdotal pieces of evidence to indicate that such events do occur.[8] And there is limited scientific research which also supports extrasensory intuition.[9]

Escape

from

the Maze

98

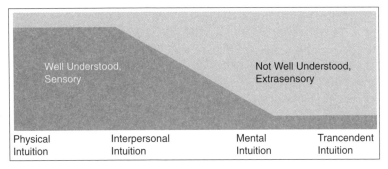

Figure 5.1 Types of Intuition

Because there are four types of intuition, you need to know which kind of intuition people are talking about when they say they used their intuition to solve a problem[10]. In more detail, these four types are[11]:

1. **Physical intuition** is a matter of paying attention to your body's signals—for example, the hair that stands up on the back of your neck when you think a prowler is in your house; or the stomach ache that comes every time you have to do that certain report, teach that safety class, or engage in some other stressful event. This is mostly a sensory recognition ability. But it is not simply recognizing incoming sensory information and its consequences, it is a matter of putting together several pieces of information and interpreting their meaning together, often in a way that uses some extra-sensory skill.

2. **Interpersonal intuition** is that which comes into consciousness through feelings. It is the ability to understand body language and other non-verbal cues. When you are sensitive to other peoples' "vibes" or "vibrations of energy," you are using interpersonal intuition. When you take an immediate dislike to someone, or you feel "love at first sight," you are experiencing interpersonal intuition. This type of intuition is stronger in women, on average, than in men.

Creating, Transcending– The Purpose of Escape– All Steps

3. **Mental intuition** is the ability to understand patterns in the current situation, to find similar patterns in previous situations, and to use related solutions from similar

Chapter 5

past problem-solving endeavors to solve current problems. When CEOs and other top managers say they use intuition to solve complex business problems, most are talking about using mental intuition.[12]

4. **Transcendent intuition** is mostly extrasensory in nature. It does not depend on sensory inputs. Transcendent intuition is knowing something without consciously thinking about it. This knowledge just comes to you. You "know" that one way of organizing the project is better than the others. You "know" that this advertising campaign will work when others don't think so. Transcendent intuition caused Dr. Edwin L. Land to market his invention, the Polaroid camera, despite the fact that extensive market research revealed there was no market for it. He knew, intuitively, that there was a market for it. Notice that both gathering information and deciding upon information can occur through mental and transcendent intuition.

Intuition and Creativity

A growing body of research indicates quite clearly that the creative/intuitive manager is a superior manager.[14] Being both rational/analytical and intuitive is critical to being a successful problem solver. Neither alone is sufficient to produce the "best" solutions or decisions. The intuitive manager can make the great leaps and bounds the singularly rational manager cannot. The latter can only continue in incremental steps along the same path. On the other hand, the singly intuitive manager may not be able to function well in the world of practicality and getting things done through people. Both skills are necessary.

Since it is going to require a series of leaps and bounds to stay competitive in the future, managers, most of whom are rational-analytics, must learn how to use their intuition.

Escape

from

the Maze

Our primary concern in this book is increasing your mental and transcendent intuition levels. Physical intuition is readily understood and interpersonal intuition is the subject of several books and articles.[15]

MENTAL INTUITION AND CREATIVITY

Mental intuition has been shown to be increased primarily through experiences requiring its use.[16] These experiences do not have to be real, they can be simulations of actual experiences. Thus computer simulations, experiential exercises, and the case method of teaching (using lengthy descriptions of organizational situations which require problem solving) are important contributors to raising the level of mental intuition.[17] This experience base can of course be obtained through actual experience. Mental intuition has been shown to be more prominent among superior CEOs, as evaluated by their peers and subordinates, than among less effective CEOs.[18] This book will help you improve your mental intuition by showing you ways to strengthen it. How important is mental intuition? As Trapped in the Maze 5.1 suggests, very!

> *Intuition is the vapor of past experiences.*
> —Joyce Hall, Founder of Hallmark

TRAPPED IN THE MAZE 5.1

Polaroid Begins Its Escape

Polaroid has been stuck in a rut and trapped in the maze. Not much new has been forthcoming from the firm, and those new products it has had have taken too long to develop and cost too much. Mac Booth, Polaroid's CEO, recently declared that speed of product development and cost had to improve. As part of that initiative, he wanted the firm to find a way not to reinvent each new camera from the ground up. Somehow, he wanted a platform that would expedite new camera development.

Suzanne Merritt, Director of Polaroid's Creativity Center, was handed the challenge of facilitating a two-day meeting of forty engineers and scientists who had been assigned this awesome task. On the morning of the first day of the meeting, Suzanne was met with crossed arms and an attitude of "If it could have been done before, we would have done it before. It's just not possible." It wasn't Suzanne's first challenge at Polaroid, but it was one of the toughest.

She states, "In that first two-day session, we had them challenge assumptions and look at things completely differently, break everything apart, come up with new materials and look for ways they could be interchangeable. By the end of the second day, they still didn't know

Creating, Transcending– The Purpose of Escape– All Steps

Chapter 5

TRANSCENDENT INTUITION AND CREATIVITY

Some people believe transcendent intuition is the logical thinking process of the subconscious. This logic of the subconscious works even on experiences that we do not remember.[19] The conscious would then apply logic to those we do remember. Others believe that transcendent intuition comes from a "universal consciousness" that we somehow tap into from time to time.[20] Transcendent intuition to many others is still unexplainable. Although we are demystifying the process, no one can yet be sure how it works. Given that transcendent intuition often occurs about issues never even remotely experienced, and that in many cases about issues never even considered, one should be open to a number of possible explanations.

> *Few people think more than two or three times a year. I've made an international reputation for myself by thinking once a week.*
> —George Bernard Shaw

Increasing transcendent intuition is not a hard and fast science. At best the process is in its infancy. But there are certain generally agreed upon ways of getting in touch with this ability, and these are the subject of three of the later chapters in this book.

The belief among many who practice and teach creativity is that utilizing the first three levels of intuition and having an open mind and practicing development of your overall intuition skills will lead to having some transcendent intuition experiences.[21]

The bottom line is that intuition leads to creativity, and creativity is critical to personal and corporate success. *So escape and use your mental and transcendent intuition.*

Escape

from the Maze

102

Great Escapes 5.3 describes how one person pursued her transcendent intuition to create a publishing hit.

GREAT ESCAPES 5.3

It's A Hit, I Just Know It

Despite the fact that everybody at Macmillan Publishing Company thought it was a "nothing book," editor Eleanor Friede knew *Jonathan Livingston Seagull* could be a hit. Despite all types of opposition, she pressed for support. Finally the book popped. It was an international success. It was made into a movie. She relied on her transcendent intuition and it paid off.

Source: Roy Rowan, *The Intuitive Manager*, (Boston, Massachusetts: Little, Brown and Company, 1986), p. 10.

> *As a result of our training as well as of our experience, most of us are disposed to approach any problem with as analytical an attitude as we can muster. We would be ill advised to do anything else, yet paradoxically, efficient, economical, and analytical perception is sometimes the enemy of creative insight.*
> — Donald W. MacKinnon, researcher of creativity

When are mental and transcendent intuition most useful in decision making? Weston Agor, creativity consultant, asked 200 highly intuitive executives when intuition was useful in business decision making.[22] The executives most frequently replied as follow:[23]

- When a high level of uncertainty exists.
- When little previous precedent exists.
- When facts are limited.
- When facts do not clearly point the way to go.
- When analytical data are of little use.
- When several plausible alternative solutions exist to choose from, with good arguments for each.
- When time is limited and there is pressure to come up with the right decisions.

Creating, Transcending– The Purpose of Escape– All Steps

Their answers reveal that mental and transcendent intuition are only two of many tools to be used in arriving at decisions. None relied exclusively on creativity nor did any recommend abandoning left brain, rational thinking.

Chapter 5

103

STRENGTHENING YOUR MENTAL AND TRANSCENDENT INTUITION

To move beyond your current level of creative problem solving, to develop and use more mental and transcendent intuition, you have to think about how you think and make any necessary changes in that process. This requires a conscious effort to find out how your brain works. You must be willing to experiment with different techniques to gain mental improvement.

Any number of techniques or processes are available to raise your level of transcendent intuition. They fall into two distinct categories—those that are primarily conscious, and those that are primarily subconscious. As you already know, one of the conscious actions involves telling yourself it is OK to be creative. It is important to do this because we have mostly learned that it's not OK to be creative. One of the conscious "permissions" to be creative I like to use is giving people the visible right to be creative through the use of a thinking visor as described in Escape Routes 5.1.

I assert that the cosmic religious experience is the strongest and the noblest driving force behind scientific research.
—Albert Einstein

Escape

from the Maze

The belief today among creativity experts is that you can increase your level of creativity by increasing your levels of mental and transcendent intuition. This is done by increasing the use of your subconscious through getting in touch with your right brain, suspending your left side, improving your thinking skills,and practicing solving complex problems. In the following chapters you will do just that. While the evidence is strong that you need to use both sides of your brain in being creative, the evidence is similarly strong that most people do not use their right brain enough and therefore could increase their creativity.

BRAIN AEROBICS 5

Part 1—Intuition Quiz[1]

Mark your answers as accurately and honestly as possible in order to measure your present level of intuitive ability. Try not to second guess how an intuitive person might respond.

Creating, Transcending– The Purpose of Escape– All Steps

	True	False
1. I feel that a logical, step-by-step method is best for solving problems.	☐	☐

[1]Reprinted by permission of Eugene Raudsepp. "The Hunch Factor," *The Executive Female.*

Chapter 5

105

2. Good hunches have provided the impetus for many of my successful projects. ▢ ▢

3. I sometimes act on a hunch out of curiosity. ▢ ▢

4. In order for me to act on a decision, it has to feel right. ▢ ▢

5. Intuition is an unreliable guide for action. ▢ ▢

6. I feel that many of my ideas seem to grow out of their own roots, as if independent of my will. ▢ ▢

7. I have little interest in problems that do not have clear-cut, unambiguous answers. ▢ ▢

8. I have the ability to penetrate to the essence of the problem. ▢ ▢

9. I tend to rely on hunches and the feeling of rightness or wrongness when moving toward the solution of a problem. ▢ ▢

10. Many of the penetrating insights I have experienced have been touched off by seemingly insignificant coincidences. ▢ ▢

THE ANSWERS

1. *False.* Only simple problems have solutions resulting from rational sequences that unfold in a straight and predictable line. Most business problems are as convoluted as the folds on the surface of the brain.

2. *True.* Success for executives who frequently must make decisions and initiate new projects on the basis of incomplete

Escape

from
the Maze

information depends largely on their capacity for good hunches. It is their ability to arrive at correct hunches combined with a willingness to take risks that determine the success of their projects.

3. *True.* Frequently a hunch is a subtle feeling supported in the mind's eye by an image of what the outcome of an action could be.

4. *True.* Although a decision may look logical on paper, it may not become an effective action because certain contingencies were overlooked. Effective decisions result from the ability to select among many alternatives the best course of action, or the one that feels right, even though none of them is a sure bet.

5. *False.* Genuine hunches are reliable in that they enable you to sense the possibilities in a situation. If an apparently genuine hunch turns out to be wrong, it did not emerge from intuition. Consider what triggered it for future reference.

6. *True.* Those moments of rare intensity when everything falls easily into place as a new idea is born or a puzzle is solved have been reported by almost every intuitive executive. So free, spontaneous and uncontrived is this process, one has the impression the ideas come from outside oneself.

7. *False.* One significant reason for the inability to produce new ideas is a strong preference for precise, clear thoughts and a tendency to reject problems that are too intangible or elusive to comprehend immediately.

8. *True.* A genuine, intuitive feeling helps an executive penetrate the complex interplay of elements to reach the very crux of the situation. Without this feeling, the central issue may become lost among a welter of irrelevancies.

9. *True.* The process whereby intuitives solve problems is held together by feelings. These people trust their feelings to tell them what belongs and what does not, what is appropriate, what is to be taken together. They can feel the direction

Creating, Transcending– The Purpose of Escape– All Steps

Chapter 5

107

of a possible solution before they actually know what the solution is.

10. *True*. Penetrating insights usually occur at the culmination of a long series of subconscious insights. What slowly has been germinating (perhaps unbeknownst to the executive) suddenly pops into full view, perceived to be a coincidence or the result of an external event. Although intuition is essentially a function of inner processes and not of outer circumstances, the telescoping of a cluster of insights into one major hunch frequently is triggered by outside occurrences.

Part 2—Intrepretation of the Quiz

If your responses match eight to ten of the answers, you tend to place a high value on intuition when making a decision. As a consequence, your greatest satisfaction is engaging in new ideas, possibilities, and directions, rather than on what already exists. Your intuitive bent leads you to approach problems in a novel and fresh manner.

A score of four to seven indicates you are flexible and effective both in the world of new ideas and when implementing well-thought-out plans and procedures. Even though you believe in the efficacy of your hunches, you tend to subject them to systematic and critical scrutiny.

A score of zero to three means that you are strongly analytical and objectively critical. You tend to value clear reasoning and logic and are suspicious of any intuitive promptings unless they can be subjected to thorough analysis and demonstrable proof.

Part 3—Taking Action

According to Dr. Frances E. Vaughn, in order to improve your intuition, you must:[24]

The more I've watched the connection between humor and increased creativity, the more I've realized that there is very little difference between "Ah ha!" and "Ha Ha."

—Roger L. Firestein, Director of the Center for Studies in Creativity, Buffalo State College

Escape

from the Maze

__1. Intend to do so.
__2. Devote time to its development.
__3. Relax.
__4. Provide your mind with periods of silence.
__5. Be honest with yourself about your intuition.
__6. Be receptive to it.
__7. Be sensitive to it.
__8. Play, non-verbally, mentally—music, drawings, clay, etc., to activate the right side.
__9. Be open to different types of experiences.
__10. Have the courage to use it.
__11. Accept, nonjudgmentally, things as they are.
__12. Be detatched.
__13. Practice it daily.
__14. Have an intuition support group.
__15. Enjoy it.

Rate yourself on a scale of 1 (low) to 10 (high) the degree to which you are able to perform to each of these fifteen actions. Place that rating in the blanks to the left of each item. Now for the five items with the lowest scores, prepare a plan of action for improvement.

Creating,
Transcending–
The Purpose of
Escape–
All Steps

Chapter 5

REFERENCES

1. John O'C. Hamilton, "Bypassing the Trauma," *Business Week* (September 4, 1995), pp. 32–34.

2. Author's personal knowledge; Eugene Raudsepp, "The Hunch Factor," *The Successful Manager: The Executive Female* (not dated), pp. 25–26.

3. Graham Wallas, *The Art of Thought* (London: J. Cape, 1926).

4. Thomas P. Murphy, "Eureka!" *Forbes* (May 7, 1984), p. 218.

5. Daniel Coleman, Paul Kaufman, and Michael Ray, *The Creative Spirit* (New York: Plume-Penguin, 1993), p. 36.

6. Roy Rowan, *The Intuitive Manager* (Boston: Little, Brown & Company, 1986), p. 11.

7. Frances E. Vaughn, "Exercises in Intuition," *Psychology Today* Tapes, 1986.

8. For a representative sample see Roy Rowan, op. cit. throughout.

9. Ibid., pp. 141–153.

10. Orlando Behling and Norman L. Echel, "Making Sense Out of Intuition," *Academy of Management Executive* (February 1991), pp. 46–54. Their study of the definition of intuition reveals six major classifications of such definitions :
    1. As a sixth sense—the way it is used here as transcendent
    2. As a personality trait—someone possesses it as part of his or her personality
    3. As an unconscious process—the way it is used here for all four types of intuition
    4. As a set of actions—the way it is used here as mental intuition
    5. As distilled experience—the way it is used here as mental intuition
    6. As a residual—if it is not rational then what is left is intuition

11. These definitions come from a number of sources. The overall scheme is that of Frances E. Vaughn, op. cit. However, I have modified her definitions and some of her labels for types of intuition to reflect a business orientation.

12. For example, see Weston Agor, "How Top Executives Make Important Decisions," *Organizational Dynamics* (Winter 1986), pp. 5–18.

Escape

from
the Maze

13. Eugene Raudsepp, "The Hunch Factor," op. cit., pp. 25–26.

14. For example, studies by author and researcher Arthur Reber, have shown that when chief executives are rated by their peers as to their ability, and are tested for their rational and intuitive skills, it becomes quite clear that those executives with high levels of creative skills as well as high levels of rational skills, are rated by their peers as the most effective, successful top executives. Those who are simply rational and analytical are evaluated as making less sound decisions. Michael A. Guillen, "The Intuitive Edge," *Psychology Today* (August 1984), pp. 68–69.

Similarly, studies of executive decision making by consultant, author, and researcher Henry Mintzberg cause him to characterize the process as requiring a "holistic thinker" —constantly relying on hunches to cope wtih problems far too complex for mere rational analysis. Henry Mintzberg, "Planning on the Left Side and Managing on the Right," *Harvard Business Review* (July/August 1976), pp. 49–58. Mintzberg also discovered in his studies of chief executives that many managerial jobs, especially those at the top of the organization, are so complex that, in his words, they defy rational, sequential thinking. His studies indicate that without intuition, chief executives are frequently lost in a maze of data they can't comprehend through analysis.

Weston H. Agor examined the 200 most intuitive executives from a sample of 3157 managers who had responded to his questionnaire on the use of intuition. All executives but one reported using intuition in making critical decisions. However, they were quick to point out that intuition was only one of many tools that they used. The study revealed that executives were more likely to use intuition when: a high level of uncertainty existed, little previous precedent existed, variables were less scientifically predictable, facts were limited, facts did not clearly point the way to go, analytical data were of little use, several plausible alternative solutions exist to choose from with good arguments for each, time was limited and there was pressure to come up with the right decision. Weston H. Agor, "How Top Executives Make Important Decisions," op. cit.

Finally, author and researcher Philip Goldberg has spent an exhaustive amount of time researching and condensing a number of studies and case observations which also support the concept of an intuitive edge. That is, the person that is intuitive has an edge in decision making over those who are not. He cites many examples, a few of the more interesting anecdotal ones are: Ray Kroc's decision, against the advice of all of his associates and advisors, to buy McDonalds because of a "funny" feeling; Marconi's insistence, despite the known laws of physics at that time, that wireless signals could traverse the ocean; and Winston Churchill's decision during a bombing raid in

Creating, Transcending– The Purpose of Escape– All Steps

Chapter 5

1941, to go against his normal behavior pattern and sit in his car on the opposite side from normal, a decision made on compelling intuition, and one that ultimately saved his life. Philip Goldberg, *The Intuitive Edge* (Los Angeles: Jeremy P. Tarcher, Inc., 1983), pp. 22, 54–55. Also see Roy Rowan, op. cit.

Numerous other research and anecdotal evidence is available from which to draw the conclusion that intuition plus rational skills are superior to rationality alone.

15. For example see: Gerard I. Nierenberg and Henry H. Calero, *How to Read a Person Like a Book* (New York: Barnes & Noble, 1993); *Fundamentals of Nonverbal Behavior*, Robert Feldman and Bernard Rim, eds. (Cambridge, England and New York: Cambridge University Press, 1991); C. Barnum and N. Wolnainsky, "Taking Cues From Body Language," *Management Review* (June 1989), pp. 59–60; Nancy Henley, *Body Politics: Power Sex and Nonverbal Communication* (New York: Simon & Schuster, 1986); David Givens, "What Body Language Can Tell You That Words Cannot," *U.S. News & World Report* (November 19, 1984), p. 100; Julius Fast, *The Body Language of Sex, Power & Aggression* (New York: M. Evans, 1977); and Julius Fast, *Body Language* (New York: M. Evans, distributed in association with Lippincott, 1970).

16. Coleman, op. cit., Kiechell, op. cit., and Ingber, op. cit.; see endnote #14 in this chapter.

17. Paul Stonham, "For and Against the Case Method," *European Management Journal* (June 1995), pp. 230–232; Elizabeth S. Niemyer, "The Case for Case Study," *Training & Development* (January 1995), pp. 50–52; for a review see Arch R. Dooley and Wickham Skinner, "Casing Case Method Methods," *Academy of Management Review* (April 1977), pp. 277–289.

18. Weston H. Agor, loc. cit.

19. Michael Ray and Rochelle Myers, *Creativity in Business* (New York: Doubleday & Company, 1986), Chapter 2.

20. Ibid.

21. Frances Vaughn, op. cit.

22. As described in his study, the intuition he examined is mostly what we call here mental intuition. To a small degree, transcendent intuition might be involved.

23. Weston Agor, op. cit.

24. Francis E. Vaughn, op. cit.

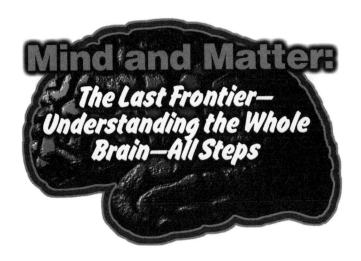

Mind and Matter:
The Last Frontier—Understanding the Whole Brain—All Steps

CHAPTER 6

The human brain represents the last frontier in human capital management.
—Weston H. Agor,
innovation researcher,
consultant, and author

It is sometimes difficult to believe, but that three-pound glob of matter that rests between your ears—your brain—controls your destiny. At its best, your brain is capable of the highest works known, but at its worst, it can mess up royally. The human brain is the most complex device on earth. It has a network that contains 100 billion neurons (nerve cells) and consumes 25 percent of your calorie intake.[1] But it functions in ways that are not easily nor fully understood. It is a bio-chemical, electrical machine—boom, flash. It works, especially in solving problems, by association, by networking sets of ideas.

The major part of the brain, the cerebrum, is divided into two hemispheres, the left and right. The left hemisphere has primary responsibility for the following functions—thinking with words, serial processing, logical thinking and analysis. The right side of the brain is primarily responsible for thinking with images, simultaneous processing, and intuitive thinking synthesis. In left-handed people, the hemispheres share tasks more equally than do those in right-handed people.

It is important to understand though, that while each hemisphere has primary responsibility for certain functions, the other hemisphere is almost always aiding in performing those functions. For example, the left hemisphere is assisting the right when it is performing intuitive synthesis, and the right side is assisting the left in verbal communication. There is a continuum of activation for each side. Thus you should not take the left brain, right brain differences too literally. Most people use both sides together for most functions.

Few minds wear out; more rust out.
—Christian Nestell Bovee

Having briefly introduced the brain, let us examine it in more detail.

THE MYSTERY OF THE MIND:[1] A PLAY ON HOW THE BRAIN WORKS

To the unitiated, the brain seems simple enough. Like other anatomical structures, the brain is composed entirely of tissue and fluid, and it is attached to the rest of the body with the usual blood vessels and musculature. But behind the scenes, an intricate network of performers and supporters are combining talents and tasks to create the continuous drama we call life. Join us now, as the "Mystery of the Mind" unfolds…

The Cast

Possibly the most mysterious players in the human brain are **nerve cells**, or **neurons**. Once developed, these specialized cells, for the most part, do not reproduce; in other words, what we have is what we get. We are born with more than 100 billion of them, so we generally do not miss the thousand or so that die off every day.

Escape

*from
the Maze*

[1]The rest of this chapter, up to the section entitled "Left-Right and Left-Right" (except for boxed materials, sections entitled " The Brain and Gender" and "Beyond Left and Right," and some minor changes), is reprinted with the permission of Corporate Communications, Orlando Regional Healthcare System, Orlando, Florida.—

The firing of nerve cells within the brain and spinal cord is constant. Through long tendrils known as dendrites and axons, chemicals called neurotransmitters dance from cell to cell, triggering a series of domino-like effects—all intricately connected, all working together toward a common goal. The brain's reactions are so sophisticated, so specific, and so directional, that one misfire, the mere stumble of a sole performer, will send the brain's choreography awry. Luckily, the talented brain usually allows us to work around these interruptions, as it continually finds new pathways where old ones have faded. What's important is to give these interconnections a chance to work as this chapter's Great Escapes 6.1 reveals.

> *I like seeing a man (or woman) with his feet up on his desk... it tells me he spends some time thinking, not just muddling around with detail and routine. It's a sign of creativity; a mind at work.*
> —J.L. Dampeu

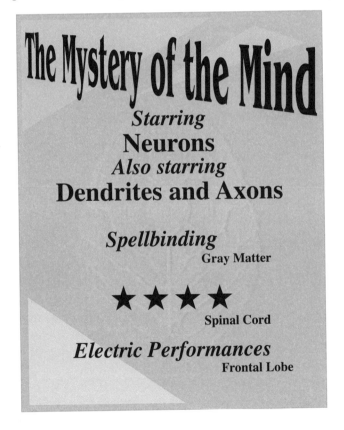

The Mystery of the Mind

Starring

Neurons

Also starring

Dendrites and Axons

Spellbinding

Gray Matter

★ ★ ★ ★

Spinal Cord

Electric Performances

Frontal Lobe

Mind and Matter: The Last Frontier– Understanding the Whole Brain– All Steps

Chapter 6

115

The Maestro

> The next time your mind wanders, follow it around for awhile.
> —Unknown

The dual functions of composer and conductor are carried out in an area of the brain called the **cerebrum**. Accounting for more than 80 percent of total brain mass, the cerebrum is the brain's most elaborate structure. Its wrinkled, furrowed surface, called the **cerebral cortex**, plays the largest role in brain function.

Escape

from

the Maze

Weighing only three pounds, the human brain can be held in one hand. But, if we were to lay the cortex flat, it would cover nearly the entire surface of an office desk. These deep folds are what sets our species apart from the rest of the animal kingdom.

Anatomically, the human body is nearly symmetrical. One side mirrors the other. But the two halves of the cerebrum, called the right and left hemispheres, are anything but alike. The nerves are situated so that the left hemisphere controls the actions of the right side of the body, and vice versa. The two hemispheres keep "in touch" through a bridge of fibers known as the corpus callosum. Without it, the left hand literally would not know what the right hand is doing.

> *Anything the mind can conceive and believe, it can achieve.*
> —Norman Vincent Peale

Solving The Mystery

Keep in "mind" that few actions and thoughts involve an isolated area of the brain. For instance, the simple act of speaking is a combination of auditory, visual and motor area activity, not to mention the deeper intellectual processes of composition and comprehension. While you may be concentrating wholly on the words that come out of your mouth, your brain has other things to think about. Unbeknownst to you, your mind is picking up background noises and activities, then filtering and prioritizing them. It is regulating your heart rate and causing your eyes to blink when necessary. It is digesting your last meal. It is even keeping you upright in your chair. The reception, absorption and coordination of many impulses and functions simultaneously is perhaps the brain's greatest feat. "We're learning new things every day," adds Dr. Michael Isley, PhD, clinical neurophysiologist and director of the Intraoperative Brain Monitoring program at Orlando Regional Healthcare System. It is here (in the cerebral cortex) that our complex thought processes take place—language, vision, hearing, movement, emotion. It is here that we experience awareness, perception and sense of self. It is here that we gain and store knowledge. Within the cerebral cortex, we shape our own personal reality. Dr. Isley observes, "We once believed we used only a small percentage of our total brain mass; we now know that just isn't so." Our minds will happily oblige with an almost endless supply of encores. Exhibit 6.1 highlights some of the key facts about the brain.

> *It's always fun to do the impossible, because that's where there is less competition.*
> —Walt Disney

Mind and Matter: The Last Frontier– Understanding the Whole Brain– All Steps

Chapter 6

117

Exhibit 6.1

Facts of the Matter

We may never fully understand how the work of the brain allows the mind to play. Could it be that our minds are too complex for our own brains to comprehend? As the 1990s unfold—termed the "decade of the brain" by former President George Bush—we can only learn more about this complex mystery.

- The brain is one of the first organs to develop in the womb. At seven weeks gestation, a human fetus measures only about one inch, but the eyes, limbs and brain are already visible.

- The brain contains approximately 100 billion nerve cells, about equal to the number of stars in the Milky Way.

- Once embryonic development is complete, nerve cells are not replaced when they die. However, the remarkable resiliency of the brain allows damaged or severed areas to develop alternate pathways.

- Although we lose brain cells from the moment we are born, the mass of the brain at birth is only about one-fourth of its adult size. Why? The brain grows as the neurons become bigger in size and increase their interactions.

- For the signal to "jump" from one neuron to another, chemical compounds called neurotransmitters are needed.

- By age eight, the human brain reaches its maximum weight of about three pounds.

- Neurons conduct information in the form of brief electrical signals, caused by increasing and decreasing concentrations of sodium, calcium and potassium. There are at least fifty known neurotransmitters, a few of which are norepinephrine, acetylcholine, and endorphins. Many physical and psychological disorders are attributed to too much or not enough of these vital chemical compounds.

- Each neuron communicates with at least 10,000 other neurons within the body.

Escape

from
the Maze

- Neurons transmit information at a rate of about 100 meters per second, or 200 miles per hour.

- From the brain stem, nerves travel the length of the spinal cord, transmitting impulses from the brain to all areas of the body.

- Tests have shown that blood flow in the brain shifts to different locations depending on what task is being performed.

BOTH SIDES NOW—THE MUSIC OF THE HEMISPHERES

At this very moment your brain is registering a thousand distinct impressions most of which are being processed in the twin halves of your cerebral cortex.

These groups of letters are being seen by the visual cortex, then recognized as words by your left brain within a millisecond. If someone were to ask what you are doing, you would reply, "I am reading." Yet that is only a small part of what is keeping your brain busy.

> *It helps to have a wide knowledge base.*
> —Nolan Bushnell, founder of Atari and Chuck E. Cheese

As your left brain begins the language process we call reading, your right brain is sensing how this page looks and feels in your hand. Your right brain is also aware of sounds in the background, a car passing, the hum of an air conditioner. This kind of "white noise" is often filtered out before it can interfere with your concentration.

Depending on your emotional response to what you are reading, both hemispheres can implant the information into memory. The more right-brained (or emotional) your response, the more likely it is to be stored in long-term memory.

Mind and Matter: The Last Frontier– Understanding the Whole Brain– All Steps

As you can see, each side of the brain concerns itself with certain kinds of tasks. By studying each half separately, scientists have discovered many interesting differences that have

Chapter 6

improved our understanding of the whole brain. What works best in problem solving is to use both sides of the brain. Most people do not. This is true in other countries, not just in the United States as Trapped in the Maze 6.1 suggests.

TRAPPED IN THE MAZE 6.1
When It Comes to Innovating New Products, The Japanese and Germans Basically Don't

Japanese and German economies have made tremendous strides since World War II. Economic successes have occurred largely through the superior implementation skills of their firms. Firms in these countries took the products of other countries, and did a superior job of manufacturing. Their competitive strategies were largely based on high quality (and in the case of the Japanese, low cost). Firms in both countries, especially the Japanese, were good at incremental product and process improvements, but most of these firms did not base their strategies on leading-edge technologies and products. There were a few exceptions, of course, Sony and Hitachi, and more recently, Mercedes and BMW, for example. Recognizing their comparative disadvantage, firms from both nations are striving hard to bring more innovation into their everyday operations, and the governments of both nations are trying to increase the levels of innovation nationwide.

In both countries this means that the national culture must change—not just organizational cultures. Why? Because the Japanese and Germans are both ritualistic, hierarchical, left brain dominated societies. There's more to it than just the way they think and interact in organizations. Both societies and their organizations function best in stable environments, which have all but disappeared from the business situation. In the 1970s and 1980s, Germany dominated Europe and Japan dominated the Pacific Rim and much of U.S. industry. With the European Union, Germany is more subject to competition. So is Japan with the emergence of Korea, Taiwan, Singapore, Hong Kong, and China. Their national and organizational cultures function best where competition is limited.

These countries will be trapped in the maze until they change the way their citizens think. As is common today around the globe, it is business that is leading the effort to change. To compete, businesses must change the way their employees think. The rest of the country will follow.

Sources: Teruyasu Murakami, "Creativity and the Next Generation of Japanese-Style Management," *Creativity and Innovation Management* (December 1994), pp. 211–220; "German Innovation: No Bubbling Brook," *Economist* (September 1994), pp. 75–76; Daniel Benjamin, "The Trailing Edge: Some Germans Feel They're Falling Behind in High-Tech Fields," *Wall Street Journal* (April 27, 1994), pp. A1, A6.

Escape

from
the Maze

WHAT DOES WHAT

Have you ever been called "left-brained" or "right-brained"? Chances are, your right brain perceived that this comment was made with some degree of sarcasm, while your left brain wondered, "But what does that mean?"

Most scientists believe that left/right dominance is learned—the result of nurture rather than nature. While it is commonly believed that left-handed people are usually right-brained, the truth is that approximately 70 percent of all people have a dominant left hemisphere, be they left-handed or right-handed. What is important is to be able to use predominantly one or both sides of the brain as necessary as Great Escapes 6.2 helps demonstrate.

> *Why can't you ever use the same side of the brain I'm using?*
> —Wife to husband in *"Lockhorns,"* a feature cartoon by Bunny Hoest

GREAT ESCAPES 6.2

How Disney Did It

Walter Elias (Walt) Disney gave us Mickey Mouse, Fantasia, Disneyland, and Walt Disney World for starters, and a whole host of other characters and ideas that have made our lives more pleasant and fun than they might otherwise have been. How did he do it? First of all, he was a "dreamer." An associate of his recalls, "When Walt was deep in thought, he would lower one brow, squint his eyes, let his jaw drop, and stare fixedly at some point in space... No words could break the spell." Psychologist Robert Dilts has studied many of the great creative geniuses including Disney. Dilts suggests that as just described, Disney was in a psychological state known as synesthesia—drawing on the memory of two senses at once—he was letting his mind see and hear his proposed new creation. This visualization, accompanied by sound, was a major contributor to Disney's success. Note, both are right-brained activities.

One of his more mundane innovations, yet one ever so critical, was the one used to solve the following problem: What kind of device do you create which allows you to analyze and plan the actions of animated cartoon characters? These characters will move at the rate of 24 frames per second, each frame being different from the previous one. You have only a nickel in your research and development budget. Walt's solution was a simple one—a very large rubber band. By drawing the character on the rubber band and then stretching it, Walt could see how the character might look.

Mind and Matter: The Last Frontier– Understanding the Whole Brain– All Steps

Chapter 6

Disney also gave us an important creativity technique which he devised to solve the following problem: How do you keep track of the story told by drawings now that the studio is using four times as many frames per second as our competition uses in a cartoon feature? Historically, sets of frames had been laid in a stack, and it was relatively easy to flip through them to see how the story was progressing. But Disney decided that quality of product would be a good competitive mechanism, so he quadrupled the number of frames per second to be used in a cartoon to make the characters move in a more realistic fashion. The solution to his problem was the first version of storyboarding. The frames were placed in the order of the story on the walls around the studio, thus making it easy to keep track of the action. Later, Mike Vance, then head of Disney University, modified this technique into a verbal creativity technique which has proven, in my opinion, to be the best creativity technique for groups when solving complex problems. (See Chapter 4.)

Sources: James M. Higgins, *101 Creative Problem Solving Techniques: The Handbook of New Ideas for Business* (Winter Park, Florida: The New Management Publishing Company, Inc. 1994), pp. 161–176; Bryan W. Mattimore, "Strategies of Genius," *Success* (October 1992), pp. 26–27.

Table 6.1 contains a list of characteristics commonly associated with the left and right hemispheres. Keep in mind that this is how your brain *prefers* to think. The majority of us are quite agile in shifting from one hemisphere to the other. It helps to know which hemisphere is considered the "seat" of certain brain functions (in order to help you better manage your brain.)

As you can see, both halves of the cerebral cortex are devoted to "higher" thinking, which occurs as a result of more basic information—the raw data we receive through our senses, the movements we make by choice or reflex. These relatively primitive abilities are handled in other, less evolved portions of the brain.

TABLE 6.1

Your Left Brain Likes To:	Your Right Brain Likes To:
• Think in words rather than pictures.	• Think visually and spatially.
• Take an intellectual approach to problem-solving.	• Solve problems using intuition rather than logic.
• Remember names more easily than faces.	• Recall faces rather than names.
• Operate in a planned and structured manner.	• Work in a fluid and spontaneous manner.

Escape

from

the Maze

• Take multiple-choice tests rather than essay tests.	• Answer open-ended questions.
• Keep a tight reign on emotions.	• Express feelings freely.
• Make objective judgments.	• Make subjective judgments.
• Compare differences.	• Compare similarities.
• Experiment systematically.	• Experiment by intuition.
• Break a problem into parts before solving it.	• Look at the whole problem then try to note patterns and solve the problem on a hunch.
• Respond to verbal instructions and explanations.	• Learn by demonstration, illustrations or symbolic instruction.
• Use concrete facts to describe things.	• Use metaphor and analogy to explain things.
• Overlook body language and focus on words.	• Interpret a message through body language.
• Talk and write in order to communicate.	• Communicate by drawing or manipulating objects.
• Operate amid ranked authority systems.	• Work within level authority structures where all participate equally.
• Do what others are doing.	• Do whatever it wants to do regardless of what others are doing.
• Respond to sounds and pictures.	• Respond to movement and action.
• Analyze information by taking it apart point by point.	• Synthesize information by understanding how it fits with other information already stored in the brain.

Mind and Matter: The Last Frontier– Understanding the Whole Brain– All Steps

EXTREMES OF LEFT & RIGHT

Much of what we know about left–right dominance was learned by studying cerebral hemispheres that had been

Chapter 6

damaged surgically, separated or put to sleep. Only then could physicians and scientists find out what still worked and what did not.

"Roger Sperry was the one who pioneered split-brain experiments," notes Michael Isley. He cut the corpus callosum, the bundle of fibers that join the left and right hemispheres, to study the effects on each severed half. Similar studies of people with brain damage have yielded a wealth of information. Doug Hennig, PhD, is a neuropsychologist working with brain-injured patients at the Brain Injury Rehabilitation Center at Sand Lake Hospital, in Orlando, Florida. He points out that a person with an injury to the right brain tends to become indifferent and adopts coping strategies such as joking and denial to deal with their injury (left-brain responses). Those with damage to the left brain, he says, react more emotionally, often crying, cursing and refusing to cooperate (right-brain responses).

> *The only reason some people get lost in thought is because it's unfamiliar territory.*
> —Paul Fix

THE BRAINS AND GENDER

Do not forget that what is done on the left and right sides varies, sometimes significiantly, when gender is taken into account. As discussed in more detail in Appendix 1 to this book, men's and women's brains are hard-wired differently, causing men and women to often gather, process, and act on information differently. For example, in a recent study, when men and women performed language tasks, brain scans (PET—positron emission tomography) revealed that women use both sides of their brain to process the meaning of words, while men used only the left side.[2] This suggests, but only suggests, that women might be adding intuitive interpretations to the words, while men might take them more literally.

Escape

from
the Maze

BEYOND LEFT & RIGHT

Science has produced new ways of investigating the brain. This technology has not only confirmed what was suspected about the brain, but has yielded richer findings as well. One is that significant differences also exist in the ways the front and back of the brain work.

The frontal lobe, for instance, contains a much higher concentration of opiate receptors than do other sections of the brain. *For this reason, neuroscientist Candace Pert at the National Institute of Mental Health believes that the frontal lobe plays the premier role in creative thought.* Opiate receptors will filter out distracting sensory input, which allows the mind to be open to higher consciousness. An excellent example is the runner's high. Because exercise stimulates endorphins (the brain's natural opiates) it can produce an altered state in the runner. Many runners report a burst of creativity after exercise. This may also be due to the fact that during repetitious activity, the left side gets bored, and almost literally falls asleep, allowing the right side to take over. (See left-side suspenders, Chapter 9.)

> *Man's mind, stretched by a new idea, never goes back to its original dimension.*
> —Oliver Wendell Holmes

THE WHOLE-BRAINED APPROACH

Whether your brain tends toward the left or right, front or back, it has an amazing ability to compensate for its own deficits. When either half of the brain is removed in infancy the child can mature normally by developing the entire range of functions in a single hemisphere. This process is understandably more difficult in adults but damage to one hemisphere can cause the neurological impulses to find detours around the affected area while achieving the same end result.

The vast majority of us enjoy whole, intact brains. Yet we may discover a need to nurture or develop skills that are associated with one hemisphere or the other. Take the classic examples of a painter who cannot keep his checkbook balanced, or an accountant who cannot relate to his family.

Mind and Matter: The Last Frontier– Understanding the Whole Brain– All Steps

Chapter 6

125

Change is quite possible, given the brain's elastic powers. In maturing, most adults strive toward a balanced "whole-brain" system of thinking. Modern technology actually shows that while certain activities may begin in the predicted side of the brain, the whole brain is utilized before that activity is finished. Some people, for example, can create a beautiful piece of art, then eloquently explain why it is visually arresting. Einstein's essential creative act was visualizing the theory of relativity. However, his mental genius would have gone unrecognized had he been unable to express this visualization as a written formula.

Author and researcher, Ned Herrmann, in a series of studies that he has often repeated, found that project teams worked best when "brain-balanced"—with roughly an equal number of left-brain dominant and right-brain dominant members. Project teams with only left brainers came back with neatly typed reports devoid of ideas. Project teams with right brainers came back with lots of ideas, but often disorganized with little concept as to implementation or applications. Balanced teams came back with innovative ideas, presented in an organized fashion, and on time.[3]

GETTING MORE FROM YOUR BRAIN

You have probably heard the claim that most people use only 10 percent of their brain. An image comes to mind of a beautiful three-pound organ in which only a small segment is active; the rest lies dormant, waiting for its owner to wise up and start using it. This image also suggests that we could all become geniuses if only we *tried* a little harder. But, the image is inaccurate. More of the brain is used than has previously been believed.

Escape

from

the Maze

There is another popular notion that the physical properties of the brain—size, weight, shape—are related to intelligence. This is true, but only to a point. In some cases, enlarged areas of the brain may indeed correspond to the specific

126

intellectual gifts. A person with perfect pitch might have an extra-thick auditory cortex. Or someone with a photographic memory could have a visual cortex roughly twice the thickness of a normal person's.

However, physical size isn't everything, according to author and neurophysiologist Richard Restak, MD. In his book, *The Brain Has a Mind of Its Own,* Restak points out that Charlemagne had a larger brain than Einstein, plus a bigger liver, heart and pancreas.[4] What Einstein did possess, however, was an abnormal abundance of glial cells—the cells that help other neurons stay healthy. It is possible that Einstein's brain was super-nourished and able to accomplish more because of its superior support system.

More important than physical properties, however, are the networks of cells that exist throughout the brain, says Dr. Restak, "It's believed more likely that the psychobiological basis for genius may be the number of networks or the intricacy of their interweaving."[5]

Researchers have used PET scans to compare the brains of those with very high IQ scores with those who have average scores. These scans show rainbow-colored maps of energy within the brain. "Like light bulbs," says Dr. Restak, "the brains of 'bright' people were expected to illuminate more intensely than those of 'dimwits" with a reduced wattage." Just the opposite happened. The brains of intelligent subjects displayed subdued patterns of blue and green, while those of the less gifted subjects "lit up like miniature Christmas trees" in hot reds and oranges. The cause, experts claim, is that a brain of average intelligence has to work harder to achieve less, while those in the gifted realm achieve more with little effort.[6]

The person who has no imagination has no wings.
—Muhammed

Mind and Matter: The Last Frontier– Understanding the Whole Brain– All Steps

A greater number of cell connections appears to be an indicator of intelligence. This means that the brain is more efficient because it has more ways to do its work. Instead of more cells or bigger cells, the high-IQ brain simply has more communication channels between cells.

Chapter 6

127

How are these new pathways created? Experts suggest that environment has a great influence, especially what they call an "enriched environment," one that provides more things to do, to talk about, to study, to look at, to touch, hear and smell. Even rats in challenging cages respond to their enhanced homes by developing more nerve cell extensions. What appears to work, then, is not learning to use more than ten percent of your brain, but rather *stimulating* more than ten percent, thereby creating more connections.[7]

> *Think left and think right, and think low and think high. Oh the things you can think up, if only you try.*
> —Dr. Seuss

In Chapters 8 and 9 you will learn several brain aerobics exercises which will help you get more from your right brain. Meanwhile read Escape Routes 6.1 and 6.2 which describe how some organizations from those countries discussed in Trapped in the Maze 6.1, are trying to escape by having members use both sides of their brains.

ESCAPE ROUTES 6.1
Keio University Tries an Unusual Experiment: Teaching Its Students How to Think Creatively

The Japanese educational system is known for its degree of difficulty up through the completion of high school, and for its lack of difficulty thereafter. It is also known for its emphasis on uniformity, and preparation for standardized tests through high school, and its emphasis on socializing in college. Learning has, until recently, been almost irrelevant in college. "That's where you go to make friends and future business contacts," observes one graduate. But privately funded Keio University is trying to change all of that.

At its four-year-old Shonan Fujisawa campus, educators stress creative-problem solving and interdisciplinary learning. Keio's leaders believed that they had to create a university system in Japan that better trained its youth for positions of the future which would value ideas and service as much or more than diligence. "We wanted students to grow out of old orthodoxies," says Hideo Aiso, dean of the school's environmental-information faculty. He continues, "We wanted them to define problems to be solved and to find tools and ways to solve them."

Students actively use computers, and are encouraged both to participate actively in class, and to debate issues with professors. These

Escape

from
the Maze

128

actions are in sharp contrast to practices at other Japanese universities where students sit sullenly in class. Learning is also an objective at the University. "People here are a lot more interested in studying than at other schools," says twenty-one year-old student, Tamaki Amae. Japanese industry is excited by what is happening at Keio. Akio Hosono, president of fast-growing memory board-maker, IO Data Device, says that, "The biggest problem we face is that we can't find graduates who can think for themselves." Hosono, who recruited from Keio's first graduating class, excitedly commented that Keio, "is just about the only place in Japan that is turning out interesting students." Keio's approach is meeting with resistance from Japan's Education Ministry, and from Japan's professors, who don't want to give up their autonomy (and who, many feel, aren't that excited about teaching anyway). Nonetheless, it appears that Keio is going to have a major impact on Japan's educational system as other universities have begun to copy their process.

Source: Jonathan Friedland, "Learning to Think," *Far Eastern Economic Review* (June 30, 1994), p. 50.

ESCAPE ROUTES 6.2

Siemens Begins to Learn to Innovate

Heinrick von Pierer, CEO of Germany's Siemens, is bringing a cultural revolution to the firm. Under his direction they have developed new teams to speed products to market, they are trying workshops to find ways of producing ideas, they are trying to please the customer, they are encouraging risk taking, and most importantly, they are learning how to innovate. Von Pierer comments, "It's a completely different way of thinking. This is exactly what we need," he continues. "People are no longer afraid to speak out with an idea."

Von Pierer's most critical challenge has been to change entrenched management practices. His first step was to win over senior management, but he failed to do the same with the rest of the company. He turned to board member Walter Kunerth, who had recently completed a spectacular turnaround at Siemens' automotive unit. Kunerth launched the TOP program—Time Optimized Processes. The program encouraged speed, creativity, and a keen focus on the market. He accompanied this with a high-profile educational program aimed at all levels of company employees. Under TOP, Siemens has forced managers to take radical approaches in order to meet market demands. TOP has proven effective.

Von Pierer's efforts to change the firm's mind-set have propelled Siemens past most of its German and European competitors who have focused on cost-cutting. He is preparing his firm to take on global firms such as General Electric and Asea, Brown, Bavari. As part of that process, he restructured, eliminating two whole layers of management,

Mind and Matter: The Last Frontier– Understanding the Whole Brain– All Steps

Chapter 6

129

and empowering managers to make things happen. Subordinates have even begun to evaluate their managers, something very un-German. One typical result of all this was the development of a new machine tool control system by the automotive division in just two years—a third the usual time—for one-third the cost of previous systems.

Source: Karen Lowry Miller, "Seimens Shapes Up," Business Week (May 1, 1995), pp. 52–53.

LEFT-RIGHT AND LEFT-RIGHT

To develop or improve any part of the brain, work in the language of that part of the brain.
—Win Wenger, author on creativity

Research by creativity expert Ned Herrmann suggests that not only is the brain's cerebral area divided into two hemispheres, but that the deeper limbic system is too. He believes that the right half of the limbic system is concerned with the expression of emotions and feelings while the left half is concerned with the dimensions of control, organization and structure. Based on his work, the four stages of the creative process can be linked to the left and right dominance pattern—preparation and verification are left-brain modes, incubation and illumination are right-brain modes.[8] Figure 6.2 shows Herrmann's model.

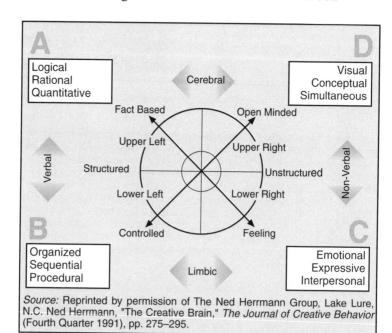

A
Logical
Rational
Quantitative

Cerebral

D
Visual
Conceptual
Simultaneous

Fact Based   Open Minded

Verbal

Upper Left   Upper Right

Structured   Unstructured

Lower Left   Lower Right

Non-Verbal

Controlled   Feeling

B
Organized
Sequential
Procedural

Limbic

C
Emotional
Expressive
Interpersonal

Escape

from

the Maze

Source: Reprinted by permission of The Ned Herrmann Group, Lake Lure, N.C. Ned Herrmann, "The Creative Brain," The Journal of Creative Behavior (Fourth Quarter 1991), pp. 275–295.

Figure 6.2 Herrmann's Four-Part Model of the Brain

130

According to Herrmann, the "whole-brained creativity" perspective attributes these skills to each of the four parts of the brain:[9] (I have placed the type theory thinking style characteristic that seems to fit his descriptions after each of them.)

1. Cerebral left—logical thinking, analysis of facts, processing numbers (Thinking)
2. Cerebral right—visualization, daydreaming, conceptualization (Intuitive)
3. Limbic left—planning approach, organizing facts, detailed review (Sensor)
4. Limbic right—gut reaction, sensory response, interpersonal relations (Feeler)

As you discovered in Chapter 3, people have preferences for the way they gather and process information, and for their general style of making decisions. I suspect that Herrmann's research may indicate clues as to how brain dominance is related to these preferences. For instance, the sensor-thinker would be dominant cerebral left and limbic left; the intuitive-feeler would be dominant cerebral right and limbic right. But it is too soon in his research effort to know as yet.

IMPLICATIONS

We have spent a lot of time discussing the brain because it is the source of creativity. By now, we know, for example, about how boom-flashes work, about building connections between neurons, gender differences in brain functioning, and that at least seven key parts of the brain are involved somehow in creativity– the cerebral right, cerebral left, limbic right, limbic left, frontal right, fontal left, and the corpus callosum. Now that you understand how the brain works, let us find out more about how you use your brain to increase your creativity. The next chapter explores your preferences for left or right brain usage and the implications of these.

Mind and Matter: The Last Frontier– Understanding the Whole Brain– All Steps

Chapter 6

BRAIN AEROBICS 6

Part 1—Your Imagination Room[2]

In Chapter 1, you learned to visualize. In this chapter, we want to put that skill to use in increasing your creativity. Please follow the visualization routine from Chapter 1—relax in a comfortable setting, lean back, close your eyes, count backwards from ten, increasing your re-laxation with each number. When you are relaxed, create a creativity room in your mind. You can furnish it any way you like. You can paint it black, blue, peach, green, mauve, any color that you feel makes you more creative. It can be equipped with the latest computers, or none at all. So relax, and visualize this room. When you are finished creating, close the door to the room. Now you know that any time you want to be creative, you can return to this imagination room, a retreat in your mind.

Variations: If you don't want a room, create what-ever environment you feel you could retreat to and become creative. Perhaps it's a warm day at the beach with blue sky and puffy clouds, or perhaps it's a day in the mountains with the cold air biting your cheeks, maybe it's a waterfall, or a golf course. It can be whatever you want it to be. *So escape, by creating a place in your mind to retreat to for creativity.*

Part 2—Using Your Creativity Room or Other Creativity Place

Now think of a problem that needs solving. Gather informa-tion. Identify the true problem. Make assumptions, concen-trate. Now go to your creativity room or other creative place and let the solutions flow.

Escape

from
the Maze

[2]*Source*: Suggested by, but different than, Barrie Konikov, "Creative Thinking," audio tape (Grand Rapids, Michigan: Potentials Unlimited, 1979).

REFERENCES

1. Sharon Begley, et. al., "Mapping the Brain," *Newsweek* (April 20, 1992), p. 66.

2. Sharon Begley, "Gray Matters," *Newsweek* (March 27, 1995), pp. 48–54.

3. Duncan Maxwell Anderson, "Reviews, Books and Tapes," *Success* (September 1995), p. 74, relating a story told on an audio tape entitled "Mind Mapping" by Michael Gelb.

4. Richard Restak, *The Brain Has a Mind of Its Own: Insights From A Practicing Neurologist* (New York: Harmony Books, 1991), pp.138–139.

5. Ibid.

6. Ibid.

7. For futher information see:Marilyn vos Savant and Leonore Fleisher, *Brain Building: Exercising Yourself Smarter* (New York: Bantam, Dell, Doubleday, 1990); Moniques le Poncin, Lowell Blair, trans., *Brain Fitness* (New York: Random House, 1990); and Jacquelyn Wonder and Priscilla Donovan, *Whole Brain Thinking: Working from Both Sides of the Brain to Achieve Peak Job Performance* (New York: William Morrow and Company, 1984).

8. Ned Herrmann, "The Creative Brain," *The Journal of Creative Behavior* (Fourth Quarter, 1991), pp. 275–295.

9. Ibid.

*Mind and
Matter:
The Last
Frontier–
Understanding
the Whole
Brain– All Steps*

Chapter 6

BRAIN BREAK 2

WHAT IF'S

One of the fastest ways to increase your brain's creativity is to ask "what if's." Simply begin asking yourself "What if _____" happened? What would result? What should I do? What should our organization do? It is very important that you give yourself permission to imagine wild and crazy possibilities in order for this to work. You can then go back and evaluate your brain stormed ideas later.

Why don't you give "what if's" a try right now? Here are some for you to munch on for five to ten (or more) minutes. Now just imagine...

1. What if your unit was ordered to cut costs by 12%?
2. What if your organization's chief competitors created a product or service that leap-frogged your own?
3. What if you could turn your product into one that was ordered, and order fulfilled, on demand?
4. What if you could create a product or service that enabled your organization to leap frog the products or services of its competitors?
5. What if the depth of the world's oceans increased two feet? (It is possible although not necessarily probable with global warming.)
6. What if the world's supply of fish were to disappear over the next ten years. (The supply has been severely over fished in recent years, and is therefore much smaller than it used to be.)

Maybe you and/or your organization ought to run a "What if's of the Week." Mull it over; talk it up.

What if you tried some of your own "what if's" right now?

Escape

from
the Maze   134

BEING OF SOUND (RIGHT) MIND–STEP 5

CHAPTER 7

From now on the big fortunes in this world will be made by selling thoughts instead of things.

—George Gilder,
researcher and author on
entrepreneurship and economic trends

By all accounts, the most successful manager of his right brain is Japanese inventor Yoshiro Nakamats. Nakamats goes to great extremes to get in touch with his right side using specially designed rooms, various mental exercises, symphonic music and underwater contemplation. (See Great Escapes 8.1.) Does it work? You bet it does. With over 3000 patents, Nakamats has three times as many as Edison (1093). His inventions include the floppy disk, which he licensed to IBM for $75 million; the compact disk; the compact disk player; a digital watch; and a water powered engine.[1]

The major purposes of getting in touch with your right brain are two fold—first to build the strength of your right brain and secondly, so you can perform what is known as whole-brain, or androgynous, thinking, that is, using both sides of your brain. Before you begin a series of exercises to achieve these ends, let us find out if you have a preference for using one side of the brain or the other. Take the whole-brain thinking test which follows, then score it as directed. Give

135

some thought to what the implications of the results of this test are for you.

PREFERRED THINKING TEST

Researchers and authors have performed extensive analyses of the left-brain, right-brain phenomenon.[2] As a consequence of years of efforts, there are several tests available that measure your preference for left or right brain dominance. One of them follows. It is useful to know your preferences, especially at the extremes. If you have a strong preference for either half, it suggests that you need to work on the other side. Now complete the survey in Where Are You Now? 7.1.

Where Are You Now? 7.1
Test Your Thinking Style

On page 137 are matched pairs of words or phrases—one word or phrase from each pair appears on Side A, the other on Side B. For each pair of words or phrases, first pick the one that best describes your thinking style, then for that word or phrase, circle the number under the adjective (Often or Sometimes) that seems closest to your preferred thinking style. Remember to heed your initial preference. (This does not mean you never use the opposite strategy.) Simply choose the one that seems most comfortable to you at first glance. Next add up the four columns of scores. Then add the totals of the four columns together and interpret with the scale given below.

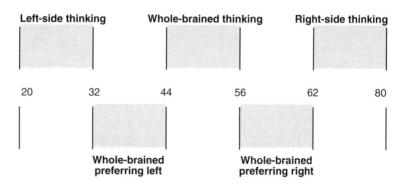

Escape

from
the Maze

SIDE A	Often	Sometimes
1. breaks problem into parts for analysis	1	2
2. oriented toward time	1	2
3. easygoing and spontaneous	4	3
4. thinks about movement and form	4	3
5. alert	1	2
6. uses intuition to solve problems	4	3
7. focuses on words being communicated	1	2
8. remembers faces, dress and motion	4	3
9. chooses words carefully	1	2
10. makes choices based on facts	1	2
11. abstract	4	3
12. works best in a structured work setting	1	2
13. insight	4	3
14. notices differences first	1	2
15. emotional	4	3
16. words and numbers	1	2
17. imagination	4	3
18. neat	1	2
19. challenge and the unusual	4	3
20. focus on the process	4	3

Totals: ___ ___

SIDE B	Often	Sometimes
1. assembles parts into whole for synthesis	4	3
2. not concerned with time	4	3
3. cautious and purposeful	1	2
4. thinks about formulas and structure	1	2
5. dreamy	4	3
6. uses logic to solve problems	1	2
7. concentrates on body language	4	3
8. remembers names and facts	1	2
9. uses gestures to communicate	4	3
10. makes chioces based on feelings	4	3
11. concrete	1	2
12. works best in a free-form work setting	4	3
13. observation	1	2
14. notices similarities first	4	3
15. rational	1	2
16. space and form	4	3
17. intellectual inquiry	1	2
18. sloppy	4	3
19. stability and the familiar	1	2
20. focuses on the product	1	2

Totals: ___ ___

Source: Reprinted by permission of Corporate Communications, Orlando Regional Healthcare System, *On Center*, Fall 1993.

Being of
Sound
(Right) Mind–
Step 5

Chapter 7

137

Interpreting Your Scores

Most of those who take this survey score between 32 and 56. Obviously if you score less than 32, you have work to do on the right side. A score of 32-44 also suggests that you have work to do. On the other hand, if your score is between 56 and 80, you probably need to give some work to the left side. The general belief is that an approach balanced between left and right is the most appropriate. However, some say there is no such thing as too much right-side strength. It can always be increased, making you even more creative. Unfortunately, as we discussed in Chapter 2, our institutions thwart right-side development as this chapter's Trapped in the Maze 7.1 suggests.

TRAPPED IN THE MAZE 7.1
Budding MBAs Not Creative Enough to Save Kool-Aid

When General Foods held a competition for budding MBAs, it was looking for creative solutions to this problem—"Develop a marketing plan to stem the plunging sales of sugar-free Kool-Aid." The results of competition among six of the nation's best business schools—Harvard, Chicago, Stanford, Northwestern, Michigan, and Columbia, were disappointing.

Students had an entire day to develop strategies. Each team was allotted 20 minutes to present its solutions. Judges from General Foods, its advertising agency and one of its consulting firms, evaluated these presentations over a five hour period. The criteria used were understanding of the business situation, feasibility, and creativity of solutions and the quality of presentations. Students did well on virtually all areas except creativity. The judges eventually named Michigan the winner on the strength of its strategic thinking.

Douglas Smith, Marketing Manager for Beverages at General Foods comments, "There were a couple of ideas that were of interest but nothing we haven't looked at before." Mr. Smith continues, "Business schools deal with the left side of the brain, with analysis and facts, but they don't help people much to use the other side which is judging and intuitive."

Source: Trish Hall, "When Budding MBA's Try to Save Kool-Aid, Original Ideas Are Scarce," *Wall Street Journal* (November 25, 1986), p. 31.

If Edison had had an MBA, he would have invented a bigger candle instead of a light bulb.
—Bennett Goodspeed, co-founder of Inferential Focus

Escape

from
the Maze

The good news is that some MBA programs are trying to shift that balance, as this chapter's Escape Routes 7.1 suggests.

ESCAPE ROUTES 7.1

Some Schools Strive to Innovate and To Teach Innovation

Not every MBA is totally deficient when it comes to creativity. A number of schools today offer courses in creativity and innovation, among them Stanford, Harvard, and Wharton. Typically such courses are electives, but a sizeable number of students take them. Effective the fall of 1996, every MBA student at the Roy E. Crummer Graduate School of Business at Rollins College in Winter Park, Florida, will be taught CPS, and receive at least some exposure to creativity techniques. The school has offered an elective "The Management of Innovation," since 1985.

Source: Lori Bongiorna, "Ivy and Innovation: B-Schools That Try Harder," *Business Week* (June 7, 1993); author's personal knowledge.

Most of us can improve in both right and left brain functioning. While most books on problem solving focus on rational processes, this book focuses on what can be done to raise the levels of creativity in problem solving.

Being of Sound (Right) Mind– Step 5

Chapter 7

GETTING THE FEEL OF LEFT AND RIGHT

Now that you have an idea of whether you are left or right brain dominant, the following sections will help you become more familiar with your left and right sides. These exercises are taken from *Whole Brain Thinking* by Jacquelyn Wonder and Priscilla Donovan. Read the following paragraphs and follow the instructions provided.

Exhibit 7.1

Left and Right

It is 2010 and the long-threatened World War III has started ... this time on American soil. Considering the size of the country and the years of preparation for war, it has been sickeningly easy for troops from China to permeate even the most remote areas of the United States. All Army, Air Force, Navy and other military forces have been mustered, and the President has announced that a million troops have been dispersed to strategic sites around the country. The governor has announced that seventy thousand well-trained reservists are in place around the state. A civilian-defense warning siren went off about an hour ago and has been wailing constantly since. Your office radio is tuned to station KODE, and your staff is gathered around listening to the mayor report what measures have been taken to protect citizens, what strategies are to be used for evacuation. In mid-sentence, the broadcast is interrupted by loud thuds and muffled cries. Suddenly your office door bursts open and six enemy soldiers armed with machine guns and carbine rifles storm into the room. They shout orders and questions excitedly, shoving your staff members against the wall for body searches. One soldier drags the youngest of your file clerks out of the office. She screams as she is buffeted down the hall. You raise an arm in protest, automatically saying "Wait!" and you see a rifle butt coming down on you!

Please write the answers to these questions without referring back to the above paragraph:

Escape

How many troops did the President command into battle around the country? _____

from
the Maze

How many reservists did the Governor call up? _____

What were the call letters of the radio station your office was tuned to? _____

How many soldiers burst into the office? _____

How were they armed? _____

If the World War III story was of compelling interest to you and you answered the questions immediately afterward, you just experienced a shift from your right brain to your left. The story is designed to set a malevolent scene and then focus it on you personally to move you to your emotional, visual hemisphere. Then the sudden switch to writing down facts and figures abruptly forces you left.

Did you feel the difference? Even a slight one? If you felt anything at all, focus on the process. Try to capture a notion of what is was like to be on the right, then on the left side. At first you may have been emotional, taking in the whole picture—seeing, hearing, and feeling all at the same time. Then, when you were asked to recall figures, names and details, your state of mind probably was quite different. The left-brained tasks focused your mind on the non-emotional aspects of the scene, and you probably calmed down quite a bit.

If a visual scene is particularly strong—whether pleasant or unpleasant—you may experience difficulty shifting brain modes. You might resist leaving the picture you were viewing or the emotions you are feeling. This resistance occurs because your body is experiencing the scene as reality with all the biochemical processes under way. Sometimes adrenaline rushes in and produces excitement or fear. In joyful situations, the brain's pleasure center releases endorphins and enkephalins, producing warm, fuzzy feelings.

On the other hand, if you have been working hard on a left-brain problem, you may become so engrossed with "the" solution or the next step in the plan that you are unable to shift right for a wider view. You know you are not getting anywhere, but you still feel irritation and resentment when someone suggests another tack or a broader view.

Being of Sound (Right) Mind– Step 5

Chapter 7

Just as some have difficulty switching modes, others shift too easily. Like a car with a bad transmission, some can not seem to stay in gear. They slip in and out of tasks, moods and thoughts so quickly and constantly that they have no perceivable point of view or direction. It is frustrating to deal with this type of person; it is frustrating to be this type of person. An awareness of your shifting patterns can help you overcome these and other thinking problems.

The sensation of shifting may at first elude you, but if you begin to pay attention to these feelings, you will come to know them. There are subtle, internal clues you can learn to identify. You can then use these to create and recreate specific body and mind reactions.

Yogis and other Eastern philosophers have been exercising this kind of internal control over so-called autonomic (automatic) body functions for centuries. Their breathing exercises have been shown to cause hemispheric shifts. (See Chapters 8 and 9)

Answers: a million, seventy thousand, KODE, six, machine guns and carbine rifles."

Source: Adapted by permission of William Morrow & Company, Inc. Jacquelyn Wonder and Priscilla Donovan, *Whole Brain Thinking* (New York: Ballantine Books, 1984), pp. 43–45. Copyright ©1984 by Jacquelyn Wonder and Priscilla Donovan.

Job Shifts[3]

If you operate successfully on your job, the chances are that you shift sides well. But if there are times when you are not happy with your performance, try developing your awareness of shifting and what provokes it so that you an do it at will.

Escape

from
the Maze

Shifting on the job:

– enables you to use more of your brain power by consciously selecting the appropriate brain style.
– helps you to understand the behavior of others and alter or adapt to it.
– shows you ways to change or adapt to your job, resulting in higher performance and personal fulfillment.
– increases energy levels and releases creative abilities.

MAKING SHIFTS FROM LEFT TO RIGHT OR RIGHT TO LEFT

There are additional actions you can take to get the feeling of shifting from left brain to right brain or right brain to left brain. Jacqueline Wonder and Priscilla Donovan suggest the following:

Exhibit 7.2

Left to Right	Right to Left
1. visualizing, daydreaming	1. taking notes, writing on flip chart
2. discovering patterns, the big picture, connections	2. organizing, setting priorities
3. opening up to "irrelevancies"	3. evaluating, eliminating extraneous ideas, setting goals
4. responding to body language, tone of voice, hug, smile, laugh	4. analyzing body language, tone of voice
5. talking to yourself in a positive, supportive way; using colorful, playful, childlike language	5. practicing your rational opinions and presentations

Being of Sound (Right) Mind– Step 5

Chapter 7

6. seeing through others' eyes, trying to feel their point of view	6. taking practice run, comparing, judging
7. moving, exercising, recreating, experiencing, playing, enjoying	7. deciding, recalling, questioning, checking progress, goals, time
8. shifting phone to your left ear (controlled by right brain) for *emphatic* listening	8. shifting phone to your right ear (controlled by left brain) for *analytic* listening
9. doodling, drawing, printing	9. writing, outlining, listing, working crossword puzzles, solving math problems
10. singing rounds, humming, recalling, joking, chuckling	10. asking questions, making puns
11. breathing deeply, saying or thinking "maaa" with each exhale; doing this until you feel relaxed; taking stroll to no place in particular	11. striding purposefully, touching toes or performing some other calisthenic activity, counting out loud until you have completed pescribed number
12. carrying a clipboard, notes or other comforting symbol	12. using dictating machine, picking up pointing of some symbol of authority
13. taking a minivacation at your desk; leaning back, relaxing, closing eyes; daydreaming	13. going off alone, writing a memo describing anger, concern, problem
14. visualizing green for freedom to glide, experience, enjoy, soar	14. thinking amber or yellow to slow down, considering consequences
15. making eye contact with others to feel their point of view	15. reporting experience to boss or spouse (preplan it with lists)

Escape

from
the Maze

144

16. relating to someone or something you know or have experienced	16. connecting with time, schedule, historic moment; looking at watch, mentally planning trips, or day's acivities
17. being aware of the colors, space, aromas, sounds, emotions around you	17. estimating value of your precision, economies, foresight
18. seeing the whole situation, how each person and element is related	18. breaking problem into separate parts, revisiting policies until consistency prevails

Source: Adapted by permission of William Morrow & Company, Inc. Jacqueline Wonder and Priscilla Donovan, *Whole Brain Thinking* (New York: Ballantine, 1984), pp. 52–53. Copyright ©1984 by Jacquelyn Wonder and Priscilla Donovan.

Moving from left to right (and right to left) is an important skill. One way to make this switch, and to do so in a way that truly unleashes creativity is to use a CAVE, a Cave Automatic Virtual Environment. Great Escapes 7.1 describes how CAVEs work and how one company has used these to improve the services it offers to its clients.

GREAT ESCAPES 7.1
Want to Be Innovative, Go Into a CAVE

There are seven CAVEs strewn across the United States. CAVEs are chambers, about 10-by-10-by-10 foot structures, within larger darkened rooms, say 30-by-20-by-15 feet. The CAVE chambers consist of a ceiling, a series of walls and a floor used as screens for multiple projectors. These projections create the illusion of reality for those inside the chambers. A series of supercomputers allow CAVE dwellers to change the environments inside the chambers according to a series of "What if," or "If then," statements. Huge amounts of information can be processed by these supercomputers allowing companies to investigate all kinds of industrial design and service situations. CAVE users do not need the complicated and bulky head sets and hand ware normally associated with virtual reality software, but rather can wear light weight stereo glasses and operate imaginary controls verbally or with small hand held controls.

Being of Sound (Right) Mind– Step 5

Chapter 7

CAVEs do not come cheap—a $million or more for complex problem solvers, but $200,000 bare-bones units are already coming on the market. The good news is you can rent one if you need to, or you can time share through financial contribution.

A typical CAVE session might go something like the following: You feel like you are standing inside the inferno of a giant industrial boiler. Looking down inside the boiler (actually looking at projections of the boiler against a wall and the ceiling and floor of the chamber), you almost get vertigo looking down the 400-foot drop to the blazing bottom. Suddenly, combustion gases, represented by multicolored arrows, literally dart past you as Lori Freitag, a modern electronic sorceress fires up the boiler using a hand held control line. Freitag next introduces pollution control chemicals through ports in the side of the boiler's simulated brick walls. Refreshingly, the electronic blizzard of gases abates somewhat, as the noxious nitrogen oxides are converted to harmless water and nitrogen. Within minutes Freitag can run simulations determining the effects of hundreds of different pollution control chemical droplets. Freitag's employer is the Argonne National Laboratory near Chicago, and her client in this simulation is Nalco Fuel Tech of Naperville, Illinois, a joint venture of Nalco Chemical Company and Fuel Tech of Stamford, Connecticut.

Fuel Tech is annually called in to some 250 companies around the world to solve pollution problems in boilers similar to the one being simulated. CAVE "technology makes it possible to find in a little as a day solutions that used to take a month," says William F. Michaels, Nalco Fuel Tech's manager of advanced computing systems. "With virtual reality," Michaels enthuses, "we now can see the result instantly," and in 3-D, and in motion, and without the need for hundreds of pages of printouts. Fuel Tech hopes not only to double its pollution control business through the use of this technology, but also to create new services to offer its customers, for example, determining where slag might build up and finding ways to head it off. Other companies are already using CAVEs for product design and for process redesign.

Source: Gene Bylinsky, "To Create Products, Go into a CAVE," Fortune (February 5, 1996), pp. 80A–80E.

> *Creativity and change are two sides of the same coin... creativity is needed to respond successfully to changes and creativity, in turn, results in change.*
> —J.L. Adams, Author of *The Care and Feeding of Ideas: A Guide to Encouraging Creativity*

TWO KINDS OF THINKING

Problem solving is a cyclical process. Within this cycle, there are two distinct kinds of thought processes: divergent and convergent.[4] **Divergent thinking** means expanding the picture of the problem. It is essentially a right-brain activity and involves stating the problem in various forms, looking at it from various points of view, gathering information, and generating numerous options for solving it. For example, think of the orange. Now think of twenty disparate uses for this fruit that don't include eating it. This is

Escape

from

the Maze

146

divergent thinking. Divergent thinking leads to escape. **Convergent thinking** means narrowing down the problem and related parts of it's solution, to a more manageable size and perspective. It is essentially a left-brain activity and

involves evaluating the selected options in preparation of making choices. For example, if you now determine which of your twenty uses for the orange is "best," then you would be engaging in convergent thinking. Convergent thinking is reductive because it creates smaller and more detailed pictures from which to prepare for action. Too much convergent thinking and you are trapped in the maze.

Both types of thinking are important to effective creative problem solving. One of the most important skills in problem solving is knowing when to use each. If you can combine divergent and convergent modes of thinking and use them flexibly according to the situation, you will be progressing toward mental integration—combining the skills of an innovator with the skills of the practical realist. Both divergent and convergent modes of thinking utilize both conscious and subconscious thought processes.

In our schools and organizations we mostly teach convergent thinking. We are, as a society, weak in divergent thinking. This book is about increasing your divergent thinking— *So escape and use both sides of your brain.*

Being of Sound (Right) Mind– Step 5

Chapter 7

147

BRAIN AEROBICS 7

Part 1—What Corrective Actions Do You Need to Take to Become Better in Each Type of Thinking?

	Action	Completion Date
1. Divergent–		
2. Convergent–		

Unfortunately, since we are taught to not be creative, we often can't when we really need to.

Part 2—Using Your Divergent Thinking Skills

If you are a manufacturer of ink-jet printers for PCs, there might be any number of reasons why your latest model isn't selling well. List 10 reasons now.

1.   2.

3.   4.

5.   6.

7.   8.

9.   10.

Escape

from
the Maze

If you said price, then what might contribute to having too high of a price? Perhaps, too many parts, even too many screws. If you said quality, then what might contribute to having too low of quality? You could guess too many parts, too many screws again, and be correct again. You might also look to subassemblies, paint, inspection, design, solders, chips, and so forth. This has been an exercise in divergent problem identification.

Try it now for one of your company's products or services. What makes it sell well, or more poorly than the sales targets?

Part 3–Making the Shifts From Right to Left and Left to Right

Practice moving from the right side to the left, and from left side to the right as shown in Exhibit 7.2.

*Being of
Sound
(Right) Mind–
Step 5*

Chapter 7

149

REFERENCES

1. Anonymous, "Japan's Amazing Inventor," *The Economist* (November 25, 1995), p. 38; Charles (Chic) Thompson, *What a Great Idea* (New York: Harper Perennial, 1992), pp. xi–xviii.

2. Jacquelyn Wonder and Priscilla Donovan, *Whole Brain Thinking* (New York: Ballantine, 1984), pp. 22–32, 40–41.

3. Ibid., pp. 47–48.

4. For an in-depth discussion see Gordon S. Bonner, *Implementing Innovative Solutions: Harvesting Acres of Diamonds* (Buffalo, New York: Creative Education Foundation, 1990), pp. 2–31.

Escape

from
the Maze

MANAGING THE RIGHT SIDE
—STEP 5

CHAPTER 8

The demands on our creative abilities have doubled in every generation.
—Peter F. Drucker

Much of creativity occurs through association—one boom, flash meets another boom, flash—one idea from a specific area of thought meets another idea from a different area of thought. Suddenly, the right brain is engaged, and the creative thinker recognizes that what works in one place could work in another. In 1989, Alda Ellis decorated bars of soap with colorful designs and gave them as Valentine's Day gifts. Those who received these gift bars were quite pleased, but Alda was not. The paper images that she had cut from gift wrap, wrinkled and fell off the soap bar when it was put in water. Pondering the problem a few days later, she remembered from her college chemistry class how she might make these images last until the soap ran out. Boom, flash. After a little experimentation, Red Oak Hill Inc., the designer soap company owned by Ellis and her husband, Buddy, was born. Sounds simple, but no other firm had ever developed such a product. Sales were about $10 million in 1994.

Managing the Right Side– Step 5

Chapter 8

The Ellis's did not stop innovating with this first step of design application. They created a special "triple French milled" soap which lasts three times as long as normal soap. They are now pursuing additional product ideas. They have already found other outlets for their products. They appear not only on the shelves of thousands of upscale specialty stores and department stores, but are also given away by companies and individuals wishing to advertise their names.[1]

DRAWING ON THE RIGHT SIDE[1]

Betty Edwards has revolutionized the way in which individuals learn to draw. She has cut the time it takes to go from beginner to artist by two-thirds. At the heart of her methodology is the belief that people have trouble drawing because they draw what they perceive, not what they really see. The left brain, you see, is in charge of perception and dominates the right side's visual perspectives with stored interpretations rather than letting the actual data through. The key is learning how to use your right side more, hence, the title of her book, *Drawing on the Right Side.*[2]   The next few pages contain exercises from her book. Although she reveals how to use your right side more effectively to be creative in only one endeavor—drawing–you can use these exercises and many other of the exercises in her book to learn to be more creative by enhancing your ability to use your right side—right brain aerobics.

Getting the Feel of Left and Right[3]

L–MODE

1.   Image the foursquare, bold L. See it with your mind's eye with its straight sides and right angle. Now enlarge the image, adding another form so you can see the comparison of sizes: image the L as large as a pyramid or the Empire State Building. Now see the L in color, any

Escape

from
the Maze

[1]Most of the material beginning at this point and continuing to "The Relexation Response," is reprinted by the permission of The Putnam Publishing Graoup/Jeremy P. Tarcher, Inc. from *Drawing on the Right Side* by Betty Edwards. Copyright ©1979, 1989 by Betty Edwards.

color. Now attach to the L, in any way you like, the characteristics of the **L-mode** style: words, numbers, time, mathematical equations, diagrams, maps, books; perhaps images of mathematicians, lawyers, scientists, accountants. The image can be whatever you decide on. You will remember the images longer and more clearly if you make them up yourself. Most important, locate the L-mode in your own skull by placing your hand (either hand will do) on the left side of your head: reduce the size of the image and imagine that you are placing the L-mode inside the left half of your brain.

If you do not expect the unexpected you will not find it, for it is not to be reached by search or trial.
— Heraclitus, philosopher

$\mathcal{R}$-MODE

2. Now image the curvy $\mathcal{R}$. See it in your mind's eye with its complex curves. Enlarge it or make it smaller if you wish. Add other forms so you can see the relationship of sizes. Then attach the functional characteristics of the **$\mathcal{R}$-mode,** right-hemisphere style: perhaps images of persons who are painting, drawing, playing melodies, sculpting, dreaming with a sense of timelessness. Because these functions are less distinct—in true right-hemisphere style—than the L-mode functions, this may tax your imaging powers. How do you image nontime? Perhaps, as a surrealist artist such as Dali would, as a clock without a face. How do you image analogs, things that are alike? How do you image the ah-ha! response? Take some time for this, until you can call up a picture in your mind of the $\mathcal{R}$-mode. Then place your hand on the right side of your skull and image again the $\mathcal{R}$-mode inside the right half of your brain.

You have to have a coyote inside you and you have to get it out.
—Chuck Jones, creator of Wiley E. Coyote

Now shift the images to opposite sides: the mathematician, scientists, etc., can move across the corpus callosum to the $\mathcal{R}$-mode in order to image and dream of new inventions; the artist and musician, to the L-mode in order to analyze aesthetic problems.

Managing the Right Side– Step 5

3. Do this several times until you can feel yourself shifting from one image to the other, first to the left side of your brain with the L-image, then to the right side with

Chapter 8

153

the $\mathcal{R}$-image. This practice in making a mental shift from L to R will help you during the drawing exercises to make the mental shift to drawing mode ($\mathcal{R}$-mode). Exhibit 8.1 describes how to do this.

Exhibit 8.1

A COMPARISON OF LEFT-MODE AND RIGHT-MODE CHARACTERISTICS	
L—MODE	**$\mathcal{R}$—MODE**
Verbal—Using words to name, describe, define	Nonverbal—Awareness of things, but minimal connection with words.
Analytic—Figuring things out step-by-step and part-by-part.	Synthetic—Putting things together to form wholes.
Symbolic—Using a symbol to stand for something. For example, the drawn form stands for eye, the sign + stands for the process of addition.	Concrete—Relating to things as they are, at the present moment.
Abstract—Taking out a small bit of information and using it to represent the whole thing.	Analogic—Seeing likenesses between things; understanding metaphoric relationships.
Temporal—Keeping track of time, sequencing one thing after another: Doing first things first, second things second, etc.	Nontemporal—Without a sense of time.
Rational—Drawing conclusions based on reason and facts.	Nonrational—Not requiring a basis of reason or facts; willingness to suspend judgment.
Digital—Using numbers as in counting.	Spatial—Seeing where things are in relation to other things, and how parts go together to form a whole.
Logical—Drawing conclusions based on logic: one thing following another in logical order — for example, a mathematical theorem or a well-stated argument.	Intuitive—Making leaps of insight, often based on incomplete patterns, hunches, feelings, or visual images.
Linear—Thinking in terms of linked ideas, one thought directly following another, often leading to a convergent conclusion.	Holistic—Seeing whole things all at once; perceiving the overall patterns and structures, often leading to divergent conclusions.

Escape Routes 8.1 describes how Disney provides the opportunity for feature movie animation employees to engage their right brains, to shift from left to right.

Escape Routes 8.1

A Creative Gong Show

How does the Feature Animation Division of Walt Disney Studios encourage right brain thinking—with a gong show where the risks are low, but the potential rewards are high. Three times a year the division holds a gong show for its staffers, ranging from secretaries to animators. About forty people present at each show. They have three to five minutes to make their pitch. They receive advice and assistance from other staffers in preparing their presentations. The gongers consist of Michael Eisner, CEO of Walt Disney Companies; Peter Schneider, president of Feature Animation; Roy Disney, Jr., major shareholder and Disney board member; and Schneider's executive VP, Tom Schumacher.

Though the gongers provide a scary audience at first glance, considerable effort is made to provide a free spirited, low threat environment for the presenters. Once the presenters are finished, the team talks about which ones they liked, and which parts of others they liked. The team may pick and choose ideas from different presentations. Feedback is instantaneous—"Great idea," or "That story line will never work." But part of creating the low threat environment is that the gongers often disagree among themselves, and tell each other out loud for all the participants to hear. For example, other members of the team might say,"Michael, you're wrong, and here's why." This then allows the presenters to feel that they can say the same thing. Over the years, the Gong Show's credibility has been established. Employees know they will get a fair shake, and that there will be no grudges held by anyone afterwards.

Once ideas have been selected, they are moved forward through a development process that depends on much debate, but eventually on consensus. When asked how effective the Gong Show was, Schneider replied, "Most of Disney's animated features have come from this process." The rewards to the presenter can be significant. The person with an original idea that is eventually put into the development process is given a "first treatment" fee which, according to the industry standard, is about $20,000.

Source: Joe McGowan, "How Disney Keeps Ideas Coming," *Fortune* (April 1, 1996), pp. 131–134.

Managing
the Right
Side–
Step 5

Chapter 8

How could your organization use a "gong show" or something similar to air employee ideas for new products or processes?

Imaging Crossover Connections: Brain and Body

The drawing exercises to come, designed to help you gain access to the ℛ-mode, will be more effective if you clearly understand the crossover connections of the brain halves and body halves. By doing these exercises you will be able to evoke easily an image of these connections, rather than having to think about them in words.

1. Imagine connections between your left brain and the right side of your body. Imagine the connections in any way you wish—as tubes, electrical currents, wires, whatever. Now imagine pathways in a color, say blue or red, going from the left brain to every part of the right side of your body.

2. Next, shift to the other side. Imagine the connections between your right brain and the left side of your body in a different color, perhaps green or yellow.

3. Now imagine the whole system and its crossover connections.

The Enchanted Loom

One of the most famous word pictures of the brain was formed by the English scientist Sir Charles Sharrington. He pictured the brain as "an **enchanted loom** where millions of flashing shuttles weave a dissolving pattern, always a meaningful pattern though never an abiding one...."

1. Visualize in your mind's eye the magic loom inside your head, with its myriad flashing shuttles now coalescing in one part of your brain—dissolving, darkening, then streaming across to another part in an ever-changing pattern: glowing and subsiding, glowing and subsiding.

Escape

from
the Maze

156

2. Now imagine that you can control the pattern and can cause the flashing shuttles to gather in one part, then dissolve and gather in another part. Imagine them gathering first on one side then on the other. Imagine that this gathering causes an actual physical sensation inside your brain, a slight change in pressure, a minute shift in weight, a faint buzzing sound, a slight warming or cooling.

Watching the Loom

Psychologists have reported that many people seem to be able to "stand back" and become aware of their varying mental states as if they were watching their brains at work. These imaging exercises and some of the drawing exercises will help you develop this hidden "Observer," psychologist Charles Tart's term, thus becoming more aware at a conscious level of slightly shifting brain states. This in turn will help you to "turn on" the *R*-mode state that enables artists to see and draw.

Fuzziness is an essential part of human thinking.
— Lofti A. Zadeh, Professor of Science, University of California, Berkeley

Using the Loom

Unfortunately, not all organizations want to have their employees engaging the right side as this chapter's Trapped in the Maze 8.1 suggests.

Trapped in the Maze 8.1

Oh No, Not the Pit

One of the Innovative Thinking Network's two 1996 George Land World Class Innovator Awards went to Ford Motor Company's Material Planning & Logistics' (MP&L) Team Learning and Creativity Center. Accepting the award for Ford was Rick Gutherie, supervisor of the center. The MP&L division was the first at Ford to embrace the company's new employee involvement and participation program in 1981.

To further this concept they embraced a "family work team"

Managing the Right Side– Step 5

Chapter 8

157

training program to encourage teams to learn new skills and challenge old paradigms together.

In the late 80s, as part of this emphasis on training, the MP&L Team Learning Center was established in an Italian-style monastery, surrounded by open land and forests. The center remains the longest running Organizational Change effort in the automotive business. However, in 1991 it's viability was challenged when a corporate edict was issued eliminating offsite training. The Center circumvented this policy by renegotiating its lease as a "warehouse, storage-only lease." During that time, Center associates were "stored" at Duns Scotus Monastery for their Team Learning sessions.

The recently renamed Team Learning & Creativity Center began specific innovation training in 1987 when each associate attended a four-day seminar that defined the environment, skills and leadership traits necessary to encourage innovation. This program provided the pivotal structure that helped transform the role of the Learning Center from just skills training to the application of skills and new learning to support key business issues, strategies and goals.

During the past year, all 600 MP&L employees have had a minimum of two non-technical training days focused on roles and responsibilities and Ford's new Vision and Key Strategies; and over the years, MP&L has saved millions of dollars working on innovation goals that have improved quality and reduced costs. Additionally, employee satisfaction, as measured by Employee Involvement surveys, shows a level 65% higher than the average corporate norm.

Ford MP&L defines innovation as the "relentless application of our natural ability to create new and better ways of enjoying life and working together. Successful innovation lies in our willingness to harness the power of chaos at the individual, team, and organizational level. The innovative spirit is truly in every one of us and it can only be fully released in a supportive, team oriented culture.

Clearly the focus of 21st century business will be the transformation of its workforce into a culture that brings out the most innovative and collaborative thinking of everyone at every level—harnessing the power of chaos."

But life at Ford has not always been so accepting of empowerment, new ideas, and innovation. When Rick first came to Ford as a full-time college student and full-time employee in the late 1960s, he worked in an assembly plant. At that time Ford had no suggestion program, but Rick had plenty of suggestions about how to improve the operation. Within a few weeks he had relayed several of these to his boss, and implemented some on his own. One day, after telling his boss of his latest idea to help save money, his boss said, "I am the manager. I have the ideas. You are the subordinate. You don't have ideas. I think a stay in the pit would be good for you." Rick thought, "Oh no, not the pit." But since he had a family to support, he followed his orders gloomily.

Escape

The pit was a work area used as much for punishment of troublesome subordinates as for assembling automobiles. The pit was just that, a pit dug into the factory floor at a level below the assembly line, but not far enough below it that workers could stand upright. They had to crouch all

from
the Maze

day as they put parts into the underbody of the cars as they moved down the assembly line. After the first day in the pit, Rick was so sore that he had begun to question the value of new ideas. After three weeks in the pit, Rick promised his supervisor that he would not have any more ideas to offer, and thereby secured his release from the pit.

Although Rick has gone on to show that new ideas can be valuable—he has documented substantial savings, improvements in customer service (product innovation), higher productivity levels, and higher employee satisfaction rates, some areas of Ford still seem disinterested in creativity and innovation. Other higher priority issues seem to capture their attention. Despite the fact that Rick has on several occasions offered to help other divisions create such centers and train employees in innovation, he has had no takers. Could Ford still be trapped in the maze? Two years ago the answer would have been yes. Now, with the company-wide transformation called Ford 2000, Rick believes this maze will be solved.

Sources: Parts are quoted directly from "George Land World Class Innovator Award Winners Announced," *MindPlay: Creativity and Innovation in Today's Business Environment,*" The Newsletter of the Innovative Thinking Network," April/May 1996, pp. 1, 3; and Rick Gutherie, "Acceptance Speech for the George Land World Class Innovator Award," (Santa Barbara, California: February 29, 1996).

Drawing Right

Now please complete a drawing exercise from Edward's *Drawing on the Right Side.* This exercise is known as a vase-faces exercise. You first draw a face, which when mirrored, can be turned into a vase. Through this exercise, you will experience both left and right side modes.

Exhibit 8.2

Vase-faces Drawing
The Baroque Vase and Monster Face

Draw a Vase-Faces drawing, following the directions below. Read all the directions before you begin.

1. On the left side of a blank sheet of paper if you are right-handed, or the right side of the piece of paper if you are left-handed, draw a human profile. Draw the profile of the oddest face you can conjure up—a witch, a ghoul, a monster. Name the parts of the face as you go down the profile, naming also whatever embellishments you add, such as wrinkles, moles, double chins, etc. The figures below provide examples, but make up your own profile if you wish.

2. After you finish this first profile, add the horizontal lines at the top and bottom to help form a vase.

3. Now draw the profile in reverse, completing the vase, a baroque vase.

Managing the Right Side– Step 5

Chapter 8

159

The first monster profile is an L-mode drawing of symbolic forms that represent the features of the face. Especially in this complex Vase-Faces drawing, the second profile can best be done—even, perhaps, can only be done—by shifting to right hemisphere mode. The complexity of the

For Left-handers   **For Right-handers**

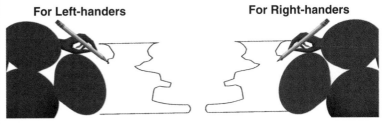

form forces the shift to right-hemisphere mode. The point of this exercise is not how perfectly you do the drawing but rather that you try to feel the shift from left-mode to right-mode. Try to be aware of the difference between the modes. As you begin to recognize when you have shifted cognitive modes, you will be taking a first step toward learning to control consciously which side of your brain you use for a given task.

Trying to draw a perceived form by using the verbal left mode is like trying to use a foot to thread a needle. It doesn't work. You need to be able to "turn down" the left hemisphere and activate the right. This requires unblocking the right, or, as Aldous Huxley phrased it, "opening the Door in the Wall."

THE RELAXATION RESPONSE

Traditionally in many Eastern cultures, one of the ways that you become more in touch with your subconscious is meditation. Thus one of the ways in which you become more intuitive, more creative, is through meditation. Meditation allows you to change from **beta brain waves** to **alpha brain waves** and **theta brain waves**. These are more likely to allow you to be creative than the beta waves that you would typically be using in day to day activities. Meditation puts you in alpha, and when you reach deep meditation (or in near sleep), you will be in theta. Table 8.1 shows the various wave patterns of the six principle types of brain wave ranges.

Escape

from
the Maze

160

Table 8.1

BRAIN WAVE LEVELS

Brain wave levels are described in terms of Hertzes, a quantification of the electric charges emitted by the brain and measured by an electroencephalogram. Following is a table indicating six ranges from the slowest, delta, to the most frequent waves of beta.

Hz.	Name of State	Characteristics
0.5-4	delta	Deeper states of sleep
4-8	theta	Drowsiness, dreaming, also occurs during such alert behaviors as sudden insight or recognition of event in memory. A trance state unless drug-induced. Used for *twilight learning (also occurs during deep meditating).*
8-14	alpha	Relaxed wakefulness. Brain not actively engaged in any specific mental or emotional activity. Can be present when mental activity is habitual and does not require concentration; when focusing inward; when receptive, or conversely, when blocking emotional responsiveness. Neutral, resting, meditating. Achieved best with eyes closed.
14-22	beta	Ordinary beta where alert behavior and concentrated mental activity occur. Also anxiety and apprehension.
22-33	high beta	Revving up, increased anxiety or hyper responses and thinking.
over 33	K-complex and unnamed	Short burst of high frequency occurring when short-term memory consolidation and problem-solving occur.

These ranges are approximate and vary among individuals because of differing response levels and location in specific parts of the brain. The matter is further complicated by the difficulty in measuring such minute amounts of electricity and screening out artifact (interference from unrelated sound and movement).

Source: Reprinted by permission of William Morrow & Company, Inc. from Jacqueline Wonder and Priscilla Donovan, *Whole Brain Thinking* (New York: Ballantine Books, 1984), pp. 114–115.

Managing the Right Side– Step 5

Chapter 8

161

As shown in the above table, you normally use beta in day–to–day activities, but in alpha and theta you are most likely to be creative.[4]

Meditation—a process of contemplation and reflection that often involves special breathing techniques—is a foreign concept to many Americans and conjures up all sorts of images which typically are not readily acceptable in our society. However, Dr. Herbert A. Benson developed a technique now used by millions of Americans to relieve stress that produces the same effects as meditation. He analyzed various forms of meditation including yoga, transcendental meditation, and self hypnosis, and determined that they all have common ingredients. His studies clearly indicated definite changes in brain waves and physiological patterns, such as galvanic skin response and blood pressure, as a consequence of meditating. He formulated an approach which combined all the major facets of the various forms of meditation. He calls this technique the **relaxation response.**

Miracles do not happen in contradiction to nature, but only in contradiction to that which is known about nature.

—St. Augustine

This technique produces the brain wave changes that are necessary to get you more in touch with your subconscious and your right brain. When your left brain is dominant, your brain is functioning mostly with beta waves. When the right brain is dominant, it functions mostly with alpha waves. Engaging in this relaxation technique changes the dominant brain wave pattern from beta to alpha and even to theta in near sleep. While conceptualized mainly as a technique for relieving stress, it well serves our purpose for getting more in touch with our subconscious and raising our levels of intuition. The belief is that by doing so, we can increase our creative abilities. A description of the technique follows in Exhibit 8.3.

Escape

from
the Maze

Exhibit 8.3

THE RELAXATION RESPONSE TECHNIQUE

1. A Quiet Environment

One should choose a quiet, calm environment with as few distractions as possible. Sound, even background noise, may prevent the elicitation of the response. Choose a convenient, suitable place — such as at an office desk in a quiet room.

2. A Mental Device

The meditator employs the constant stimulus of a single syllable sound or word. The syllable is repeated silently or in a low, gentle tone. The purpose of the repetition is to free oneself from logical, externally oriented thought by focusing solely on the stimulus. Many different words and sounds have been used in traditional practices. Because of its simplicity and neutrality, the use of the syllable "one" is suggested.

3. A Passive Attitude

The purpose of the response is to help one rest and relax, and this requires a completely passive attitude. One should not scrutinize his performance or try to force the response, because this may well prevent the response from occurring. When distracting thoughts enter the mind, they should simply be disregarded.

4. A Comfortable Position

The meditator should sit in a comfortable chair in as restful a position as possible. The purpose is to reduce muscular effort to a minimum. The head may be supported; the arms should be balanced or supported as well. The shoes may be removed and the feet propped up several inches, if desired. Loosen all tight-fitting clothing.

Eliciting the Relaxation Response

Using these four basic elements, one can evoke the response by following the simple, mental, noncultic procedure that subjects have used in my laboratory.

- In a quiet environment, sit in a comfortable position.
- Close your eyes.
- Deeply relax all your muscles, beginning at your feet and progressing up to your face — feet, calves, thighs, lower torso, chest, shoulders, neck, head. Allow them to remain deeply relaxed.
- Breathe through your nose. Become aware of your breathing. As you breathe out, say the word "one" silently to yourself. Thus: breathe in ... breathe out, with "one." In ... out, with "one" ...
- Continue this practice for 20 minutes. You may open your eyes to check the time, but do not use an alarm. When you finish, sit quietly for several minutes, at first with your eyes closed and later with your eyes open.

Managing the Right Side– Step 5

Chapter 8

163

Remember not to worry about whether you are successful in achieving a deep level of relaxation — maintain a passive attitude and permit relaxation to occur at its own pace. When distracting thoughts occur, ignore them and continue to repeat "one" as you breathe. The technique should be practiced once or twice daily, and not within two hours after any meal, since the digestive processes seem to interfere with the elicitation of the expected changes.

With practice, the response should come with little effort. Investigations have shown that only a small percentage of people do not experience the expected physiological changes. (It has been noted that people who are undergoing psychoanalysis for at least two sessions a week experience difficulty in eliciting the response.)

A person cannot be certain that the technique is eliciting these physiologic changes unless actual measurements are being made. However, most people report feelings of relaxation and freedom from anxiety during the elicitation of the relaxation response and during the rest of the day as well. These feelings of well-being are akin to those often noted after physical exercise, but without the attendant physical fatigue.

The practice of this technique evokes some of the same physiologic changes noted while practicing other techniques. These physiologic changes are significant decreases in body metabolism (oxygen consumption and carbon dioxide elimination) and rate of breathing. Decreased oxygen consumption is the most sensitive index of the elicitation of the relaxation response.

Source: Reprinted by permission of *Harvard Business Review.* An excerpt from "Your Innate Asset for Combating Stress," by Herbert Benson, (July/August 1974). Copyright ©1974 by the President and Fellows of Harvard College: all rights reserved.

If your mind is empty, it is always ready for anything; it is open to everything. In the beginner's mind there are many possibilities, in the expert's mind, there are few.

—Shunryu Suzuki,
*Zen Mind,
Beginner's Mind*

You want to start with the relaxation response and practice it a couple of times as described. Then move to what is known as creative relaxation. In creative relaxation, you concentrate on a problem before you begin the relaxation response. Next, you relax deeply. Then you let thoughts come into your mind about the problem. The relaxation response helps you incubate. Ideas will follow. Almost every time I have used this approach, it has produced at least a few worthwhile ideas in just twenty minutes. Sometimes lots of ideas result.

Once you feel comfortable with the relaxation response, envision yourself being creative while you are in that response. You might, for example, want to see yourself in your creativity room. You construct that room in your mind but when you feel the need to be creative at work or at home or whatever you are, you can retreat to that room in your mind. (See

Escape

*from
the Maze*

164

Brain Aerobics 6)   Put yourself in your relaxation response, get into your right side, and retreat to that room and become creative.

Yoshiro Nakamats goes to great extremes to make the shift to the right side possible for himself.   Great Escapes 8.1 describes how.

GREAT ESCAPES 8.1
Dr. Yoshiro Nakamats' Creative Environments

Dr. Yoshiro Nakamats is arguably the most innovative person who ever lived, with almost three times as many patents, over 3,000, as Thomas Edison, 1,093. The next closest inventor holds only 400. Nakamat's inventions include the floppy disk (which he licensed to IBM), the compact disc, the compact disc player, the digital watch and a water powered engine.

Nakamats uses a three part process to spark his creativity, each part involving a separate environment which he has developed. The first step is free association.   To do this, he uses his "static room."   It has white walls, except for the one which is glass and overlooks the Tokyo skyline, and it contains only natural things—a rock garden, running water in a little stream, a five-ton boulder, plants, and wood.   There is no concrete or metal.

Next, he goes to his "dynamic room" to begin focusing, concentrating. This room is the opposite of the static room.   It is dark, with black-and-white striped walls.   It has dark leather furniture and special audio and video equipment to help him create.   He always starts out listening to jazz, then easy listening, and finally completes his creative sessions with Beethoven's fifth symphony, "good music for conclusions," he notes.

Finally, he engages in creative swimming. He has developed a special way of breathing and swimming underwater that enables him to really focus.   "That's when I come up with my best ideas."   He has created a special plexiglass writing pad so that he can record his ideas while underwater.

Some of Nakamats' personality characteristics that might also be of interest are these: He takes naps to help him come up with good ideas; he only sleeps four hours a day; he believes that creativity lies in a balance of freedom and regimentation and he is, in 1996, 66 years old;

Managing the Right Side– Step 5

Chapter 8

165

Nakamats' environments help him significantly increase his incubation potential by activating his right side. Since most of the time, you must concentrate to create, most of the time you must also have time to incubate, to let creativity happen.[5] So you may want to set aside a creative environment for yourself—a quiet room, a hammock in the shade of an old oak tree, or some other place to which you can retreat. (In group creativity sessions, concentration often is not as important as the interaction dynamics which function to produce ideas.)

Brain Aerobics 8

Breathing Right and Left

In addition to the value of getting on the right side, many creativity experts also agree that it is a very good idea to be able to use both sides together more intentionally than just starting on the right side and letting the left side assist naturally. There is a breathing process known as **centering** which accomplishes this end.

CENTERING

Sit comfortably, close your eyes, and relax, counting backward from ten, relaxing more with each decreasing number. Begin feeling the difference between your left and right nostril. Try to identify sensations on each side.

Escape

from
the Maze

Now, breath in through your left nostril and out through your right nostril.

166

Now reverse this process, breath in through your right nostril and out through your left nostril.

Repeat these steps seven to ten times. At the end of this period, assuming you have been able to achieve this process, you will be centered. Now you can begin to work on a problem and expect to be more creative.

COMMENTS AND OBSERVATIONS

This is not an easy process at first, but with practice, you can achieve the physical breathing in and out. You will have to use it a few times before you can determine for yourself whether it helps your creativity or not.

*Managing
the Right
Side–
Step 5*

Chapter 8

REFERENCES

1. Michael Barrier, " Innovation as a Way of Life," *Nation's Business* (July 1994), pp. 18, 19.

2. Betty Edwards, *Drawing on the Right Side* (Los Angeles, California: J.P. Tarcher, Inc., 1979).

3. The material beginning at this point and continuing to "The Relaxation Response," with the exception of Escape Routes 8.1 and Trapped in the Maze 8.1,is reprinted by the permission of The Putnam Publishing Group/Jeremy P. Tarcher, Inc. from *Drawing on the Right Side* by Betty Edwards. Copyright ©1979, 1989 by Betty Edwards.

4. Some experts say alpha, some theta, so I have included both.

5. Pierce J. Howard, *The Owner's Manual for the Brain* (Austin, Tex.: Leornian Press, 1994), p. 4.

CHAPTER 9

Intuitive decisions come from a capacity to integrate and make use of information coming from <u>both</u> the left and right sides of the brain. It is a product of both factual and feeling ones—unclouded by deep personal ego involvement in the issue at hand.

—Weston Agor,
innovation researcher,
consultant and author

Doug Hall is a master at freeing up the right side in himself, and in others. His companies, Richard Saunders International and AcuPoll Research, are among the leading new product invention firms in the United States. He states that his firms test more new product ideas in one year than Procter & Gamble tests in ten.[1] He uses a variety of techniques to "loosen up" an audience. One of those is the whoopee cushion. When 125 hard-nosed, Anheuser-Busch executives whooped all at once, somehow their childhood began to return.[2]

Reinforced with other techniques, creativity usually follows this process of letting go and getting whacky, just one of the right-brain techniques we will study in this chapter. Others include listening to creativity tapes, blue skying, biofeedback, and certain breathing exercises.

169

The chapter then discusses the activities which you can use to increase mental and transcendent intuition through suspending the left side. Suspending the left side includes listening to music; cloud watching and day dreaming; mindless activity where the left side gets bored, such as jogging, showering and driving; sleeping on it and getting alone.

One thing is for sure, firms in the toy industry could benefit from teaching their employees activities for getting more in touch with their right side and for managing the left side. Why? Because, "The toy business, in the view of many who work in it or watch it, is suffering from a chronic creativity shortage."[3] Trapped in the Maze 9.1 describes this apparent shortage, and some of the problems that this industry faces.

TRAPPED IN THE MAZE 9.1
There Is Not Much Creativity in this Creativity Business

When the average adult thinks about the toy business, he or she thinks about lots of new, exciting toys coming to market—toys that stir the imagination and bring new perspectives. But in the U.S., apparently nothing could be further from the truth. Few toys are new, and few stir the imagination. True, many are exciting, but they provide few new perspectives.

Of the 5000 "new" toys displayed at a recent toy fair, by and large most of them were extensions of existing products. Only three of the top 15 toys sold in the U.S. have been created within the last year. Barbie, a well preserved doll of thirty-seven years, and related product extensions, is the largest selling toy product at $1.4 billion. Of course, if toy makers had not given up on electronic games, one of those would undoubtedly be the best selling "toy" since Japanese firms now sell over $6 billion of them each year. Many new toys are the result of extending movie characters and their "toys" or other paraphernalia into the toy field, for example, Batman and his Batmobile. Frank Reysen, editor of the an industry magazine, *Playthings*, ponders, "One wonders if toy makers are running out of ideas?"

Toy makers of course deny this, but they spend a lot more on advertising than they do on R&D, three times as much at Hasbro, and five times as much at Mattel, for example. Mattel spokesman, Glenn Bozarth notes, "Marketing is the name of the game in the toy industry. Our success has been concentrating on time-tested products that endure from year to year." Perhaps that is why that sales of traditional

---

Escape

from
the Maze

toys are sluggish, with only a one-half percent growth rate after considering inflation. Industry observers point out that following a conservative strategy of licensing movie characters and extending tried and true products causes toy makers to lose out on the possible revenues that blockbusters such as the Cabbage Patch Kids and Frisbie's can create.

Kids toys today do not stir their users' imaginations very much either. Nancy Carlsson-Paige, professor of early-childhood education at Lesley College in Cambridge, Massachusetts, comments that a common complaint among her colleagues at the teacher-training institution is that, "when kids as young as first grade get drawing assignments, they all end up drawing toys they see on TV, instead of coming up with their own creative ideas and symbols." Apparently toys made from movie and cartoon features do little for the child's creativity.

The position the industry appears to be taking on creativity can perhaps be summed up by an experience that game inventor Bruce Whitehill had when he first reported to work at Milton Bradley, a division of Hasbro. He was told two things. 'Invent games with the head buyer at Toys "R" Us in mind, not the consumer; and don't create games that can't be explained in a 30-second commercial on TV." Whitehill goes on to explain that the most valued people in a toy company's development department "aren't idea guys but people who can draw," because they can sketch new prototypes for old characters.

Source: Joseph Pereira, "Playground Safety: Toy Business Focuses More on Marketing and Less on New Ideas," *Wall Street Journal* (February 29, 1996), pp. A1, A8.

MORE ACTIVITIES FOR GETTING IT MORE RIGHT–STEP 5

This section of the chapter covers creativity-increasing tapes, blue skying, biofeedback, breathing exercises, letting go and getting whacky, and brain tune-ups.

Listening to Creativity Tapes

For achievement-oriented people, who often have numerous thoughts running through their heads, the relaxation response is often difficult to elicit properly by themselves. If you are having difficulty performing the relaxation response to its fullest extent, try a **creativity enhancing audio tape.** What you are looking for in a tape

More Managing the Right Side, and What's Left of It– Steps 5 and 6

Chapter 9

171

is a guided relaxation effort. Several of my most productive idea sessions came when using such a tape.

There are a limited number of self-hypnotic tapes available in bookstores and elsewhere, which can lead you to a creative experience. Typically these tapes attempt to put you in a relaxed state much like the relaxation response would, and then have you see yourself being creative. The difference between doing creative relaxation alone or with a creativity enhancing tape, is that the tape will, 95 times out of 100, enable you to be more relaxed than you would on your own. Later, you can do just as well on your own. You may have to try a couple of tapes before you find the one you like. I have created such a tape to help guide you to higher levels of creativity. To obtain a copy of "Releasing Creativity," call 1-407-647-5344 or 1-800-2-N-O-VATE. For an alternative, try "Creative Thinking" by Barrie Konicov. Call 1-616-891-0410 to order it.

Blue Skying

Blue skying is a technique in which you simply let your mind roam to its level of wildest imagination about your personal or organizational objectives, or any other subject of interest to you. Fantasize, create, imagine fantastic objectives that you would like to achieve, fantastic things that you would like to do. Think about what you would like to become. Think of things that you would like to see made.

Some men see things and say, "Why?" I dream of things and say "Why not?"
—George Bernard Shaw

Many good ideas usually come from this exercise. This is essentially personal brainstorming, but with much more fantasy added to it.

Biofeedback

Escape

Biofeedback is informative feedback about one's biological conditions given to someone that he or she be able to respond to, replicate, or modify those biological conditions. In building creativity levels, biofeedback is used primarily as a way of replicating biological and/or mental actions which lead to

from the Maze

172

creativity. For example, if you are attempting to learn how to elicit the relaxation response, the biofeedback machines will "show" you when you have reached the proper brain wave pattern. You would, upon examination of biofeed- back information about your mind and body at that time, know how you "felt," and what you did to "feel" that way. Thus, you would be able to repeat that behavior in the future in order to repeat the brain wave level de- sired.

"Biofeedback uses sophisticated electronic equipment to measure such body responses as skin moisture, muscle ten- sion, and electrical emissions of the brain. As brain waves shorten or lengthen and as temperature and muscle tension rise and fall, the biofeedback machine to which the person is attached signals these changes either visually or with sound. The person then devises internal strategies for achieving the desired body reaction. Like the children's game of blindman's bluff, as you get closer to the object, you receive signals tell- ing whether you are getting hot or cold. Then you change directions based on this feedback.

However, the biofeedback client has an advantage over the game player. A person who has developed a strategy for achieving warmer fingers or less muscle tension can perform the feat over and over again without further feedback.

Your feelings are *your* feedback, and by becoming sensitive to them, you will be able to shift and integrate your brain's activities as the situation demands. Like the person in bio- feedback therapy who learns to control tension, perspiration, heartbeat, temperature and other responses, you can develop inner strategies for moving between your brain's hemispheres or integrating the thinking powers of both."[4]

Breathing Exercises

Breathing exercises that effect hemispheric brain dominance can raise creativity levels. "Research shows that by altering primary breathing from one nostril to the other, short-term hemispheric control is accomplished. (This allows you to call on the right side when you need it.)

More Managing the Right Side, and What's Left of It– Steps 5 and 6

Chapter 9

One swami was able to heat opposite sides of one of his palms to temperatures five to seven degrees apart through breathing and mental exercises. He noted that it had taken him twenty years of training to accomplish this, but biofeedback, called the "Yoga of the West," has enabled people to perform the same feat after several weeks of training.[5]

> *At the boundary, life blossoms.*
> —James Gleick, author of *Chaos*

Ancient yoga techniques for changing mental or psychological states prescribed alternating one's breathing between the two nostrils. Research at the Salk Institute for Biological Studies, San Diego, indicates that the nose is more than a mere olfactory device, it is an instrument for altering brain activity. Electroencephalograph (EEG) tests show a consistent relationship between nasal airflow and cerebral dominance.

The researcher, David Shannahoff-Khalsa, feels that his work demonstrates the individual's ability to noninvasively, selectively, and predictably alter cerebral activity and associated physiological processes and also implies that humans need not be helpless victims of a given emotional state. If you want to alter an unwanted state, just breathe through the appropriate nostril.

Escape

from the Maze

174

Dr. I. N. Riga, an ear, nose and throat specialist from Bucharest, Romania, discovered that surgically correcting nasal deformities had the simultaneous benefit of curing physical and emotional ills. Of four hundred patients with nasal obstructions due to deviated septa, those who had breathed through the left nostril suffered from stress-related diseases (89 percent left-nostril breathers versus 29 percent of right nostril breathers). Once their right-nasal passages were open, these former left-nostril breathers were relieved of their stress illnesses. This concurs with other research that indicates that the right brain usually is the source of negative stress."[6]

Letting Go and Getting Whacky

As the chapter's opening paragraph on Doug Hall suggested, sometimes, you just have to **let go and get whacky.** Normally, this helps free up the right brain. A number of companies have provided different settings to encourage this to happen. For example, a number of companies have creativity rooms complete with punching bags, trampolines, play dough, children's games and other fun stuff. Employees go there to have fun to trigger the creative process. Other firms allow spontaneity throughout the firm. This chapter's Escape Routes 9.1 describes one of these settings.

More Managing the Right Side, and What's Left of It– Steps 5 and 6

Chapter 9

175

ESCAPE ROUTES 9.1

Getting Completely Whacky At Southwest Airlines

When was the last time you were sitting on an airliner when a stewardess dressed in a bunny costume popped out of the overhead baggage compartment? Or how often have you flown in a plane painted like Shamu, the whale. Or how often have you had your pilot say, "Folks, you need to sit down so I can see to back up?" If you fly any company other than Southwest Airlines, probably never, but if you fly Southwest, such events may have happened to you more than once this past year. Southwest has created a culture in which it's ok to be whacky, within the limits of good taste, of course. The objective is not just to have fun, but to create ways of serving the customer better.

CEO, Herbert D. Kelleher—dubbed by *Fortune* magazine as the "High-Priest of Ha-Ha"— wants his employees to have a sense of humor and work in an environment that builds a strong sense of community. Creativity aimed ultimately at improving customer relations is found throughout the company. For example, Southwest encourages unions and company personal to research issues and survey employees before contract negotiations. "If we treat employees the right way, they will naturally treat our customers the right way," offers Elizabeth Pedrick Sartain, vice-president of the "People Department."

The results—impressive. Southwest won the 1996 Triple Crown Award (customer satisfaction, baggage handling, and punctuality) given by the U.S. Department of Transportation. It has the lowest employee turnover in the industry, and it has managed to make money in recent years when most other airlines were reporting losses. So the next time a Southwest stewardess asks you to, "Please pass your empty plastic cups to the end of your aisle so they can be washed and used on the next flight," or gives you a rubber cockroach in your drink, or you see a bunch of Southwest ticket agents dressed in costumes for Halloween, remember, it's all in creatively good fun aimed at improving customer service.

Sources: "ABC Evening News" (April 18, 1996); Cathy Lynn Grossman, "Making the Skies Friendlier: These Pilots Like to Travel Lighthearted," *USA Today* (March 13, 1996), pp. D1, D2; Brenda Paik Sunoo, "How Fun Flies at Southwest Airlines," *Personnel Journal* (June 1995), pp. 62–73.

Escape

from

the Maze

Brain Tune-ups

One way of improving your brain functioning, according to its proponents, is a **brain tune-up**. Such tune-ups consist of

being hooked up to sound and light machines which balance your two hemispheres. Most such programs use
goggles to provide the light images and
headsets for sound.[7] Variations include
earphone-only cassettes which prom-
ise to synchronize your brain.[8] Clinics
or brain centers in a few major cities
offer brain tune-ups.

For most people, the best way of achieving a brain tune-up, is
through the purchase of a brain tune-up system for use at
home. Most of these are priced in the $300–$400 range for
audio-visual systems, and the $100 range for audio only sys-
tems. Zygon International, Inc. of Redmond, Washington
(1-800-865-7575), is the most frequent advertiser of such
products that I have seen. I have not used their system, so I
am unable to comment on it, but they will send you information on their product if you call them.

USING LEFT-SIDE SUSPENDERS–STEP 6

Certain types of activities suspend the left side and put the
right side in control–**left side suspenders**. You may already
know some left-side suspenders: driving a car, taking a
shower, meditating (already discussed in a more active format as a right-brain aerobic), jogging, or drinking alcoholic
beverages. The first four of these activities are mental, the
last one is physical. Mental suspenders suspend the left side's
control of the brain in two ways: by overloading it with details (such as might happen in a cross-examination by an at-
torney), or by starving it to death for information, such as
occurs while driving, showering, meditating, or jogging; as a
result, the left brain becomes bored and the right side takes
over. Physical suspenders work to change the chemistry of
the brain. Alcohol, which changes chemistry, works primarily to remove social inhibitions, but the chemical changes
may also function somehow to make idea associations easier.

> *The basis of
> creativity has
> always been a
> new
> connection.
> To make
> connections
> would take
> hours using
> words. Your
> subconscious
> has to use
> pictures.*
> — William
> J.J. Gordon

*More
Managing
the Right
Side,
and What's
Left of It–
Steps 5 and 6*

Chapter 9

The following paragraphs examine several left-side suspenders.

Driving, Taking a Shower, Jogging, and Other Non-Thinking Activities

Non-thinking activities such as driving a car are good for incubation and illumination. The left side falls asleep and the right side is engaged. Ned Herrmann, creativity researcher and author (see Chapter 6), discovered the integrating principal for his whole-brain thinking concept while driving the thirty-five curvy mountain miles from his office to his home. He had been concentrating on the problem, when, eureka, the solution appeared right in front of him, fortunately on a straightaway and not in a curve. Hence was born the four parts of the brain theory—the left and right cerebral and the left and right limbic.[9] (Don't forget frontal right and left.)

Jogging, taking a shower, rowing, swimming, and other monotonous exercises also put the left side to sleep. Wayne Green of Peterborough, New Hampshire, a publisher of computer magazines and owner of several software-related enterprises, swears by the process. "When I get into the shower, the light goes on for me."[10] Stanford's Hugh Lusted, inventor of Biomuse—a device that makes music from brain waves—got the idea for Biomuse while taking a shower.[11] When you take a shower, another creativity enhancing event is taking place—negative ions coming from the water, charge your environment in such a way that you may become more creative. Part of using the shower to be creative has to do with having thought about the problem before you take the shower, much like sleeping on it. Also, because of your wet environment, you may want to purchase a plastic notepad and appropriate pen to record your ideas.

> *Why is it I get my best ideas in the morning while I'm shaving?*
>
> —Albert Einstein

John Sculley, former CEO of Apple Computers, claims that he got his best ideas on his three-mile morning jog. Jain Benham, founder of Capital Preservation Fund, and his own performing jazz band, comments on his own creative process, "I really do get a lot of great ideas when I play the

Escape

from
the Maze

178

horn. ... I'll be playing my horn and all of a sudden some business thought pops into my head. I'll go write it down. I don't know how to explain it, but that's just what happens."[12]

Or how about a nice sauna? Or a massage? Ralph S. Heath, president of Ovation Marketing, Inc., provides his employees with an exercise room complete with sauna and masseuse.[13] The creative results, he believes, have been worth the cost.

Watching lava lamps, wave machines, bubbling water towers, waterfalls, getting lost in your PC's screen-saver pattern, and other repetitive, no thinking required phenomena also suspends the left side, and lets the right side take over.

Cloud Watching and Daydreaming

Remember back when you were a child and you used to lie on the ground and watch the clouds go by and make all sorts of fantasies about what the clouds represented— lobsters, cattle, people, faces, trees. Doing that evokes the visual side of your brain, your right side. Watching clouds causes you to create fantasies which are important in getting those atrophied brain "muscles" back into shape. So go out and lay down and look up, watch the clouds and fantasize about what you see. Now think about a problem and watch the ideas flow. This happens in two main ways. First, cloud watching causes you to get on your right side—which helps you incubate and improve your creativity. Secondly, fantasies about the clouds may suggest solutions to your problem. Sitting out at night and gazing at the stars and looking into space has somewhat the same affect.

The uncreative life isn't worth living.
— Ted Nierenberg, founder, Dansk International Designs, Ltd.

More Managing the Right Side, and What's Left of It– Steps 5 and 6

Chapter 9

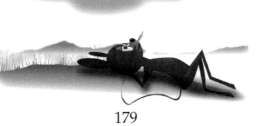

179

Listening to Music

Music puts many people into their subconscious. They begin to visualize, to make associations, to drift. Music is a right-brain activity, so that also aids creativity. Not all types of music assist creativity, and what helps seems to vary but soft, not overly loud music, seems best.[14]

James Cameron and his wife, Gale Anne Hurd, produced and directed "Aliens," the summer movie hit of 1986. Cameron was responsible for drafting the basic story. He secluded himself for four days, listening to music, appropriately Gustav Holst's *The Planets*. The results were both artistically and financially successful.[15]

Sleeping on It–What Happens When We Sleep?[1]

You can use sleep productively as an incubation period. Before we address that issue, let us discuss sleep in general.

"In my dream, I was standing in an art gallery. As I walked down the hall, I began to count the paintings. As I came to the sixth and seventh, I realized they had been ripped from their frames."

This recollection of a dream came from a Stanford University student the day after he and 500 others were asked to solve the following riddle: The letters O, T, T, F, F form the beginning of an infinite sequence. What are the next two letters in the sequence? The students were to ponder the riddle and record any dreams they had that night.

When the conscious mind cannot come up with the language to communicate a solution, says Richard Restak in his book

Escape

from
the Maze

[1] This section, up to the point "Getting Alone," with the exception of boxed material and certain modifications, is reprinted by permission of the Communications Department, Orlando Regional Healthcare System, Orlando, Florida

180

The Brain Has a Mind of Its Own, it must rely on help from the subconscious.[16] Although the student was consciously unable to solve the riddle, his (subconscious) mind knew the answer. Consider the letters in the riddle. If we assign numbers — one, two, three, four, five — to them, we can then, using the dreamer's clues, identify the next two letters in the sequence as S, S — six and seven.

We spend one-third of our lives sleeping, and not all of it is spent problem-solving. The exact purpose of sleep has long been a subject for debate. As a necessary bodily function, we could say that sleep is our brain's vehicle for performing preventive maintenance on our entire system. The brain is selective when choosing which areas work the night shift. For instance, those tracts responsible for attention and learning are at rest during sleep. Sensorimotor neurons—those governing movement and sensation —are also inhibited. Once the body is resting comfortably, the real action begins.

THE ART OF DREAMING

> *If one advances in the direction of his (or her) dreams, one will meet with success unexpected in common hours.*
> —Henry David Thoreau

Sleep follows a well-charted course through the waters of the night, traveling through a series of channels appropriately termed "cycles." As we lose consciousness, the brain, with a quickening of pulse and breathing, suddenly bursts into electrical activity. In the telltale sign of rapid eye movement (REM) sleep, our eyes begin to mirror the intense activity occurring within, as they begin to dart back and forth, right and left. Let the dreams begin.

During REM, the brain stem fires bursts of impulses into the area of the brain that processes visual information, probably inciting the images we experience during dreaming. At the same time, activity is triggered in a critical part of the brain known as the hippocampus, where our recent experiences are encoded for long-term memory.

From a scientific standpoint, we can guess that, aside from their often nonsensical content, dreams perform a physical function as well — a kind of "housecleaning" of our memory

More Managing the Right Side, and What's Left of It– Steps 5 and 6

Chapter 9

banks. Experiences from the day are sorted through and decisions are made to file them away or pitch them out. Daily puzzles (problems) are pondered and sometimes solved.

Carrying this notion one step further, we can say that the brain is "creative" even during the nighttime hours. In our dreams we become writers, painters and filmmakers, combining extraordinary characters, plots and locations into strangely coherent experiences. Once coined the "royal road to the subconscious" by psychoanalyst Sigmund Freud, dreams are now believed to be simply part of a normal physiological process. Dreams are of emotional consequence, and most dreams are a result of pre-sleep feelings that trigger our brains to search our memory banks for similar experiences.

Think hard about your problem and then go to sleep on it. Charles Goodyear dreamed that a man told him to add sulfur to the product he was working on. Following this advice, Goodyear eventually developed the vulcanization process for rubber.[17] Fredrich August Kekulé was able to discover the chemical structure for the benzene ring in a dream. It was during sleep that Edison found the key to inventing the light bulb. Great Escapes 9.1 discusses some of these great creative sleepers.

GREAT ESCAPES 9.1

To Sleep, Perchance to Dream, Perchance to Problem Solve

Fredrich August Kekulé, a German scientist, had worked many weeks on the structure of benzene but couldn't figure out how it was bonded. Having thought about it all day he went to sleep one night in his chair in front of his fireplace. He had a dream about the sparks from the fire dancing in a snakelike way. Suddenly they formed a whirling circle which appeared to be six snakes each biting the tail of the next snake. The sparks (snakes) formed an approximate circle, but more than a circle, they formed a hexagon. (Another version of the story reports a snake biting its own tail.) When he awoke from the dream, he knew immediately that the benzene molecular formula was a ring with six sides.

Escape

from
the Maze

182

Thomas Alva Edison recognized that being asleep or in near sleep was vital to his creativity. He would often work through the night on a project. He would take catnaps, sleeping sitting up in a chair. In both hands he would hold ball bearings. As he fell fully asleep, the bearings would fall into metal pie pans that he had placed beneath each hand. The noise from the bearing hitting the metal would wake him. Often he would have a new insight upon awakening which he would instantly write down.

More recently, French entrepreneur Pierre Alan-Cotte went to bed wondering why we still had all the paper in our offices even though computers were supposed to eliminate the paper overload. In the middle of the night, the solution came to him—an inexpensive scanner. So off to Silicon Valley he headed. His $500 PaperMac hit the market in 1994.

Computer whiz, Alan Huang, head of Bell Labs Opitcal Computing Research Department, had been working for years on an optical computer. He had made some headway, but couldn't seem to find the breaththrough he needed. The goal was certainly worthy—a laser-based computer would be much faster than a Cray supercomputer because light travels faster than electricity. But traditional computer engineering was not getting Huang very far. Then, for a period of several months, he kept having a reocurring dream—two armies marched towards each other, stopping just short of confrontation; or on some nights they would run into each other tying themselves into a big red knot. Then one night, they marched right through each other, but with no collision. When Huang awoke, he knew there was a way to make the laser computer work. Unlike electric currents, laser beams can pass right through each other unchanged, thus making normal circuitry paths irrelevant.

Sources: For the six snake version see William D. Dement, *Some Must Watch While Some Must Sleep: Exploring the World of Sleep* (New York: Norton, 1978), p. 98; David Goleman, Paul Kaufman, and Michael Ray, *The Creative Spirit* (New York: Penguin/Plume, 1993), pp. 23, 59, for the one snake version and the material on Edison; and Richard Brandt, "Heavenly Valley," *Business Week-Enterprise*, special edition (1993), pp. 169–170 for the material on Pierre-Alan-Cotte. Jason Forsythe, "The Deam Machine: Use the Powers of Your Unconscious," *Success* (October 1990), p. 36, for material on Huang.

To make the most of your sleep, you should:

1. Pick an appropriate night when you are not too tired, and when you have not consumed any alcohol nor taken any drugs that might affect brain function.
2. Write down notes on the events of the day, especially the problem you want to solve.
3. Concentrate on your problem just before going to sleep, talk about it with yourself.
4. Condense or synopsize your discussion into a couple of sentences—your problem statement.
5. Repeat your problem statement until you fall asleep.
6. Sleep.

More Managing the Right Side, and What's Left of It– Steps 5 and 6

Chapter 9

7. Record your dreams and/or solution ideas when you awake.[18] If you have dreams rather than straight solutions, interpret these in light of your problem. Record those solutions that emerge.

GOOD NIGHT

More than a mere recovery from today's wear and tear, tonight's sleep will be an active and dynamic preparation for the challenges of tomorrow, and you can thank your brain for this renewal. Until then, sweet dreams!

Getting Alone

Sometimes it pays to just get alone and think about other things, not about the problem you have been working on and thinking about. It is amazing how often, when you are thinking about other things, your mind begins to tie thoughts together, to make connections on previous thoughts and problems that you had been concentrating on.

Closing Your Eyes

Closing your eyes acts to suspend your left side by shutting off one of its primary functions—perception. It gets bored, and the right side takes over.

Sensory Deprivation Tanks

Much the same occurs when using sensory deprivation tanks. All senses are cut off and the right side takes over. The tanks are expensive and potentially dangerous for some users.

LEARNING TO INCUBATE

Escape

from the Maze

There are a number of techniques that you can use to facilitate the incubation stage of the creative process. One of the key factors in being creative seems to be the ability to allow your thoughts to connect by allowing them to incubate. They seem to have to bang around in there for awhile before they

184

can get together. Sometimes incubation takes six minutes and sometimes it takes six weeks, six months, or six years. You can improve your incubation through right-side aerobics and through suspending the left side.

BRAIN AEROBICS 9

Using the Right Side, Suspending the Left

USING THE RIGHT SIDE

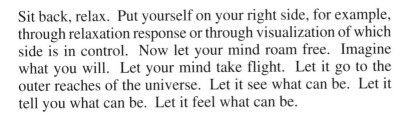

LISTENING TO CREATIVITY TAPES

Purchase a creativity tape. Now use it.

BLUE SKYING

Sit back, relax. Put yourself on your right side, for example, through relaxation response or through visualization of which side is in control. Now let your mind roam free. Imagine what you will. Let your mind take flight. Let it go to the outer reaches of the universe. Let it see what can be. Let it tell you what can be. Let it feel what can be.

Once you have done this, use blue skying to solve a problem, to set personal goals, to fantasize, to create.

BIOFEEDBACK

If you have the money (it is not inexpensive), you can obtain biofeedback equipment through ads in various magazines, for example, *Psychology Today,* or through various mail order catalogs which sell such items, for example, *Self-Care.* Or you can call the psychology department of a local college or university to find out if they would assist you in developing your capabilities.

If you want a surrogate biofeedback measure of your brainwave management effectiveness, you can take your pulse and/or blood pressure, before and after a relaxation response

More Managing the Right Side, and What's Left of It– Steps 5 and 6

Chapter 9

185

exercise. Odds are that if your pulse drops five to ten points, or your blood pressure drops a similar amount on the low side, then you are affecting your brain-wave activity to some extent. However, if you get a lot of heart-lung exercise every week (twenty minutes, four times a week), these surrogates are not going to be as indicative—pulses and blood pressures are already pretty low and cannot drop much further.

BREATHING EXERCISES

See Brain Aerobics 8.

LETTING GO AND GETTING WHACKY

Go to a toy store. Find something intriguing. Take it home. Now, it's up to you. If it's a punching bag, punch it. If it's a model plane, put it together. If it's play dough, make wild and crazy figures. If it's a humorous video, watch it. Have fun.

Now be creative. Try to solve that problem you've been working on.

BRAIN TUNE-UPS

Brain tune-up facilities exist in only a few cities. If you want to do this, your best bet is to order either audio-visual equipment and tapes, or audio tapes.

USING LEFT-SIDE SUSPENDERS

The next time you take a shower, jog, swim, or engage in other monotonous activities, be aware of what is occuring. Feel your left side falling asleep. Feel the right side taking control. Become aware of how this transition occurs. Now take advantage of it. Solve a problem. (Often, before you can begin to consciously take advantage of this transition, your mind will have already moved on to solving a problem.)

CLOUD WATCHING AND DAYDREAMING

Take off twenty minutes some partially cloudy afternoon, go outside, lie down in a comfortable position, in a lounge chair or on the ground, and watch the clouds go by. When you are finished, record your feelings. Record what you saw. Record your new ideas. Think about how the process occured. Note how your left-side fell asleep, and your right side engaged.

Now when you need new ideas, give it a try.

Now repeat these instructions for daydreaming, but you need not go outside to do so. Any comfortable position will usually lead to day dreaming if you let your mind wander.

LISTENING TO MUSIC

Most people enjoy listening to music so this should be an easy one for most of you reading this book. However, it is important that the music you choose for being creative, be soft, for example, easy listening or most classical music. Listen, then feel your mind wandering. Try to solve some problem while listening to this music. Let the ideas flow. When completed, record what happened using the same instructions as for previous exercises in this section.

SLEEPING ON IT

It is very important to think hard about your problem for a few minutes just before you fall asleep. Think of the key ingredients to the problem, think of possible solutions. Then let your self drift off into sleep. Be sure to have something to write with and some paper on your night stand. When you awake, either during the night or in the morning, record your thoughts at that moment. Do not be discouraged if you do not immediately have brilliant ideas. Give it time.

OTHER LEFT-SIDE SUSPENDERS

Next time you need to solve a problem creatively, get alone or close your eyes and let the right side take over, or maybe even try a sensory deprivation tank (caution: can be dangerous).

More Managing the Right Side, and What's Left of It– Steps 5 and 6

Chapter 9

REFERENCES

1. Doug Hall with David Wecker, *Jump Start Your Brain* (New York: Warner Books, 1995), p. 31.

2. Ibid., pp. 32–33.

3. Joseph Pereira, "Playground Safety: Toy Business Focuses More on Marketing and Less on New Ideas," *The Wall Street Journal* (February 29, 1996), pp. A1, A8.

4. Jacquelyn Wonder and Priscilla Donovan, *Whole Brain Thinking* (New York: Ballantine, 1984), pp. 46–47.

5. Ibid, p. 46.

6. David Shannahoff-Khalsa, "Rhythms and Reality: The Dynamics of the Mind," *Psychology Today* (September 1984), pp. 72–73.

7. Joshua Cooper Ramo, "Putting the High In High Tech," *Newsweek* (November 8, 1993), p. 73; John Patrick Zmiark, "Workplace Utopia," *Success* (March 1993), pp. 35–36; Mark Alpert, "How Japan's Workers Relax," *Fortune* (April 23, 1990), p. 17; Joseph Pereira, "How Many People Would Shell Out $20 To Listen To Static?" *Wall Street Journal* (April 13, 1990), pp. A1, A6; Carrie Dolen, "Try a Brain Tune up to Keep Your Mind Off the Stock Market," *Wall Street Journal* (October 21, 1987), pp. 1, 31.

8. I have not tried their products, but one such company is the John-David Learning Institute. 1-800-437-5646. *Psychology Today* has several ads for such items in each issue.

9. Ned Hermann, "The Creative Brain," *Journal of Creativity* (Fourth Quarter, 1991), pp. 275–276.

10. Author's personal knowledge.

11. Brian Mattimore, "Breakthrough Ideas—Part 3," *Success* (October 1990), p. 61.

12. Michael Ray and Rochelle Myers, *Creativity in Business* (New York: Doubleday, 1986), p. 7.

13. Greg Hinderyck, "Creative Process Often Starts With a Good Massage," *Marketing News* (April 15, 1991), pp. 8–9.

14. For a partial review see Jill E. Adaman and Paul H. Blaney, "The Effects of Musical Mood Induction on Creativity," *Journal of Creative Behavior* (Second Quarter, 1995), pp. 95–109; William F. Allman, "The Musical Brain," *U.S. News & World Report* (June 11, 1990), pp. 56–62; Anne H. Rosenfeld, "Music, The Beautiful Disturber," *Psychology Today* (December 1985), pp. 48–56.

15. Richard Schickel, "Help! They're Back!" *Time* (July 28, 1986), p. 57.

16. Richard Restak, *The Brain Has a Mind of Its Own: Insights From a Practicing Neurologist* (New York: Harmony Books, 1991), pp.138–139.

17. Thomas P. Murphy, "Eureka," *Forbes* (May 7, 1984), p. 8.

18. Gayle Delaney, *Living Your Dream: Using Sleep to Solve Problems and Enrich Your Life,* Revised Edition (San Francisco, California: Harper, 1988), pp. 55–58.

More
Managing
the Right
Side,
and What's
Left of It–
Steps 5 and 6

Chapter 9

BRAIN BREAK 3

Time for some more fun.

One of the most important aspects of developing your intuitive thinking style is to expand your perspectives. One of the best ways of doing this is to play what are commonly called "wordies." The idea is to see what phrase is represented by an arrangement of words. Try the following pair of wordies to see if you get the gist of it

$$\frac{\text{MAN}}{\text{BOARD}}$$ LEG Quartre ION

If you answered "man overboard," and French Foreign Legion (French four on Legion), bravo. So now let's see how good you really are at this game. (Answers may be found in Appendix 3.)

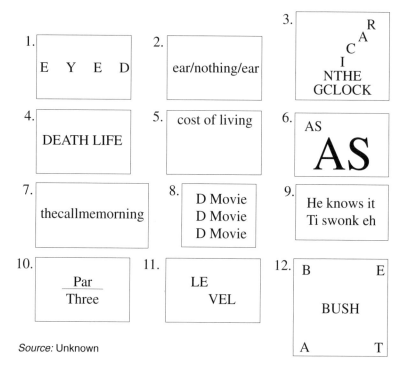

1. E Y E D

2. ear/nothing/ear

3.
```
            R
          A
      C
    I
   NTHE
   GCLOCK
```

4. DEATH LIFE

5. cost of living

6.
AS
AS

7. thecallmemorning

8. D Movie
D Movie
D Movie

9. He knows it
Ti swonk eh

10.
$$\frac{\text{Par}}{\text{Three}}$$

11. LE
VEL

12.
```
B              E

        BUSH

A              T
```

Escape

from
the Maze

STILL MORE MANAGING THE RIGHT SIDE—STEPS 7, 8 AND 9

CHAPTER 10

Creativity isn't a destination, it's a journey.
　　　　　　　　　　—Michael Ray and Rochelle Myers,
　　　　　　　　　　authors and consultants on creativity

Ed Katz had built Choice Courier into one of the premier messenger services in the northeast. But then along came faxes. No, the courier business did not go away, but its market potential was clearly limited, and it offered no real hope of growth. So Katz began Twilight Express—the first regional next-day delivery service. About one-third of all overnight service takes place in the northeast. By limiting his service area to the northeast, Katz was able to offer what Federal Express could offer but at half the price. Then Katz realized that he could offer both storage and delivery services for his customers. For example, in New York City, one of his customers is a computer company. Rather than lugging parts all over town, service technicians now just call Choice and the part is delivered immediately to the location where it is needed. As Katz notes, "The innovative hot button is third-party logistics." Katz is expanding this storage and delivery service nationwide.[1]

Recognizing and identifying complex problems are difficult tasks. Solving them can be even more difficult. One of the most difficult challenges an entrepreneur faces is recognizing when his or her business or industry is maturing. The next major challenge is what to do about this problem. Ed Katz saw his problem as an opportunity. He made something happen. If he had not been a sound creative thinker, and if he had not had considerable experience at solving complex problems, he might have missed this perspective. This chapter discusses three important steps to escape—improving your thinking skills, practicing solving complex problems, and recording your creative thoughts.

IMPROVING YOUR THINKING SKILLS— STEP 7

Edward de Bono, one of the leading authorities on thinking, suggests that we have not really made much progress in our thinking modes since the Greeks.[2] "We still use their kind of dialog and dialectical ideas. As tools these are very limited, they are absolutely useless for resolving conflict which is why we are still fighting so many wars. Dialectics, math, logic, data processing are all second-stage thinking. Perception comes first and we have yet to improve on perception."[3]

De Bono suggests that the brain is really not designed to function as a thinking machine but rather as a recognition machine. He feels the mind is simply, brilliantly routine and uncreative. It sorts, it recognizes but it does not do very much with it. The key for you to be successful, he feels, is to do much more with your brain than others do.

De Bono observes that business people, more than anyone else, are very interested in thinking. "Businessmen (and businesswomen) the world over are more interested in thinking than anyone else because their's is the one area where defense is not a sufficient strategy for survival. In politics, the academic world or anywhere else if you can defend your point of view, that is enough. In business you can defend your idea

Escape

from
the Maze

192

until you are blue in the face but if no one buys your product, you are out of business...."[4] De Bono suggests that there are three major types of thinking.[5] The two most critical for this discussion of creativity are lateral thinking and vertical thinking.

1. **Lateral Thinking** (Insightful Thinking): "The steps leading up to the solution are not all apparent. The solution seems to come about by virtue of a sudden jump in thinking. It's more a matter of finding the right approach than of care in pursuing an approach." Lateral thinking asks you to dig more holes instead of digging the same hole deeper.

2. **Vertical Thinking** (Sequential Thinking): "The solution follows a progressive sequence of steps (modification, improvement, mistakes, new ideas, etc.) The sequence need not be a logical sequence; nevertheless, the steps occur one after another."

One of de Bono's greatest concerns is that you increase your lateral thinking abilities. He believes that most people follow vertical thinking to its extreme, ignoring the opportunities that lateral thinking provides. He has written several books of exercises to help you increase your lateral thinking.

Vertical thinking is concerned with digging the same hole deeper. Lateral thinking is concerened with digging the hole somewhere else. The aim of both is effectiveness.
—Edward de Bono

De Bono provides twelve lateral thinking techniques in his book, *Serious Creativity*.[6] The best known of these is his **"Six Thinking Hats"** in which different colored hats are used by a group to discuss an idea. Many organizations use the Six Thinking Hats approach to manage their problem solving efforts. I have summarized the key issues relative to each of the hats in Exhibit 10.1.

Still More Managing the Right Side– Steps 7, 8 and 9

Chapter 10

193

Exhibit 10.1

Wearing this color hat or asking for this color of thinking:	means you focus on:
white	information–what do we know? What don't we know? What do we need to know? How do we get this information?
red	feelings, intuition, hunches, and emotions–about the ideas
black	being critical, using judgement, seeing difficulties and problems, being cautious.
yellow	feasibility, optimism, logically positive perspective, values.
green	creative thinking, new ideas, alternatives, suggestions, other explanations.
blue	overviews, organizational control, conclusions, the agenda for thinking, leadership, asking for other hats.

Inexpensive plastic hats of the different colors can usually be found in party stores. Each of the six thinking hats is worn by a different individual in a problem-solving session. Each person plays the role suggested by the hat's color as the problem is discussed. This allows a problem to be seen from several different perspectives. This process also allows people to escape from their own usual thinking style. Hats may be rotated among the decision making group during a problem-solving session, or as the group tackles each new problem. (Roles can be played without hats.)

Insanity—doing the same things over and over again expecting different results.
—Anonymous

Escape

from the Maze

Another focal point of de Bono's work is how you seek alternatives in a situation. Do you always follow the rational, step-by-step approach—vertical thinking—or do you look for non-traditional, insightful means of solving a problem—lateral thinking? De Bono suggests that by practicing solving problems that require insightful solutions, you will improve your skill at such endeavors. Where Are You Now? 10.1 is an example of just such a problem. Try your insightful thinking skills on this problem.

Where Are You Now? 10.1

The Merchant's Daughter

Many years ago when a person who owed money could be thrown into jail, a merchant in London had the misfortune to owe a huge sum to a money-lender. The money-lender, who was old and ugly, fancied the merchant's beautiful teenage daughter. He proposed a bargain. He said he would cancel the merchant's debt if he could have the girl instead.

Both the merchant and his daughter were horrified at the proposal. So the cunning money-lender proposed that they let Providence decide the matter. He told them that he would put a black pebble and a white pebble into an empty money-bag and then the girl would have to pick out one of the pebbles. If she chose the black pebble she would become his wife and her father's debt would be cancelled. If she chose the white pebble she would stay with her father and the debt would still be cancelled. But if she refused to pick out a pebble her father would be thrown into jail and she would starve.

Reluctantly the merchant agreed. They were standing on a pebble-strewn path in the merchant's garden as they talked and the money-lender stooped down to pick up the two pebbles. As he picked up the pebbles the girl, sharp-eyed with fright, noticed that he picked up two black pebbles and put them into the money-bag. He then asked the girl to pick out the pebble that was to decide her fate and that of her father.

Imagine that you are standing on that path in the merchant's garden. What would you have done if you had been the unfortunate girl? If you had had to advise her what would you have advised her to do?

What type of thinking would you use to solve the problem? You may believe that careful logical analysis must solve the problem if there is a solution. This type of thinking is straight-forward vertical thinking. The other type of thinking is lateral thinking.

Vertical thinkers are not usually of much help to a girl in this situation. The way they analyze it, there are three possibilities:

Still More Managing the Right Side– Steps 7, 8 and 9

Chapter 10

195

1. The girl should refuse to take a pebble.
2. The girl should show that there are two black pebbles in the bag and expose the money-lender as a cheat.
3. The girl should take a black pebble and sacrifice herself in order to save her father from prison.

None of these suggestions is very helpful, for if the girl does not take a pebble, her father goes to prison; and if she does take a pebble, then she has to marry the money-lender.

OOPS!

The story shows the difference between vertical thinking and lateral thinking. Vertical thinkers are concerned with the fact that the girl has to take a pebble. Lateral thinkers become concerned with the pebble that is left behind. Vertical thinkers take the most reasonable view of a situation and then proceed logically and carefully to work it out. Lateral thinkers tend to explore all the different ways of looking at something, rather than accepting the most promising and proceeding from that.

The girl in the pebble story put her hand into the money-bag and drew out a pebble. Without looking at it she fumbled and let it fall to the path where it was immediately lost among all the others.

"Oh, how clumsy of me," she said, "but never mind — if you look into the bag you will be able to tell which pebble I took by the color of the one that is left."

Since the remaining pebble is of course black, it must be assumed that she has taken the white pebble, since the money-lender dare not admit his dishonesty. In this way, by using lateral thinking, the girl changes what seems an impossible situation into an extremely advantageous one. The girl is actually better off than if the money-lender had been honest and had put one black and one white pebble into the bag, for then she would have had only an even chance of being saved. As it is, she is sure of remaining with her father and at the same time having his debt cancelled.

Vertical thinking has always been the only respectable type of thinking. In its ultimate form as logic it is the recommended ideal towards which all minds are urged to strive, no matter how far short they fall. Computers are perhaps the best example. The problem is defined by the programmer, who also indicates the path along which the problem is to be explored. The computer then proceeds with its incomparable logic and efficiency to work out the problem. The smooth progression of vertical thinking from one solid step to another solid step is quite different from lateral thinking.

Escape

from
the Maze

If you were to take a set of toy blocks and build them upwards, each block resting firmly and squarely on the block below it, you would have an illustration of vertical thinking. With laterial thinking the blocks are scattered around. They may be connected to each other loosely or not at all. But the pattern that may eventually emerge can be as useful as the vertical structure.

Lateral thinking is easiest to appreciate when it is seen in action, as in the pebble story. Everyone has come across the sort of problem which seems impossible to solve until suddenly a surprisingly simple solution is revealed. Once it has been thought of, the solution is so obvious that one cannot understand why it was ever so difficult to find. This sort of problem may indeed be difficult to solve so long as vertical thinking is used.

Lateral thinking is not only concerned with problem-solving; it has to do with new ways of looking at things and new ideas of every sort.

Source: Excerpts from pp. 11–13 from *New Think: The Use of Lateral Thinking in the Generation of New Ideas* by Edward de Bono. Copyright ©1967 by Edward de Bono. Reprinted by permission of BasicBooks, a division of HarperCollins Publishers, Inc.

One company which recognizes the importance of improving its employees' thinking skills in an age of complex turbulence is British Airways (BA). Much of its success has been due to its visionary leadership, employee involvement, employee empowerment, and innovation.

ESCAPE ROUTES 10.1

The Power of Innovative Thinking

Sir Colin Marshall, BA's chairman since 1993, and CEO from 1983 to 1993, has presided over the transformation of British Airways from a firm that mostly disdained customers to one that strives to please them. Marshall laughingly notes that in 1983, most people he knew thought BA stood for bloody awful, but now, his competitors believe it stands for bloody awesome. At the center of that transformation was Marshall's and former chairman John King's common vision for the firm—to privatize the firm, and then to create a firm that would serve the customer.

To achieve the latter goal, King and Marshall knew that they had to totally change corporate culture. To create a concern for

Still More Managing the Right Side– Steps 7, 8 and 9

Chapter 10

the customer they knew they had to get employees involved and to have them solve problems, especially some of the complex ones that they would have the keenest insight into. Empowering employees who had never before been asked to solve problems meant numerous hours of training and development in problem solving, team building, and the ways and whys of adding to customer satisfaction. Once service became world class, the thrust became one of adding value. To do that, creativity was encouraged to blossom in the organization. Innovations resulted.

"Most of the major U.S. airlines have not been very innovative or creative," Marshall recently declared. He adds, "Compared with international flying anyway, the flying experience in the United States today is pretty ghastly." He goes on to say that he believes that much of the problem lies in the singular focus by U.S. carriers on price. BA has found, however, that a large number of passengers, not just first-class passengers but economy passengers as well, will pay a small extra amount for significant added value. So BA has gone about creating significant added value items that do not cost passengers very much, and are included in the ticket price. Among the more recent innovations have been: the addition of showers to four major European destination lounges so that passengers who arrive after an overnight flight can freshen up, the serving of breakfast to those just arriving after long flights, fast-track channels at Heathrow and Gatwick to speed premium and full-fare passengers through customs and immigration, "real" meals served in the various (first-class and frequent flier) lounges before the plane takes off on long flights allowing passengers to slip into "sleeper suits" once they have boarded.

> *Sit in reverie,*
> *and watch the*
> *changing color*
> *of the waves that*
> *break upon the*
> *idle seashore of*
> *the mind.*
> —Longfellow

Earlier innovations included upscale lounges with virtually everything for free including phone calls, special attention to animal transportation, the CARESS (Customer Analysis and Retention System)—a specially designed system to increase customer retention, various customer service process redesigns, the establishment of twelve different listening posts to hear customer complaints ranging from post cards to video interview machines at airport exits so that any disgruntled passenger can register a complaint immediately.

The results—in an era when most airlines are losing money, BA is making a nice profit and has been voted the number one international carrier over the past several years. Market share is growing and employees are more satisfied.

Sources: Steven E. Prokesch, "Competing on Customer Service: An Interview with British Airways' Sir Colin Marshall," *Harvard Business Review* (November–December, 1995), pp. 101–112; Charles R. Weiser, "Championing the Customer," *Harvard Business Review* (November–December, 1995), pp. 113–116; Alan Osborn, "Ahead of the Competition," *Europe* (October, 1995), pp. 20–24; Sir Colin Marshall, "From Bloody Awful to Bloody Awesome," speech to the Strategic Management Society (London: October 15, 1992); Patricia Sellers, "How to Handle Customers' Gripes," *Fortune* (October 24, 1988), pp. 88–97; and Kenneth Labich, "The Big Comeback of British Airways," *Fortune* (December 5, 1988), pp. 163–174.

Escape

from
the Maze

Unfortunately, not all organizations realize the importance of improving employees' thinking skills. Some firms seem forever locked into restructurings and reengineerings that cause employees to wonder, "Who's next," rather than "What can I contribute to the future of this organization?" One such organization is the former Scott Paper Company. As this chapter's Trapped in the Maze reveals, at some point, the CEO of Kimberly-Clark, Scott's new owner, must turn this situation around.

TRAPPED IN THE MAZE 10.1
Needed: A New Outlook

During his less than two year tenure as CEO, "Chainsaw Al" Dunlap claims to have saved the life of Scott Paper Company (the merger of which into Kimberly-Clark Corporation was approved by stockholders in December 1995). To "save" the company, he eliminated a lot of it—35 percent of the workforce, more than 11,000 employees. This included 71 percent of the headquarters staff, 50 percent of the managers, and 20 percent of the hourly workers. Dunlap likes to describe what he did as surgery to save a dying patient. His detractors felt he should have used a scalpel instead of a chainsaw. His cuts, most analysts believe, went far too deep.

At first glance, the claims he makes about the results of his leadership are impressive—an increase in the market value of the stock of $6.3 billion; an increase in stock price of 225 percent; the sale of subsidiary printing unit, S.D. Warren; the sale of the entire firm to Kimberly-Clark; 107 new products; a major new, innovative product that combines baking soda with bath tissue; and the signing of joint-production pacts in India, China, and Indonesia. Closer examination, however, reveals a number of problems in the corporation left behind by Dunlap, and a number of questions about just how effective he was personally.

There is no denying the numbers on stock and market values, but how much Dunlap's actions were responsible for these gains is hard to say. He did cut enough employees to enable the company to be profitable, but some of his other claims are highly inflated. Initiatives to sell S.D. Warren, develop the baking soda/toilet tissue product, and the groundwork for the Chinese deal, had all commenced long before Dunlap came on the scene. And half of the 107 supposed new products are accounted for by packaging changes to two product lines. Furthermore, Dunlap cut R&D by 50 percent. The company now is losing market share in major markets despite growth in these markets, and is having trouble getting new products to market. And finally, social costs were very high for both former and remaining employees, and to the communities that lost jobs and philanthropic contributions. Kimberly-Clark has a tough task facing it in trying to restore motivation among those who became Kimberly employees as a result of the merger. One example of Dunlap's

Still More Managing the Right Side— Steps 7, 8 and 9

Chapter 10

199

Achieving a high level of insightful thinking is critical in today's volatile business and personal environments. As organizations demand more of their employees, individuals must be able to deliver. As more and more complex problem solving is pushed down the organization hierarchy in order for the organization to be more competitive, employees must acquire this type of thinking skill. A lot of this skill depends on perception, another important ingredient in the de Bono approach to thinking.

> *Take advantage of the ambiguity in the world. Look at something and think about what else it might be.*
> —Roger von Oech, author and consultant on creativity

Put simply, what you see is your reality. But seeing what you see in another way, and then acting on this new reality is the essence of this part of the skill. A very popular series of books—*Magic Eye, Magic Eye 2,* and *Magic Eye 3*—asks you to look at a page of what appear to be random dots, other random small figures or splotches of color in such a way that you see the imbedded 3-D image. Looking at a situation—a problem or an opportunity—in another way, is the essence of the business application of this skill. It's just as if you were looking for the 3-D image in a *Magic Eye* book. The different perspective is there, you just have to find it.[8]

A few years ago, Chemical Bank ran an advertisement that is simulated here in part so that you can get a feel for how this skill translates into creative business activity.

Look at the illustration in Figure 10.1. What do you see in this figure?

Escape

from

the Maze

Figure 10.1 What Do You See?

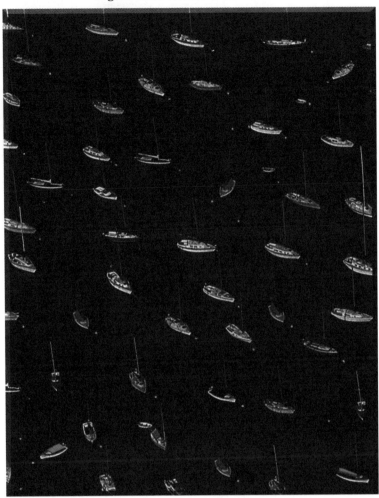

What did you see? Boats? That is what everybody else saw too. But at Chemical Bank, they saw these boats, and more importantly, the loans they had on them, as a marketable financial instrument. So they created the instrument, sold it, and product innovation occured.

Still More Managing the Right Side– Steps 7, 8 and 9

Chapter 10

Lateral thinking is part of escape thinking—one more way to escape from the maze. You use a jet pack, a hot-air balloon, a pole vault, a ladder, a saw—you do not keep going down the same old paths in the maze. *So escape and use lateral thinking.*

PRACTICING SOLVING COMPLEX PROBLEMS—STEP 8

The general belief is that the more you solve complex problems, the more likely you are to become good at this process. We also know that the more complex the problem, the more difficult it is to use simply rational approaches. Researcher, author, and consultant, Henry Mintzberg discovered in his studies of chief executives that many managerial jobs, especially those at the top of the organization, are so complex that, in his words, they defy rational, sequential thinking. His studies indicate that without intuition, chief executives are frequently lost in a maze of data they cannot comprehend through analysis.[9]

Furthermore, the general belief is that the more you solve complex problems, the more likely you are to increase your mental intuition skills. There may be some hard wiring requirements involved, that is, certain levels of intelligence, knowledge, and experience may be required before such efforts bring rewards. We just do not really know for sure yet. Two research studies provide intriguing clues as to how mental intuition works.

> *Implicitly or explicitly, creativity always begins with a question. In both your business and personal lives, the quality of your creativity is determined by the quality of your questions.*
> —Michael Ray and Rochelle Myers, authors and consultants on creativity

WESTIN H. AGOR'S STUDY OF INTUITION

Escape

from
the Maze

Westin H. Agor, researcher, author and consultant on brain management, studied the use of intuition by 3157 managers in various types of business and government organizations. The intuition he was examining was essentially what I have designated as mental intuition, but transcendent intuition might have been used by some or even all of these managers to some degree. Agor used a questionnaire to measure the probable intuition skill levels of managers. This questionnaire was not too different from the one on Sensing Versus Intuition found in Chapter 3 of this book.[10] Agor found that the ability to use intuition varied by organizational level, gender, ethnicity, and functional specialty.[11]

He found that top managers were more likely to have higher levels of intuition than were middle-level managers. He indicated that this was probably due to the fact that top managers operate in much more turbulent environments and face much more complex, unstructured problems than do middle-level managers. His work suggests that top managers gain the skill as they move upward, as they face these more complex, unstructured problems.[12] In essence, they learn by doing.

Agor also found that women were more likely to have higher levels of intuition than men. He indicated two possible explanations. First, brain studies indicate that there are some differences in men and women's brain physiology that might account for these different levels of skill.[13] Secondly, it is more culturally acceptable for women to use their intuition in our culture than it is for men who have historically been culturally bound to controlling their feelings and acting rational.[14] Agor also reported that Asian Americans appeared to have higher levels of intuitive ability than did members of other ethnic groups. This is attributed to the cultural rearing practices in Asian families that emphasize more intuitive thinking than do typical Western rearing practices.[15]

Those in certain positions, primarily administration and policy areas, possessed higher intuition levels than those in functional specialty areas such as finance and engineering. Here the explanation focused on the kind of training people receive as well as the requirements of their jobs—financial staff and engineers receive training that is very rational-analytically oriented, and they work in jobs that require a narrow focus on accuracy. As noted previously, those in administration and policy areas have jobs that are complex and unstruc-

Still More Managing the Right Side– Steps 7, 8 and 9

Chapter 10

203

tured. The functional areas of marketing and human resources were not examined.

Agor points out that when he examined the 200 most intuitive of these executives, all but one of them reported using intuition in making decisions. These executives also used intuition only after rationally working through the problem, and as one of several approaches to solving the problem. They also tended to use intuition most in highly complex, unstructured situations where information was limited.[16]

The most relevant aspect of Agor's research findings with respect to this discussion is that his research shows that people can learn to improve their skill levels of mental (and perhaps transcendent) intuition. Top managers apparently learn on the job. Agor goes on to propose a Brain Skills Management (BSM) program for companies which describes how organizations can identify, develop, and better use the brain skills of their employees.[17] He suggests using many of the techniques mentioned in chapters 7, 8, 9, and 10, as well as additional approaches, to assist the individual in increasing his or her levels of intuition, either as part of a BSM program or on ones own.[18]

SIEGFRED STRUFERT'S STUDY OF THINKING

A study by researcher, professor, and author, Siegfried Streufert of the Pennsylvania State University College of Medicine at Hershey, reveals that successful upper-level managers are better able to discern the complex interrelationships that exist between the factors in complex problems than are less successful managers. Less successful managers tend to use uni-dimensional thinking—wherein problems are seen in isolation from each other—and often hold rigidly to one overriding objective, such as profit. Successful managers use multi-dimensional thinking—wherein a decision's variable relationships and a decision's long-term consequences are taken into account in a complex manner.[19] (See Figure 10.2.) This multi-dimensional thinking is especially important in today's complex, rapidly changing environment.

Escape

from
the Maze

Figure 10.2 Multidimensional Thinking

Decisions were made by two executives during an experiment that simulated an international business situation. Asterisks show when the executives received new information. The double circles represent decisions made in response to it. Solid circles show decisions made without any new information. Horizontal lines connect decisions in the same general category(i.e., all those involving profit). The diagonal lines with arrows show when the executive linked a decision in one category to a decision in another. The successful, "multi-dimensional" executive at the bottom made decisions so that they set the stage for later ones, related decisions to others in a complex fashion and coordinated everything toward one major decision.

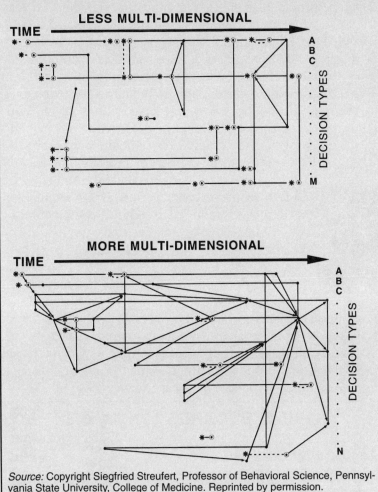

Source: Copyright Siegfried Streufert, Professor of Behavioral Science, Pennsylvania State University, College of Medicine. Reprinted by permission.

Still More Managing the Right Side– Steps 7, 8 and 9

Chapter 10

This study helps us partly understand mental intuition. I believe mental intuition and multi-dimensional thinking are related. Streufert's research does not go so far as to discuss mental intuition as such, but his research is pointing us towards a more accurate definition of this process. Clearly, mental intuition depends on the distillation of experiences, much as does the ability to think multi-dimensionally. Notice also how his research findings parallel the concepts of vertical and lateral thinking put forth by de Bono.

Streufert suggests that multi-dimensional thinking can be improved by training in complex problem solving. Since reporting his original research, Streufert and his colleagues have developed complex experimental simulations/exercises to test for and develop multi-dimensional thinking.[20] Based on our knowledge of educational techniques—complex computer business simulations, case studies, and experiential exercises—can and should be used to increase mental intuition. The more problem solving situations you expose someone to, the more experiences they will have to draw upon. Furthermore, these activities should be designed to not just encourage the use of intuition, but rather include a segment that requires the use of intuition. If executives learn by doing as Agor's and Streufert's works suggest, then everyone can learn from simulating that doing as is required in complex computer business simulations, case studies, and experiential exercises.[21]

What we do know for sure is that the brain develops connections the harder you work it; and the more connections you have, the better the brain functions. Based on all of the available research, it seems reasonable to assume that mental intuition would increase with an increase in connections. Typical of the complex problem solver is Lane Nemeth, highlighted in Great Escapes 10.1.

GREAT ESCAPES 10.1

Toying with Success

Lane Nemeth became a businesswoman almost by chance. As a day-care center administrator for the State of California, she purchased toys for the center that she wanted her own newly born child to have. She liked their quality and their educational

Escape

from

the Maze

value, something she could not find in the toys in most retail stores. But she quickly discovered that the educational supply houses would not deal directly with the consumer. So she bought her daughter's toys through the day-care center, then reimbursing the center for these purchases. But the bureaucrats did not like keeping track of all this. So her father suggested that she go into business selling quality toys. Her husband suggested that she do parties, something like Tupperware did. In November of 1977, she had a small party for friends with unopened toys. Her friends loved the toys and the concept. Her business had begun.

In 1995, her company, Discovery Toys, Inc., did $100 million in sales. The company makes many of its own products, and sells through a sales force of 30,000 spread throughout the U.S. and Canada. A few sales representatives make $350,000 to $400,000 a year. Most simply supplement their incomes in relatively small amounts. The key feature of being a sales representative for Discovery Toys is that this job allows women the freedom to spend time with their own children.

Lane Nemeth is a very capable complex problem solver. She asks tons of questions, and can quickly sort the wheat from the chaff. She recognizes when major changes are necessary and what their impacts might be. But she doesn't just use her rational mind. Intuitively, she often knows what must be done. Typical of her use of this skill was her mid-eighties experience when she knew she had to change the company's mission, a major undertaking. "We grew very heavily for fourteen years and flattened out for two years. Then I was driving home one day. Our COO had just died of cancer at 45. I had this bizarre vision: I had to change the company. My real mission isn't to sell toys—it's to be a parent educator. I wasn't doing enough to help parents realize the benefit of playing with their kids. That's how kids learn, that's what keeps communication and social life alive. With more women in the work force, there's less time for play. I felt depressed that I wasn't making enough of a difference.

It hit me that I needed product lines that would help take the stress out of raising kids, so parents and children would enjoy each other more. One of these lines is The Whole Child, an at-home seminar that gives parents warm, humorous help in raising kids. It has videos, audiotapes, and a magazine."

Nemeth's new approach has proven to be a resounding success. Revenues and profits have grown substantially. She feels she's making a real contribution. So do her customers.

Sources: Duncan Maxwell Anderson, "An Empire at Home: Discovery Toys Thrives on the Renaissance of Family Life," *Success* (June 1995), pp. 24, 26.

Still More Managing the Right Side– Steps 7, 8 and 9

ACCIDENTS DO HAPPEN

Despite all the plotting and planning, all the right-brain aerobics and left-side suspending, a lot of ideas and resultant innovations are accidents. We started out to get to X, but along the way, Z happened. Z turned out to be a pretty good

Chapter 10

idea. In fact, we found out we could make a good bit of money from it. So we ran with it. Sometimes we do both Z and X (if we ever get to X), and sometimes we just do Z. Estimates vary, but as many as 20 percent of all innovations may just be accidents waiting for someone to see their significance as Great Escapes 10.2 suggests.

GREAT ESCAPES 10.2

Accidental Escapes

Accidents do happen, and they often lead to quite important innovations. For example, "Nobel Prize-winning physicist Murray Gel-Mann, in an interview with Bill Moyers on PBS, revealed that he made one of his most important theoretical breakthroughs when he made a mistake in presenting a mathematical description of an event in a lecture and suddenly realized that this 'mistake' was not a mistake at all, but held the key to solving a problem in physics he had long been contemplating, but for which he had never found a satisfactory answer."

3M, the Minnesota Mining and Manufacturing Company, headquartered in St. Paul, is a firm that believes in innovation as a way of life. As a consequence, it has created a culture which demands and supports innovation. Its size and R&D strength allow it to be involved in many endeavors at once. Because there is always a lot of research going on, the culture encourages the sharing of ideas. The culture also allows people to make mistakes without being punished. There are, therefore, also a lot of "accidental discoveries" of importance. Probably the best known of these is the Scotchgard line of protective products. Lab technician Patsy Sherman had been working as part of a team searching for a flourocarbon-based compound that could be used as a sealant in jet engines. During a routine lab procedure, she dropped some of one of their test products on one of her tennis shoes. (The culture encourages dressing in a comfortable manner.) Trying various solutions, she could not get the sealant out of her shoe. Noting after a few days that the shoe with the spilled product on it remained clean while the other became dirty, and remembering that another 3M team was trying to develop a line of protective products, she made the connection that perhaps this sealant could be the basis of that product line. She explained her theory to lab director Sam Smith, and Scotchgard became a product.

Sources: Bryan W. Mattimore, *99% Inspiration: Tips, Tales & Techniques for Liberating Your Business Creativity* (New York: AMACOM, 1993), p. 21; John Diebold, *The Innovators: The Discoveries, Inventions and Breakthroughs of Our Time* (New York: Truman Talley Books/Plume, 1990), pp. 67–75.

Escape

from
the Maze

RECORDING THE ACTIONS OF YOUR CREATIVE SELF—STEP 9

Remember that last great idea you had, now what was it?... That's the point. Record your ideas as they happen.

A hundred thousand thoughts a day go through your mind. You have a lot of ideas that could be used, but you cannot do much about them if you forget them. You should carry a personal digital assistant, a personal organizer, a dictaphone, 3 x 5 cards or an idea notebook with you. When you have ideas, type or write them down or dictate them. Keep a notepad and pencil by your bed at night and when you have ideas during the middle of the night write them down. Keep 3 x 5 cards or a dictaphone in your car, always be prepared to record or write down your ideas and then put them into action.

> *If you don't write down random insights, you may be obliterating the most fruitful ideas of the day.*
> —Charles Atkinson, President, Whole Brain Corporation

Employee ideas are precious commodities. One company keeps a 24-hour Hot Ideas Hotline so that employees can phone in ideas at any time.[22]

BRAIN AEROBICS 10

Part 1–Improving Your Thinking Skills

There are a large number of books that discuss how to improve thinking skills. Most of these types of books can be found in a large book store in the psychology or self-help section. They are also available from mail-order catalogs such as *Mindware* and *Brainstorms*. Edward de Bono has written several such books and is easily the best known author on improving your thinking skills. The important action is to engage in thinking exercises that give you new perspectives on problem solving, especially those that build your lateral thinking. Appendix 2 contains a brief list of such books.

Still More Managing the Right Side– Steps 7, 8 and 9

Chapter 10

Part 2–Practicing Solving Complex Problems

For managers, professionals, team members, team leaders, and others interested in improving complex problem-solving skills, attending company-sponsored or college-sponsored training program which uses management simulations, case studies or experiential exercises offers the best method for learning this skill. Mentor programs also help, and, of course, there is no substitute for real experience.

Part 3–Recording Your Creative Ideas

If you do not already own a personal digital assistant, personal organizer, or dictaphone, get one—now. Start carrying it everywhere you go. Use it to record ideas. If one of these is not financially feasible, buy a pack of 3x5 notecards and put 5–10 of them in readily accessible clothing items—suits, for example, or purses, or billfolds. Use them to record ideas.

REFERENCES

1. Michael Barrier, "Innovation as a Way of Life," *Nation's Business* (July 1994), pp. 24–25.

2. Reiterated in an interview by Selina Scott, "The Selina Scott Show," CNBC-The Super Channel, London: Europe, (October 11, 1995).

3. Anthony Liversidge, "Edward De Bono: An Interview," *Omni* (March 1985), p. 75.

4. Ibid, p. 115.

5. Edward de Bono, *The Five Day Course in Thinking*, (New York: Facts on File, 1985), p. 115.

6. Edward de Bono, *Serious Creativity* (New York: Harper Business, 1992), pp. 77–81.

7. Steven E. Prokesch, "Competing on Customer Service: An Interview with British Airways' Sir Colin Marshall," *Harvard Business Review* (November–December, 1995), pp. 101–112; Charles R. Weiser, "Championing the Customer," *Harvard Business Review* (November–December, 1995), pp. 113–116; Alan Osborn, "Ahead of the Competition," *Europe* (October, 1995), pp. 20–24; Sir Colin Marshall, "From Bloody Awful to Bloody Awesome," speech to the Strategic Management Society (London: October 15 , 1992); Patricia Sellers, "How to Handle Customers' Gripes," *Fortune* (October 24, 1988), pp. 88–97; and Kenneth Labich, "The Big Comeback of British Airways," *Fortune* (December 5, 1988), pp. 163–174.

8. *Magic Eye* (Vol.1, 1993), *Magic Eye 2* (Vol. 2, 1994), *Magic Eye 3* (Vol. 3, 1994) (Kansas City, Missouri: Andrews & McMeel).

9. Henry Mintzberg, "Planning on the Left Side and Managing on the Right," *Harvard Business Review* (July/August 1976), pp. 49–58.

10. Westin H. Agor, "Test Your Intuitive Powers: AIM Survey," in Westin H. Agor, ed., *Intuition in Organizations* (Newbury Park, California: Sage Publications, 1989), pp. 145–156.

11. Westin H. Agor, "The Intuitive Ability of Executives: Findings from Field Research," in Westin H. Agor, ed., *Intuition in Organizations* (Newbury Park, California: Sage Publications, 1989), pp. 145–156.

12. Westin H. Agor, "The Intuitive Ability of Executives: Findings from Field Research," op. cit., pp. 147–149.

Still More Managing the Right Side– Steps 7, 8 and 9

Chapter 10

13. *Escape* examines this issue in more detail in Chapter 6 and Appendix 1. Agor's specific reference for this analysis was Pamela Weintraub, "The Brain: His and Hers," *Discover* (April 1981), pp. 15–20.

14. *Escape* examines this issue in more detail in Chapter 6 and Appendix 1. Agor's specific reference for this analysis was Alice G. Sargent, *The Androgynous Manager* (New York: AMACOM 1981).

15. Richard Tanner Pascale and Anthony G. Athos, *The Art of Japanese Management: Applications for American Executives* (New York: Warner Books, 1981), especially Chapter 4 on Zen and the art of management.

16. Westin H. Agor, "The Logic of Intuition: How Top Executives Make Important Decisions," in Westin H. Agor, ed., *Intuition in Organizations* (Newbury Park, California: Sage Publications, 1989), pp. 157–170.

17. Westin H. Agor, "Nurturing Executive Intrapreneurship with a Brain Skills Management Program," in Westin H. Agor, ed., *Intuition in Organizations* (Newbury Park, California: Sage Publications, 1989), pp. 205–213.

18. Ibid., p. 207; and Westin H. Agor, "How to Use and Develop Your Intuition in Management," in Westin H. Agor, ed., *Intuition in Organizations* (Newbury Park, California: Sage Publications, 1989), pp. 217–246.

19. See Daniel Coleman, "Successful Executives Rely on Own Kind of Intelligence," *New York Times* (July 13, 1984), pp. C1, C2; Walter Kiechell III, "How Executives Think," *Fortune* (February 4, 1985), pp. 127–128; Dina Ingber, "Inside the Executive Mind," *Success* (January 1984), pp. 33–37.

20. Siegfried Streufert and Klaus Breuer, "Assessment/Training of Senior Personnel with the Strategic Management Simulations," paper presented to 35th Conference of Military Testing Association (Williamsburg, Virginia, 1993); Siegfried Streufert, "Assessing and Training Senior Personnel with the Strategic Management Simulations," working paper based on a 1992 presentation to the American Psychological Association and parts of Siegfried Streufert, *Assessment and Training of Senior Personnel* (Toronto: Hogrefe, 1993).

21. Paul Stonham, "For and Against the Case Method," *European Management Journal* (June 1995), pp. 230–232; Elizabeth S. Niemyer, "The Case for Case Study," *Training & Development* (January 1995), pp. 50–52; for a review see Arch R. Dooley and Wickham Skinner, "Casing Case Method Methods," *Academy of Management Review* (April 1977), pp. 277–289.

22. Padi Selwyn, "Fostering a Creative Work Environment," *Mindplay* (October 1994), p. 4.

CHAPTER 11

Innovate or Evaporate.

> —*James M. Higgins*

In this book, you have been exposed to a large number of ideas, processes, and excercises which can improve your personal creativity level. The first action you need to take is to accept your innate creativity. You also need to unlearn what you have been taught about how not to be creative. Next, you need to expand your problem-solving style. Then you need to learn creative problem-solving techniques. Vitally, you need to work (and work is the correct word) on developing your right brain to get in tune with your subconscious; learn to suspend the left side; improve your thinking skills; and practice solving complex problems. Finally, you should always be recording your creative ideas.

213

All of these actions are what's required. Creativity will not come easily, but it will come. You too can be creative because you already are. *Just escape.*

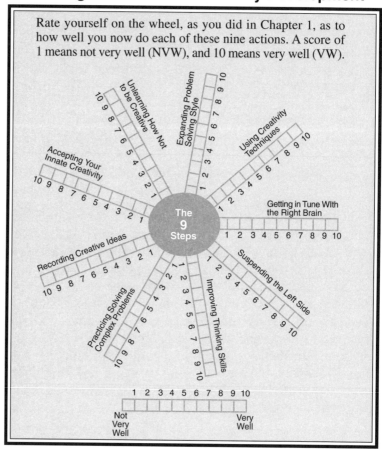

Now that you have completed this book, and now that you have begun to work on your creativity, let us examine your creativity skill levels again. Evaluate yourself using the Where Are You Now? which follows.

WHERE ARE YOU NOW? 11.1
Assessing Your Level of Creativity Development

Rate yourself on the wheel, as you did in Chapter 1, as to how well you now do each of these nine actions. A score of 1 means not very well (NVW), and 10 means very well (VW).

The
9
Steps

Unlearning How Not to be Creative
Expanding Problem Solving Style
Using Creativity Techniques
Getting in Tune With the Right Brain
Suspending the Left Side
Improving Thinking Skills
Practicing Solving Complex Problems
Recording Creative Ideas
Accepting Your Innate Creativity

1 2 3 4 5 6 7 8 9 10
Not Very Well   Very Well

Escape

from the Maze

Becoming an Imaginician

An **imaginician** is a technician of the imagination. Everyone needs to become an imaginician if he or she wants to stay ahead of the competition. Managers need to ensure that their employees become imaginicians if the firm is to survive and prosper.

I created the term imaginician to emphasize one major point—creativity and innovation are skills. As a technician you can learn the skills—the processes (techniques) and personal intuition skills, which can help you be more creative. These skills are to be used with your imagination. You can become more innovative—turn creativity into innovation—by learning innovation management. Creativity and innovation are not mystical. You can learn to be more creative and more innovative.

To escape, to become an imaginician, you have to get started. A personal contract is a good way to begin.

A new idea, like a pebble in a pond, can change the world around it... There's no end to where it can lead.
— TRW Inc. advertisement

The best way to predict the future is to invent it.
—Peter Drucker

Becoming an Imaginician

Chapter 11

215

Personal Creativity Contract

I hereby contract with myself to accomplish the following objectives through the indicated actions by the dates shown in order to significantly increase my level of personal creativity and the creativity and innovation of my organization.

Personal Creativity Objectives	Action	Date
1.		
2.		
3.		

Organizational Creativity and Innovation Objectives (things I can do to make my organization more creative and more innovative)	Action	Date
1.		
2.		
3.		

YOU ARE ON YOUR WAY TO BECOMING AN IMAGINICIAN.

GO OUT AND BE CREATIVE.

Escape

from
the Maze

APPENDIX 1

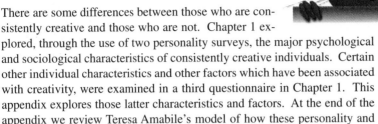

There are some differences between those who are consistently creative and those who are not. Chapter 1 explored, through the use of two personality surveys, the major psychological and sociological characteristics of consistently creative individuals. Certain other individual characteristics and other factors which have been associated with creativity, were examined in a third questionnaire in Chapter 1. This appendix explores those latter characteristics and factors. At the end of the appendix we review Teresa Amabile's model of how these personality and other characteristics fit together to describe the creative person.

INDIVIDUAL CHARACTERISTICS AND CREATIVITY

People often link creativity to various individual characteristics including intelligence, age, and gender. But no single characteristic really identifies the creative person. The following paragraphs examine creativity and a number of individual characteristics that are related to, or are commonly thought of as being related to creativity. You will note that most of these characteristics were examined in the third questionnaire in Chapter 1.

Intelligence and Creativity

Throughout the population, **creatives**, those who are consistently creative, are usually more intelligent than non-creatives, but not always. While a limited amount of intelligence is definitely necessary to be creative (many say an I.Q. of 100), the intelligence quotient measured by standard I.Q. tests does not correlate highly with creativity above this minimum level. This is probably because these tests primarily measure verbal/linguistic and logical/mathematic intelligences, and not other forms of intelligence,[1] such as the five additional kinds identified by Howard Gardner: visual/spatial, body/kinesthetic, musical/rhythmic, interpersonal, and intrapersonal.[2] Researcher Nirmal K. Sethia observes that, "Within any given field of endeavor, there are no systematic differences in the standardly measured intelligence levels of more highly creative individuals and comparatively less creative individuals."[3] In scientific and technical fields, however, IQ becomes extremely important—an IQ of 120 seems a reasonable entry level.

Experience and Creativity

A data base–knowledge and/or experience–is necessary to be creative.[5] The more experiences you have, the more knowledgeable you become, the more information you have stored in your brain, the more connections you can make. These connections are critical to creativity. Making connections between two thoughts is the essence of the creative process.

Appendix 1

217

Age and Creativity

Generally speaking, creativity and age are not significantly correlated, except as discussed in Chapter 2—all people are born with creativity–innate creativity potential is highest at age levels less than six, when we begin school. Employed middle-aged persons seem to be slightly more creative than persons in other age groups of employed people. This is largely explained by the experience factor. The most creative age in the sciences seems to be in the late 30s and early 40s when people have enough experience to be creative but aren't so vested in the system as to overlook new possibilities. Creativity may lessen somewhat in old age, but not significantly.

Gender and Creativity

Currently, men seem to produce more creative results than women, primarily because they have more opportunities to do so. Early studies found no difference in creativity potential between men and women. A number of more recent studies suggest that each gender has certain characteristics that might enable one gender to be more creative than the other. A considerable amount of research suggests that men, on average, are more right brain dominant then women, and women, on average, are more left brain dominant then men. Men, on average, tend to have more mathematical and spatial ability. Men like to tinker more. These are critical skills for scientific creativity. On the other hand, women have higher verbal skill levels, which assist in certain types of language-based creativity.[6]

The reasons for these differences are that men's brains are, on average, hardwired somewhat differently from women's brains. A man's right cerebral cortex is usually thicker and has more dense neurons than a woman's. Women usually have a thicker left cerebral cortex and less dense neurons. Furthermore, men and women often use different parts of their brains to perform the same functions.[7] Recent evidence suggests that the ability to transfer information between the hemispheres via the corpus callosum, the connecting tissue between the two hemispheres of the brain, is critical to creativity. This connection is larger in women than in men.[8]

In summary, neither gender seems to have an advantage in creativity. Because the right brain is believed to be the primary source of intuition, men might have an opportunity to be more creative since they tend to use the right brain more than women, for example, in exercising spatial abilities. Since women have a larger corpus callosum, they have an advantage because they can shift more information, and shift it faster between the two sides, than men can. To further complicate the situation, there are women who have dominant brain functions similar to men, and vice versa.

Escape

from
the Maze

218

As with most studies which analyze a large number of people with a large number of variables, it certainly is not clear whether men or women, if either, have a creative edge. The greater likelihood is that a large number of men and women, who can use both sides of the brain well, and who exercise both verbal and spatial skills, using left and right brains, will be the most creative.

Education and Creativity

The amount of education one possesses has no major impact on creativity. In one study, many people with low levels of education were highly creative while many of those with high levels of education were not creative at all. The converse was also true.[9] Again, it is the knowledge relevant to the situation that is necessary.

Note—most of our formal education is directed toward left brain functions, and most of our education discourages right brain thinking. So, education may in some ways be harmful to creativity, in addition to the negative effects of regimentation noted earlier.

Fantasy, Imagery, and Creativity

Highly creative people have a rich, sometimes almost bizarre fantasy life. They are fond of visualizing, imagining, making up stories, inventing new products in their minds, spending time on crazy projects.[10] Many scientists actively use visual imagery as part of their problem solving process.[11]

Creativity and Mental Health

Researcher Ruth Richard's review of the relevant research reveals that the extremely creative person may be more prone to mood disorders than the average person. Furthermore, research suggests that highly creative people are more likely to have psychological problems.[12] But this is apparently true of only an extremely small number of people. Moreover, whether or not the creative types tend to have more problems or those with more problems tend to enter professions that require creativity, is as yet unknown. Certainly for most people, including those using this book, these psychological problems are not likely to occur, but, this point does have certain personal and managerial implications. For example, if you are a poet, author, R&D person, musician, and so on, you may need to be attuned to your own psychological needs. Similarly, managers of creatives need to recognize that creative people may be moody from time to time, and there is a need to not make a big deal out of it.[13]

Appendix 1

219

SOME ADDITIONAL INTERESTING FACTS ABOUT CREATIVITY

When studying creativity, certain factors in addition to an individual's personality characteristics are important in understanding how to increase ones levels of creativity. Among these are the impacts of exercise, the creative's environment, early encouragement, humor, food, and drugs.

> You should pray to have a sound mind in a sound body.
> —Juvenal, a Roman poet

Creativity and Exercise

Physical exercise has been shown to increase your levels of creativity.[14] The reason is that the brain needs oxygen, a supply of blood and nutrients, and certain biochemical substances to work well. Exercise helps provide these. For instance, aerobic exercise (12 minutes of continuous, challenging but not overly demanding exercise that forces use of lower body muscle groups) causes endorphins to be released. These neurotransmitters relax us into a state of cortical alertness.[15] We also know that aerobic exercise improves memory and the making of connections. In addition neurotrophins, which help brain cells grow, are increased with aerobic exercise.[16] These then could lead to increased creativity. You may want to plan some type of exercise activity before trying to be creative, either individually or in groups. However, some creative types report having to calm down before being creative, for example by meditating or listening to music.[17]

Creativity and Your Environment

Stimulating environments apparently raise creativity levels. If you are in a dull job and/or a dull home life, you may not be as creative as someone who has an exciting job and/or exciting home life, or other interests or hobbies. Activities get the mind going, they get the blood flowing, they get the electrical impulses functioning in your brain. This seems to be very critical to increasing your levels of creativity.[16] More importantly, stimulating environments get the neurons interconnecting and these interconnections are the basis for brain power and creativity.[19]

One man who has gone out of his way to create a stimulating environment for himself is Dr. Yoshiro Nakamats, arguably the world's most creative person. Chapter 8's Great Escapes 8.1 discussed the three environments he has developed to raise his creativity level.

Escape

from
the Maze

Nakamats' environments help him significantly increase his idea incubation potential. Since most of the time, you must concentrate to create, most of the time you must also have time alone—to think, to incubate, to let creativity happen.[20] So you may want to set aside a creative environment for yourself—a quiet room, a hammock in the shade of an old oak tree, or some other place to which you can retreat. (In group creativity sessions, concentration

often is not as important as the interactive dynamics which function to produce ideas.)

Early Encouragement and Creativity

Creativity researcher Vera John-Steiner, in an extensive research effort with
over 100 creative individuals, found that a life of creativity begins early on,
usually through encouragement at home, but also sometimes by teachers.[21]
Simply undertaking creative activity causes more connections and builds brain
power. These stimulating environmental circumstances are especially important in our younger years. Teresa M. Amabile, noted creativity researcher,
comes to this conclusion, "Children's social environment (at home and in
school) can have a significant impact on their motivation (to be creative)."[22]

A Penny for Your Thoughts

About a hundred thousand thoughts a day go through your mind.
Why not make some of them creative? If you do, they will be
worth a whole lot more than a penny.

Distribution of Creativity Within the Population

*The world is
but canvas to
our minds.*
—Henry
David
Thoreau

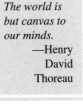

Creativity follows a normal distribution pattern throughout the population at birth. This means that before we reach adulthood, a small
number of people are not very creative at all, a large number of
people are fairly creative, a tremendous number of people have average levels of creativity, a large number of people are very creative, and finally a
small number of people are extremely creative. Almost all people possess
some amount of creativity at birth. Unfortunately, socialization—parents,
teachers, bosses and organizations—have through rules and regulations, significantly reduced our innate levels of creativity by adulthood. Thus, by
adulthood, only a small percentage of people are creative while a large percentage are not. The good news is that a large number of people can become
very creative simply by accepting their innate creativity and unlearning what
they have been taught not to do. Chapter 2 reviewed these issues in more
detail.

Creativity and Food

There is no special diet that can be recommended to increase creativity levels, per se.[23] However, eating certain foods might negatively affect creativity
through their impact on brain functioning. A number of studies have shown
that the types of foods individuals eat can raise or lower the speed with which
the brain functions.[24] The saying "You are what you eat," is a lot truer than
many people realize. Foods which many believe reduce the brain's creativity
levels include refined sugars, and simple carbohydrates and fats when consumed in excessive amounts.

Appendix 1

Brain-food research is in its early stages. We know, for instance, that eating certain types of carbohydrates might better enable you to cope with environmental circumstances, but eating other types of foods like cookies (sugar) might give you depression.[25] We also know that less effective problem solvers use more glucose than good problem solvers.[26]

Brain functions are affected by chemicals known as neuro-transmitters which carry the brain's signals. At least five of the fifty-plus known neuro-transmitters are directly influenced by specific nutrients in foods.[27] This means the nutritional aspect of physical self-development could be a prerequisite to intuitive development. Compare your diet to the one contained in Exhibit A.1. If you have an inappropriate diet, develop a plan for improvement.[28]

Exhibit A.1

Eating Right

Limit
  Egg yolks
  Organ meats
  Fried foods
  Fatty foods (pastries, spreads, dressings)
  Animal protein (has no known benefits and may cause cancer)
  Alcohol
  Certain shellfish (there is some debate over which; scallops are
  apparently okay)

Emphasize
  Fish
  Skinless poultry
  Lean meats
  Low or nonfat dairy products
  Complex carbohydrates (fruits, vegetables, starches)

Eliminate
  Dietary supplements (megadoes have no known benefits and
  may be toxic)
  Calcium, fish oil, or fiber supplements (they have no known benefits and must be taken in food)

Specific Limits
  Fat
    No more than 30% of daily calories
    (1 tablespoon of peanut butter = 8 grams = 90 calories)

  Saturated Fats
    Less than 10% of the fat allowances (includes coconut oil
    and animal fat)

Escape

from
the Maze

Complex Carbohydrates
At least 55% of daily calories

Vegetables
Five or more servings, especially of green and yellow vegetables (1 serving = 1/2 cup)

Fruits
Five or more servings, especially of citrus fruits (1 serving = 1 medium-sized fruit or 1/2 banana)

Starches
Six or more servings; includes rice, potatoes, pasta, legumes, and whole-grain bread and cereal (1 serving = 1 slice of bread)

Protein
Eight grams per kilogram of body weight (for a 180-pound man, an 8.4-ounce hamburger patty; or a 120-pound woman, a 5.6-ounce hamburger patty)

Alcohol
Less than 1 ounce daily (2 cans of beer or two small glasses of wine; none for women who are pregnant or trying to conceive)

Salt
Six grams a day (about 1 teaspoon)

Note that in general, Americans eat too much fat, cholesterol, and protein, and too few complex carbohydrates.

Source: Pierce J. Howard, *The Owner's Manual for the Brain,* Appendix B, (Austin, Tex.: Leornian Press, 1994), pp. 334-335.

Creativity and Drugs

Alcohol, drugs, and other stimulants or depressants can increase or decrease creativity levels, but often the actual impact of the chemicals on the brain is not as critical as related psychological phenomena. These substances often remove your inhibitions, and the resultant lowering of socialization against creativity makes you more creative. For example, in one group, creativity increased significantly after taking 2 ozs. of alcohol but only for those who religiously or philosophically believed that alcohol was acceptable. For

Appendix 1

those who did not, creativity did not increase. In excess, more than 2 ozs. a day, alcohol has negative effects on creativity.[29] A study by Ernest Noble of the UCLA School of Medicine reveals that two to three drinks a day, four days per week, have a detectable, negative impact on brain functioning, especially for those over forty. Furthermore, studies of alcoholic men indicate reduced blood flow to the frontal lobe of the brain—a location critical to memory, creativity, and problem solving.[30] Drugs of all types, especially in excess, are not recommended.

Having examined some of the key factors associated with creativity, and earlier, some of the personality characteristics of the creative person, let us now examine how these fit together in a comprehensive model of the creative personality.

TERESA AMABILE'S CREATIVE PERSONALITY

Distilling the type of information we examined earlier relative to the characteristics of creative people, researcher Teresa Amabile has identified three components of the creative personality: domain-relevant skills, creativity-relevant skills and task motivation. All three components must be present for an individual to be fully creative.

Innovative opportunities do not come with the tempest, but with the rustling of the breeze.
—Peter Drucker

Domain-Relevant Skills

To have domain-relevant skills, the individual must possess not only knowledge about the subject at hand, but also technical skills and special talents peculiar to the domain in which he or she is attempting to be creative. Originality may occur without these skills, but creativity is unlikely without them. This is the experience and knowledge factor.

Creativity-Relevant Skills

Amabile indicates that creativity-relevant skills must exist in three different areas: cognitive style, knowledge of heuristics, and work style.

COGNITIVE STYLE

It is especially important that the individual be able to break routine perceptual sets (the cognitive-perceptual style most conducive to creativity appears to be characterized by facility in understanding complexities and the ability to break mental sets during problem solving).[31] The individual must also be able to interpret complexity and be comfortable with it, have an accurate memory, abandon or suspend performance scripts, see things differently from others, suspend judgement rather than just reacting immediately to whatever is seen, and hold options open and not push for closure.

Escape

from the Maze

224

In this particular case, heuristics is defined as "insightful tips for coming up with new ideas."[32] One of the most famous heuristics comes from the neuro-linguistic programming literature. "If what you are doing is not working, try something different." This is based on the axiom that "if you always do what you've always done, you always get what you've always gotten."[33] Roger von Oech in *Whack on the Side of the Head*, provides heuristics to help you improve your problem solving. Some of these are discussed in Chapter 5.

> *I have no special gifts, I am only passionately curious.*
> —Albert Einstein

WORK STYLE

"The appropriate work style consists of :

- the ability to sustain long periods of concentration
- the ability to abandon non-productive approaches
- persistance during difficulty
- a high level of energy
- a willingness to work hard"[35]

Amabile indicates that two prerequisites determine each person's level of performance in these three areas of creativity-relevant skills—experience and personality traits. Experience is critical. The more practiced you are, the better you will be.

Some of the personality characteristics critical to these creativity-relevant skills are:

- self-discipline
- delay of gratification
- perserverance
- independent judgment
- tolerance for ambiguity
- autonomy
- internal locus of control
- willingness to take risks
- ability to be a self-starter
- absence of conformity to social pressure[36]
- curiosity/inquisitiveness
- positive self-image[37]

> *It requires a strong constitution to go it alone in creative matters.*
> —Howard Gardner, author and researcher on intelligence

Task Motivation

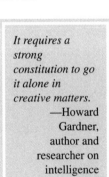

The individual must be motivated by the task, have a positive attitude toward the task, and must want to do it. If he or she does not want to do it, significantly lower creativity results. Furthermore, additional research has shown

Appendix 1

225

that internal motivation is a prerequisite for creative behavior; you must want to do something because you want to do it. It can be shown that this leads to greater relevance, spontaneity, and novelty than result from external motivation such as pay, or because the boss/teacher/spouse wants you to do it. This does not mean that external factors, such as pay, do not increase the motivation to be creative. Because of the long time it takes to see the results of their work, firms have found that money can be a very important motivator for creatives.[38] Figure A.1 shows how Amabile's characteristics just discussed, fit together in a comprehensive model.

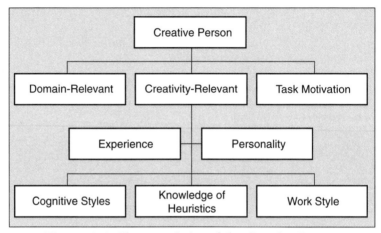

Figure A.1 Characteristics of the Creative Person

Making Use of this Information

Having learned about creativity and the individual, and other interesting facts about creativity, now use this information to increase your own levels of creativity and those of other individuals. To do so follow the nine steps.

Escape

from

the Maze

226

REFERENCES

1. Donald W. MacKinnon, "What Makes a Person Creative?" *The Saturday Review* (February 10, 1962), p. 16.

2. Howard Gardner, *Frames of Mind: The Theory of Multiple Intelligences* (New York: Harper & Row, 1983).

3. Nirmal K. Sethia, "The Shaping of Creativity in Organizations," *Proceedings: Academy of Management*, (San Francisco, California: Academy of Management, 1989), pp. 224–228.

4. F.M. Barron and D.M. Harrington, "Creativity, Intelligence and Personality," in M.R. Rosenzweig and Lyman W. Porter (Eds.) *Annual Review of Psychology* (Palo Alto, California: Annual Review Press), Vol. 32.

5. Teresa M. Amabile, *The Social Psychology of Creativity* (New York: Springer-Verlag, 1993); Herbert A. Simon, "Understanding Creativity and Creative Management," in R.L. Kuhn, *Handbook for Creative and Innovative Managers* (New York: McGraw-Hill, 1988); M.D. Mumford and S. Gustafson, "Creativity Syndrome: Integration, Application, and Innovation," *Psychological Bulletin* (103), 1, pp. 27–43.

6. Anne Moir and David Jessel, *Brain Sex: The Real Difference Between Men and Women* (New York: Dell Publishing, 1992), p. 89.

7. Ibid., pp. 46–48.

8. Ibid., p. 48.

9. Pierce J. Howard, *The Owner's Manual for the Brain* (Austin, Texas: Leornian Press, 1994), p. 275.

10. D.N. Perkins, *The Mind's Best Work* (Cambridge, Massachusetts: Harvard University Press, 1981); Howard E. Gruber, "Darwin's Tree of Nature," in J. Weschler (Ed.), *On Aesthetics in Science* (Cambridge, Massachusetts: The MIT Press, 1981).

11. Gruber, ibid.; D.N. Perkins, "The Possibility of Invention," in R.J. Sternberg (Ed.), *The Nature of Creativity* (New York: Cambridge University Press, 1981).

12. Ruth Richards, "Mood Swings and Everyday Creativity," *Harvard Health Letter* (April 1992), pp. 4–6; see also, Constance Holden, "States of Mind: Creativity and the Troubled Mind," *Psychology Today* (April 1987), p. 9.

Appendix 1

13. Pierce J. Howard, op. cit., p. 278.

14. Victor M. Parachin, "Seven Ways to Fire Up Your Creativity," *Supervision* (January 1992), p. 3.

15. Pierce J. Howard, op. cit., p. 109.

16. Susan Brink, "Smart Moves," *U.S. News & World Report* (May 15, 1995), pp. 76–83.

17. Teresa Amabile, *The Social Psychology of Creativity*, op. cit.

18. Tim Friend, "A New School of Thought on Nurturing a Better Brain," *USA Today* (November 30, 1993), p. 7D.

19. Win Wenger and Richard Poe, "Excerpts From The Einstein Factor: Proven Techniques to Boost Your Brain's Performance!" *Success* (November 1995), p. 56.

20. Pierce J. Howard, op. cit., p. 4.

21. Vera John-Steiner, *Notebook of the Mind* (University of New Mexico Press, 1985), Chapter 1; also see Tim Friend, loc. cit.

22. Teresa M. Amabile, *Growing Up Creative: Nurturing a Lifetime of Creativity* (Buffalo, N.Y.: Creative Education Foundation, 1989), p.x.

23. Pierce J. Howard, op. cit., p. 275.

24. See for example, Arthur Winter and Ruth Winter, *Eat Right, Be Bright: The Latest Techniques to Preserve, Restore, and Improve Your Brain's Potential* (New York: St. Martin's Press, 1988).

25. Rowland Stiteler, "Brain Food," *The Orlando Sentinel, Florida Magazine* (February 16, 1986), pp. 20–23.

26. Roberta Friedman, "The Hungry Brain," *Psychology Today* (June 1988), p. 9.

27. Sharon Begley, et.al., "How The Brain Works—Food for Thought: You Think What You Eat," *Newsweek* (February 7, 1983), p. 46.

28. For a more in-depth review of this issue see Arthur Winter and Ruth Winter, loc cit.

29. Author's personal knowledge.

30. Pierce J. Howard, op. cit., p. 83.

Escape

from
the Maze

31. Teresa M. Amabile, "A Model of Creativity and Innovation in Organizations," p. 131.

32. Pierce J. Howard, op. cit., p. 272.

33. Ibid.

34. Roger von Oech, *A Whack on the Side of the Head: How to Unlock Your Mind for Innovation* (New York: Warner, 1983).

35. Pierce J. Howard, loc. cit.

36. Pierce J. Howard, op. cit., p. 273.

37. The last two in this list are from Nirmal K. Sethia, loc. cit.

38. For a review see James M. Higgins, *Innovate or Evaporate: Test and Improve Your Organization's IQ—Its Innovation Quotient* (Winter Park, Florida: New Management Publishing Company, 1995), pp. 205–207.

Appendix 1

Escape

from
  the Maze

APPENDIX 2: ADDITIONAL READINGS

Chapter 1

Adams, James L., *Conceptual Block Busting* (Reading, Massachusetts: Addison-Westley, 1986).

Albrecht, Karl, *Brain Power: Learn To Improve Your Thinking Skills* (Englewood Cliffs, New Jersey: Prentice-Hall, Inc., 1980).

Conlin, Joseph, "Brainstorming: It's Not as Easy as You Think," *Successful Meetings* (September 1989).

de Bono, Edward, *Serious Creativity* (New York: HarperBusiness, 1992).

Diebold, John, *The Innovators: The Discoveries, Inventions, and Breakthroughs of Our Time* (New York: Truman Talley Books/Plume, 1991).

Gawain, Shakti, *Creative Visualization* (New York: Muff Books, 1978).

Gelman, David, et.al., "Mapping the Brain," *Newsweek* (April 20, 1992).

Henry, Jane, *Creative Management* (Newbury Park, California: Sage Publications, 1991).

Henry, Jane and Walker, David, *Managing Innovation* (Newbury Park, California: Sage Publications, 1991).

Higgins, James M., *Innovate or Evaporate: Test and Improve Your Organization's IQ—Its Innovation Quotient* (Winter Park, Florida: The New Management Publishing Company, Inc., 1995).

Howard, Pierce J., *The Owner's Manual for the Brian* (Austin, Texas: Leornian Press, 1994).

Isaksen, Scott G. and Teffinger, Donald J., *Creative Problem Solving: The Basic Course* (Buffalo, New York: Bearley Limited, 1985).

Kuhn, R. L., ed., *Handbook for Creative and Innovative Managers* (New York: McGraw Hill, 1988).

Maltz, Maxwell, *Psycho-Cybernetics: The New Way to a Successful Life* (Englewood Cliffs, NJ: Prentice-Hall, 1960).

Mattimore, Bryan W., *99% Inspiration: Tips, Tales & Techniques for Liberating Your Business Creativity* (New York: AMACOM, 1994).

Miller, William C., *The Creative Edge: Fostering Innovation Where You Work* (Reading, Massachusetts: Edison-Westley Publishing, 1986).

Parnes, Sidney J., *Source Book for Creative Problem Solving: A Fifty Year Digest of Proven Innovation Processes* (Buffalo, New York: The Creative Education Foundation Press, 1992).

Ray, Michael and Myers, Michele, *Creativity in Business* (New York: Doubleday & Company, 1986).

Rowan, Roy, *The Intuitive Manager* (Boston: Little, Brown & Co., 1986).

Sumer, Bobbe, with Mark Falstein, *Psycho-Cybernetics 2000* (Englewood Cliffs, New Jersey: Prentice-Hall, 1993).

Torrance, E. Paul, Torrance Tests of Creative Thinking (Chicago, Illinois: University of Chicago Press, 1984).

VanGundy, Arthur B., *Idea Power: Techniques and Resources to Unleash the Creativity in Your Organization* (New York: AMACOM, 1992).

Appendix 2

Wujec, Tom, *Pumping Ions: Games and Exercises to Flex Your Mind* (New York: Doubleday, 1988).

Chapter 2

Adams, James L., *Care and Feeding of Ideas* (Reading, Massachusetts: Addison-Westley, 1986).

Adams, James L., *Conceptual Block Busting* (Reading, Massachusetts: Addison-Westley, 1986).

Kuhn, R. L., ed., *Handbook for Creative and Innovative Managers* (New York: McGraw Hill, 1988).

Gawain, Shakti, *Creative Visualization* (New York: Muff Books, 1978).

Russo, J. Edward and Schoemaker, Paul J.H., *Decision Traps* (New York: Simon & Schuster, Inc., 1989).

Thompson, Charles "Chic", *Yes But: The Top 40 Idea Killers and How You Can Fight Them* (New York: HarperBusiness, 1993).

VanDemark, Noland, PhD., *Breaking the Barriers to Everyday Creativity* (Buffalo, New York: The Creative Education Foundation, 1991)

Von Oech, Roger, *A Whack on the Side of the Head: How to Unlock Your Mind for Innovation* (New York: Warner, 1983).

Chapter 3

Basadur, Min, *The Power of Innovation: To Make Innovation a Way of Life & Put Creative Solutions to Work* (London: Pitman Publishing, 1995).

Benfari, Robert with Knox, Jean, *Understanding Your Management Style* New York: Lexington Books— Macmillan, Inc., 1991).

Collier, Lindsay, *The Whack-A-Mole Theory* (West Henrietta, New York: WhaM Books, 1994).

De Porter, Bobbie with Hernacki, Mike, *Quantum Learning: Unleashing the Genius in You* (New York: Dell, 1992).

Goldberg, Philip, *The Intuitive Edge* (Los Angeles, California: Jeremy P. Tarcher, Inc. 1983).

Hirsh, Sandra Krebs and Kummerow, Jean M., "Introduction to Type in Organizations," (Palo Alto, California: Consulting Psychologists Press, 1990).

Keirsey, David and Bates, Marilyn, *Please Understand Me* (Del Mar, California: Prometheus Nemesis, 1978).

Kirby, Linda R. and Myers, Katherine D., "Introduction to Type," 5th ed. (Palo Alto, California: Consulting Psychologists Press, 1993).

Kroeger, Otto with Thriesen, Janet M., *Type Talk at Work: How the Personality Types Determine Your Success on the Job* (New York: Delacorte Press–Bantam Doubleday Dell Publishing Group, Inc., 1992).

Myers, Isabel Briggs, "Introduction to Type," 4th ed. (Palo Alto, California: Consulting Psychologists Press, 1987).

Myers, Isabel Briggs with Myers, Peter B., *Gifts Differing*, (Palo Alto, California: Consulting Psychologists Press, 1980).

Escape

from

the Maze

Parikh, Jagdish, *Intuition: The New Frontier of Management* (Oxford, England, 1988).

Rowan, Roy, *The Intuitive Manager* (Boston, Massachusetts: Little, Brown and Company, 1986).

Chapter 4

Albrecht, Karl, *Brain Power: Learn To Improve Your Thinking Skills* (Englewood Cliffs, New Jersey: Prentice-Hall, Inc., 1980).

Berger, Florence and Ferguson, Dennis H., *Innovation: Creativity Techniques for Hospitality Managers* (New York: John Wiley & Sons, Inc., 1990).

Brightman, Harvey J., *Group Problem Solving: An Improved Managerial Approach* (Atlanta, Georgia: Business Publishing Division, Georgia State University, 1988).

Buzan, Tony, *Use Both Sides of Your Brain*, (New York: E.P. Dutton, Inc., 1983).

de Vito, Joseph A., Brainstorms: How to think More Creatively about Communication...Or About Anything Else (New York: HarperCollins, 1996).

Diebold, John, *The Innovators: The Discoveries, Inventions, and Breakthroughs of Our Time* (New York: Truman Talley Books/Plume, 1991).

Dudley, Lynch, *Brain Mapping* (Fort Collins, Colorado: Brain Technologies Corporation, 1992).

Fobes, Richard, *The Creative Problem Solvers Toolbox* (Coralus, Oregan: Solutions Through Innovation Press, 1993).

Higgins, James M., *101 Creative Problem Solving Techniques: The Handbook of New Ideas for Business* (Winter Park, Florida: The New Management Publishing Company, Inc., 1994).

Michalko, Michael, *Thinkertoys* (Berkeley, California: Ten Speed Press, 1991).

Nolan, Vincent, *The Innovators Handbook: The Skills of Innovative Management* (London, England: Penguin Books, 1989).

Osborn, Alex, *Applied Imagination* (New York: Charles Scribner & Sons, 1953).

Parnes, Sidney J., *Source Book for Creative Problem Solving: A Fifty Year Digest of Proven Innovation Processes* (Buffalo, New York: Creative Education Foundation Press, 1992).

VanGundy, Arthur B., *Techniques of Structured Problem Solving*, 2ed. (New York: Van Nostrand Reinhold Company, 1980).

VanGundy, Arthur B., *Brain Boosters for Business Advantage: Ticklers, Grab Bags, Blue Skies, and Other Bionic Ideas* (San Diego, California: Pfeiffer & Company, 1995).

VanGundy, Arthur B., *Idea Power: Techniques and Resources to Unleash the Creativity in Your Organization* (New York: AMACOM, 1992).

Wycoff, Joyce, *Transformation Thinking* (New York: Berkeley Publishing Group, 1995).

Appendix 2

233

Wycoff, Joyce, *MindMapping*, (Berkeley Publishing Group: 1991).

Chapter 5

Coleman, Daniel, Kaufman, Paul, and Ray, Michael, *The Creative Spirit* (New York: Plume-Penguin, 1993).

Emery, Marcia, Dr., *Intuition Workbook: An Expert's Guide to Unlocking the Wisdom of Your Subconscious Mind* (Englewood Cliffs, New Jersey: Prentice-Hall, 1994).

De Porter, Bobbie with Hernacki, Mike, *Quantum Learning: Unleashing the Genius in You* (New York: Dell, 1992).

Donovan, Priscilla and Wonder, Jacquelyn, *The Forever Mind: Eight Ways to Unleash the Power of Your Mature Mind* (New York: William Morrow, 1994).

Goldberg, Philip, *The Intuitive Edge* (Los Angeles: Jeremy P. Tarcher, Inc., 1983).

Goleman, Dan, *Meditative Mind* (Los Angeles: Jeremy P. Tarcher, Inc., 1988).

Michaud, Ellen, Wild, Russell and the editors of *Prevention Magazine, Boost Your Brain Power: A Total Program to Sharpen Your Thinking and Age-Proof Your Mind* (Emmaus, Pennsylvania: Rodale Press, 1991).

Miller, Emmett E., Dr., *Software for the Mind* (Berkeley, California: Celestial Arts, 1987).

Minninger, Joan, PhD. and Dugan, Eleanor, *Make Your Mind Work for You* (Emmaus, Pennsylvania: Rodale Press, 1988).

Morris, Jill, *Creative Breakthroughs: Tap the Power of Your Unconscious Mind* (New York: Warner Books, 1992).

Nadel, Laurie with Haims, Judy and Stempson, Robert, *Sixth Sense* (New York: Avon Books, 1990).

Parnes, Disney J., *The Magic of Your Mind* (Buffalo, New York: The Creative Education Foundation, 1981).

Ray, Michael and Myers, Michele, *Creativity in Business* (New York: Doubleday & Company, 1986).

Rowan, Roy, *The Intuitive Manager* (Boston: Little, Brown & Company, 1986).

Silva, José, *The Silva Mind Control Method for Business Managers*, (New York: Pocket Book, 1983).

Sinetar, Marsha, *Developing a 21st Century Mind* (New York: Villard Books, 1991).

Vaughan, Francis E., Awakening Intuition (Garden City, New Jersey: Anchor Books, 1979).

vos Savant, Marilyn and Fleischer, Leonore, *Brain Building in Just Twelve Weeks* (New York: Bantam Books, 1990).

Escape

from

the Maze

Chapter 6

Adams, James L., *Care and Feeding of Ideas* (Reading, Massachusetts: Addison-Westley, 1986).

Donovan, Priscilla and Wonder, Jacquelyn, *The Forever Mind: Eight Ways to Unleash the Power of Your Mature Mind* (New York: William Morrow, 1994).

Herrman Ned *The Creative Brain* (Lake Lure, North Carolina: Brain Books, 1990).

Higgins, James M., *101 Creative Problem Solving Techniques: The Handbook of New Ideas for Business* (Winter Park, Florida: The New Management Publishing Company, Inc. 1994).

Leviton, Richard, *Brain Building!—A Lifelong Guide to Sharper Thinking, Better Memory, and an Age-Proof Mind* (Englewood Cliffs, New Jersey: Printice-Hall, 1996).

Master, Robert and Houston, Jean, *Mind Games: The Guide to Inner Space* (New York: Barnes & Noble Books, 1973).

Morris, Jill, *Creative Breakthroughs: Tap the Power of Your Unconscious Mind* (New York: Warner Books, 1992).

Restak, Richard, *The Brain Has a Mind of Its Own* (New York: Harmony Books, 1991).

vos Savant, Marilyn and Fleischer, Leonore, *Brain Building: Exercising Yourself Smarter* (New York: Bantam, Dell, Doubleday, 1990).

Wonder, Jacquelyn and Donovan, Priscilla, *Whole-Brain Thinking: Working from Both Sides of the Brain to Achieve Peak Job Performance* (New York: William Morrow and Company, 1984).

Chapter 7

Donovan, Priscilla and Wonder, Jacquelyn, *The Forever Mind: Eight Ways to Unleash the Power of Your Mature Mind* (New York: William Morrow, 1994).

Edwards, Betty, *Drawing on the Right Side* (Los Angeles, California: Jeremy P. Tarcher, Inc., 1984).

Emery, Marcia, Dr., *Intuition Workbook: An Expert's Guide to Unlocking the Wisdom of Your Subconscious Mind* (Englewood Cliffs, New Jersey: Prentice-Hall, 1994).

Hall, Doug with Wecker, David, *Jump Start Your Brain* (New York: Warner Books, 1995).

Howard, Pierce J., *The Owner's Manual for the Brain* (Austin, Texas: Leornian Press, 1994).

Leviton, Richard, *Brain Building!—A Lifelong Guide to Sharper Thinking, Better Memory, and an Age-Proof Mind* (Englewood Cliffs, New Jersey: Printice-Hall, 1996).

Mattimore, Bryan W., *99% Inspiration: Tips, Tales & Techniques for Liberating Your Business Creativity* (New York: AMACOM, 1994).

Michaud, Ellen, Wild, Russell and the editors of *Prevention Magazine, Boost Your Brain Power: A Total Program to Sharpen Your Thinking and Age-Proof Your Mind* (Emmaus, Pennsylvania: Rodale Press, 1991).

Morris, Jill, *Creative Breakthroughs: Tap the Power of Your Unconscious Mind* (New York: Warner Books, 1992).

Appendix 2

Nadel, Laurie with Haims, Judy and Stempson, Robert, *Sixth Sense* (New York: Avon Books, 1990).

Ray, Michael and Myers, Michele, *Creativity in Business* (New York: Doubleday & Company, 1986).

vos Savant, Marilyn and Fleischer, Leonore, *Brain Building in Just Twelve Weeks* (New York: Bantam Books, 1990).

Wonder, Jacquelyn and Donovan, Priscilla, *Whole-Brain Thinking: Working from Both Sides of the Brain to Achieve Peak Job Performance* (New York: William Morrow and Company, 1984).

Wonder, Jacquelyn and Donovan, Priscilla, *Whole Brain Thinking* (New York: Ballantine Books, 1984).

Wujec, Tom, *Pumping Ions: Games and Exercises to Flex Your Mind* (New York: Doubleday, 1988).

Chapter 8

Donovan, Priscilla and Wonder, Jacquelyn, *The Forever Mind: Eight Ways to Unleash the Power of Your Mature Mind* (New York: William Morrow, 1994).

Edwards, Betty, *Drawing on the Right Side* (Los Angeles, California: Jeremy P. Tarcher, Inc., 1984).

Emery, Marcia, Dr., *Intuition Workbook: An Expert's Guide to Unlocking the Wisdom of Your Subconscious Mind* (Englewood Cliffs, New Jersey: Prentice-Hall, 1994).

Hall, Doug with Wecker, David, *Jump Start Your Brain* (New York: Warner Books, 1995).

Leviton, Richard, *Brain Building!—A Lifelong Guide to Sharper Thinking, Better Memory, and an Age-Proof Mind* (Englewood Cliffs, New Jersey: Printice-Hall, 1996).

Mattimore, Bryan W., *99% Inspiration: Tips, Tales & Techniques for Liberating Your Business Creativity* (New York: AMACOM, 1994).

Michaud, Ellen, Wild, Russell and the editors of *Prevention Magazine*, *Boost Your Brain Power: A Total Program to Sharpen Your Thinking and Age-Proof Your Mind* (Emmaus, Pennsylvania: Rodale Press, 1991).

Morris, Jill, *Creative Breakthroughs: Tap the Power of Your Unconscious Mind* (New York: Warner Books, 1992).

Nadel, Laurie with Haims, Judy and Stempson, Robert, *Sixth Sense* (New York: Avon Books, 1990).

Ray, Michael and Myers, Michele, *Creativity in Business* (New York: Doubleday & Company, 1986).

vos Savant, Marilyn and Fleischer, Leonore, *Brain Building in Just Twelve Weeks* (New York: Bantam Books, 1990).

Wonder, Jacquelyn and Donovan, Priscilla, *Whole Brain Thinking* (New York: Ballantine Books, 1984).

Wujec, Tom, *Pumping Ions: Games and Exercises to Flex Your Mind* (New York: Doubleday, 1988).

Chapter 9

Dement, William D., *Some Must Watch While Some Must Sleep: Exploring the World of Sleep* (New York: Norton, 1978).

Donovan, Priscilla and Wonder, Jacquelyn, *The Forever Mind: Eight Ways to Unleash the Power of Your Mature Mind* (New York: William Morrow, 1994).

Edwards, Betty, *Drawing on the Right Side* (Los Angeles, California: Jeremy P. Tarcher, Inc., 1984).

Emery, Marcia, Dr., *Intuition Workbook: An Expert's Guide to Unlocking the Wisdom of Your Subconscious Mind* (Englewood Cliffs, New Jersey: Prentice-Hall, 1994).

Coleman, David, Kaufman, Paul, and Ray, Michael, *The Creative Spirit* (New York: Penguin/Plume, 1993).

Hall, Doug with Wecker, David, *Jump Start Your Brain* (New York: Warner Books, 1995).

Hinderyck, Greg, "Creative Process Often Starts With a Good Massage," *Marketing News* (April 15, 1991).

Leviton, Richard, *Brain Building!—A Lifelong Guide to Sharper Thinking, Better Memory, and an Age-Proof Mind* (Englewood Cliffs, New Jersey: Printice-Hall, 1996).

Master, Robert and Houston, Jean, *Mind Games: The Guide to Inner Space* (New York: Barnes & Noble Books, 1973).

Mattimore, Bryan W., *99% Inspiration: Tips, Tales & Techniques for Liberating Your Business Creativity* (New York: AMACOM, 1994).

Michaud, Ellen, Wild, Russell and the editors of *Prevention Magazine*, *Boost Your Brain Power: A Total Program to Sharpen Your Thinking and Age-Proof Your Mind* (Emmaus, Pennsylvania: Rodale Press, 1991).

Morris, Jill, *Creative Breakthroughs: Tap the Power of Your Unconscious Mind* (New York: Warner Books, 1992).

Nadel, Laurie with Haims, Judy and Stempson, Robert, *Sixth Sense* (New York: Avon Books, 1990).

Ray, Michael and Myers, Michele, *Creativity in Business* (New York: Doubleday & Company, 1986).

Restak, Richard, *The Brain Has a Mind of Its Own* (New York: Harmony Books, 1991).

Vance, Mike and Deacon, Diane, *Think Out of the Box* (Franklin Lakes, New Jersey: Career Press, 1995).

vos Savant, Marilyn and Fleischer, Leonore, *Brain Building in Just Twelve Weeks* (New York: Bantam Books, 1990).

Wonder, Jacquelyn and Donovan, Priscilla, *Whole Brain Thinking* (New York: Ballantine Books, 1984).

Wujec, Tom, *Pumping Ions: Games and Exercises to Flex Your Mind* (New York: Doubleday, 1988).

Chapter 10

Agor, Weston H., *Intuition In Organizations* (Newbury Park, California: Sage Publications, 1989).

Appendix 2

Basadur, Min, *The Power of Innovation: To Make Innovation a Way of Life & Put Creative Solutions to Work* (London: Pitman Publishing, 1995).

Collier, Lindsay, *Get Out of Your Thinking Box* (San Francisco, California: Robert D. Reed Publishers, 1994).

de Bono, Edward, *Lateral Thinking: Creativity Step by Step* (New York: Harper & Row, 1970).

de Bono, Edward, *Serious Creativity* (New York: Harper Business, 1992).

de Bono, Edward, *New Think: The Use of Lateral Thinking in the Generation of New Ideas* (New York: Basic Books, a division of HarperCollins Publishers, Inc., 1967).

de Bono, Edward, *The Five Day Course in Thinking* (New York: Facts on File, 1985), p. 115.

Diebold, John, *The Innovators: The Discoveries, Inventions, and Breakthroughs of Our Time* (New York: Truman Talley Books/Plume, 1991).

Doyle, Bruce I., III, *Before You Think Another Thought* (Winter Park, Florida: Rare Shares Limited, 1994).

Henry, Jane and Walker, David, *Managing Innovation* (Newbury Park, California: Sage Publications, 1991).

Henry, Jane, *Creative Management* (Newbury Park, California: Sage Publications, 1991).

Magic Eye (Vol.1, 1993), *Magic Eye* (Vol. 2, 1994), *Magic Eye* (Vol. 3, 1994) (Kansas City, Missouri: Andrews & McMeel).

Mattimore, Bryan W., *99% Inspiration: Tips, Tales & Techniques for Liberating Your Business Creativity* (New York: AMACOM, 1994).

Ray, Michael and Myers, Michele, *Creativity in Business* (New York: Doubleday & Company, 1986).

Sargent, Alice G., *The Androgynous Manager* (New York: AMACOM, 1981).

Schank, Roger, *The Creative Attitude* (New York: Macmillian Publishing Company, 1988).

Schultz, Ron, *Unconventional Wisdom* (New York: HarperBusiness, 1994).

Shekerjian, Denise, *Uncommon Genius: How Great Ideas are Born* (New York: Penguin Books, 1991).

Sinetar, Marsha, *Developing a 21st Century Mind* (New York: Villard Books, 1991).

vos Savant, Marilyn and Fleischer, Leonore, *Brain Building in Just Twelve Weeks* (New York: Bantam Books, 1990).

Chapter 11

Higgins, James M., *Innovate or Evaporate: Test and Improve Your Organization's IQ—Its Innovation Quotient* (Winter Park, Florida: The New Management Publishing Company, Inc., 1995).

For information on teams and creativity:

Glassman, Edward, *The Creativity Factor: Unlocking the Potential of Your Team* (San Deigo, California: Pfeiffer, 1991).

Escape

from
the Maze

APPENDIX 3

BRAIN BREAK SOLUTIONS

BRAIN BREAK 1

In Chapter 2, we discussed five major types of blocks to creativity. One of those was perceptual. The nine dot exercise helps demonstrate the perceptual block concept. The key to the nine dot exercise is not to allow your perceptual block to stop you from solving the problem. Unless you go outside what your perception routinely allows you to "see," you cannot solve this problem. If you look below, you will see a common solution to this problem. As you can now "see," your lines must go outside the perceptual square created by the dots if you are going to solve this problem. Since you have seen so many squares before, the left side of your brain thinks square when it sees the dots. Only by using your right side and seeing past this square can you solve the problem.

a. Four-line Solution

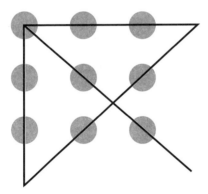

Perceptual Assumptions Overturned: You have to stay within the perceived box formed by the dots.

Appendix 3

239

b. Three-line Solution

Since the dots are sufficiently large, you can angle the three lines such that you can connect the dots with only three lines as seen at the right.

Perceptual Assumptions Overturned: the lines have to go through the center of the dots.

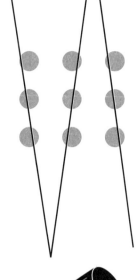

c. Two-line Solution

Perceptual Assumptions Overturned:
you have only a thin pencil or pen to use.

d. One-line Solution

There are at least three ways of connecting the dots with only one straight line. First, cut the dots from the paper, paste or tape them to another piece of paper, and draw a straight line through them.

Perceptual Assumptions Overturned: You cannot cut the pages.

Secondly, it is possible to fold and cut your paper such that all nine dots are arranged in a row. Now draw a line through them.

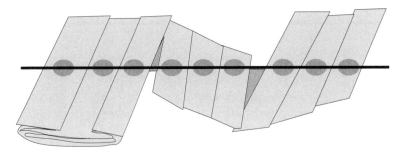

Perceptual Assumptions Overturned: you cannot fold the paper.

Thirdly, if you make a cylinder of your paper with the nine dots on it, then you can connect the nine dots by going around the cylinder with your pencil or pen. This works much like the three line solution, execpt in three dimensions, you need only one line.

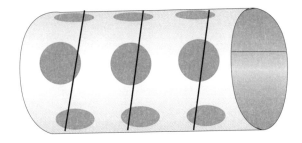

Perceptual Assumptions Overturned: the paper must be flat.

NOTE: The point of all of these solutions is that you must get outside the box (the literal box—the square—created by the arrangement of the nine dots, and the allegorical one created by your perception of the instructions to the exercise) if you are going to solve these puzzles. As long as you specifically follow the rules of the game, no one says you cannot do whatever it takes to solve the problem.

Sources of Solutions: Tom Wujec, *Pumping Ions* (New York: Doubleday, 1988), pp. 117, 118; and James L. Adams, *Conceptual Blockbusting, 3ed.* (Reading, Massachusetts: Addison-Wesley, 1986), pp. 25—31.

Appendix 3

241

1. Wide (physically wide) eyed.
2. Nothing between two ears, as in, he has nothing between his two ears.
3. Racing (leaning) against the clock.
4. Life after death.
5. High (in the box) cost of living.
6. As big as (as, [physically big] AS).
7. Call me in the morning.
8. 3 D Movies.
9. He knows it backwards and forwards.
   (Spelling of second line is backwards.)
10. Three (physically) under par.
11. Split level.
12. Beat around (physically) the bush.

Escape

from
the Maze

INDEX

Index

243

D

Index

Escape

from
the Maze

246

Index

247

Index

249

Escape

from
the Maze

Y

Z

Index

Escape

from
  the Maze

BOOK ORDER FORM

Customer Information: Date: _____

Name: _____

Address: _____

City/State/Zip: _____

Item #	Description	Unit Price	Qty	Subtotal
101	*101 Creative Problem Solving Techniques: The Handbook of New Ideas for Business*	$17.95		
102	*Innovate or Evaporate: Test & Improve Your Organization's IQ – Its Innovation Quotient*	$19.95		
103	*Escape From the Maze: 9 Steps to Personal Creativity*	$19.95		

Comments:	Sub.	
Discounts are available for volume orders	**S & H***	
Shipping and handling is single book orders*		
Sales tax in Florida is 6%	**Tax**	
If payment is by check, please pay in <u>U.S. dollars only</u>	**Total**	

CREDIT CARD INFORMATION: VISA ☐   MASTER CARD ☐   AMEX ☐

Exact Account Name _____

Card Number _____ Expiration Date _____

Signature _____

*101 Creative Problem Solving Techniques *and* Escape From the Maze *ship at $3.00 each in the U.S. and Canada.* Innovate or Evaporate *ships at $4.00 each to the U.S. and Canada. Shipping to other countries is on a cost basis.*

THE NEW
MANAGEMENT
PUBLISHING COMPANY

400 North New York Avenue, Suite #215, Winter Park, Fl 32789
407-647-5344 or 800-266-8283/fax: 407-647-5575

SURVEY

As an author, I like feedback on my books. Please take the time to fill out the three questions below and send your responses to me. As this is revised for reprinting, I will review my readers' suggestions and make changes as necessary. Thank you for taking the time to help make improvements.

What did you like about the book?

_____

_____

_____

_____

_____

What would you like to see added?

_____

_____

_____

_____

_____

What changes should be made and why?

_____

_____

_____

_____

_____

Please mail this to:
New Management Publishing Company, Inc.
ATTN: *Escape Survey*
400 North New York Avenue, #215
Winter Park, FL 32789